AF479172

Picasso.
The Women in His Life

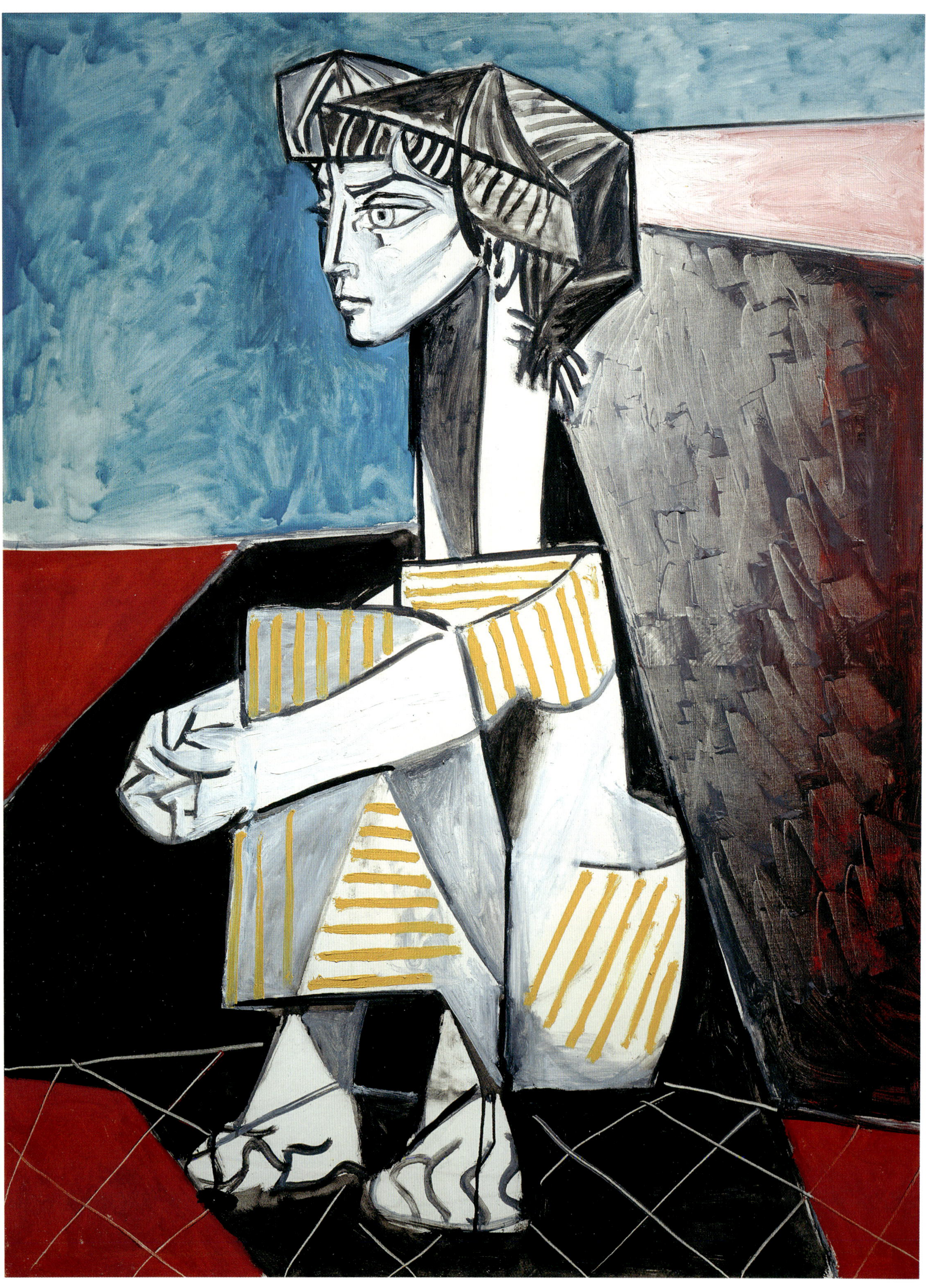

Picasso.
The
Women
in His
Life

An Homage

Edited by Margrit Bernard

**With texts by
Marilyn McCully and Markus Müller**

HIRMER

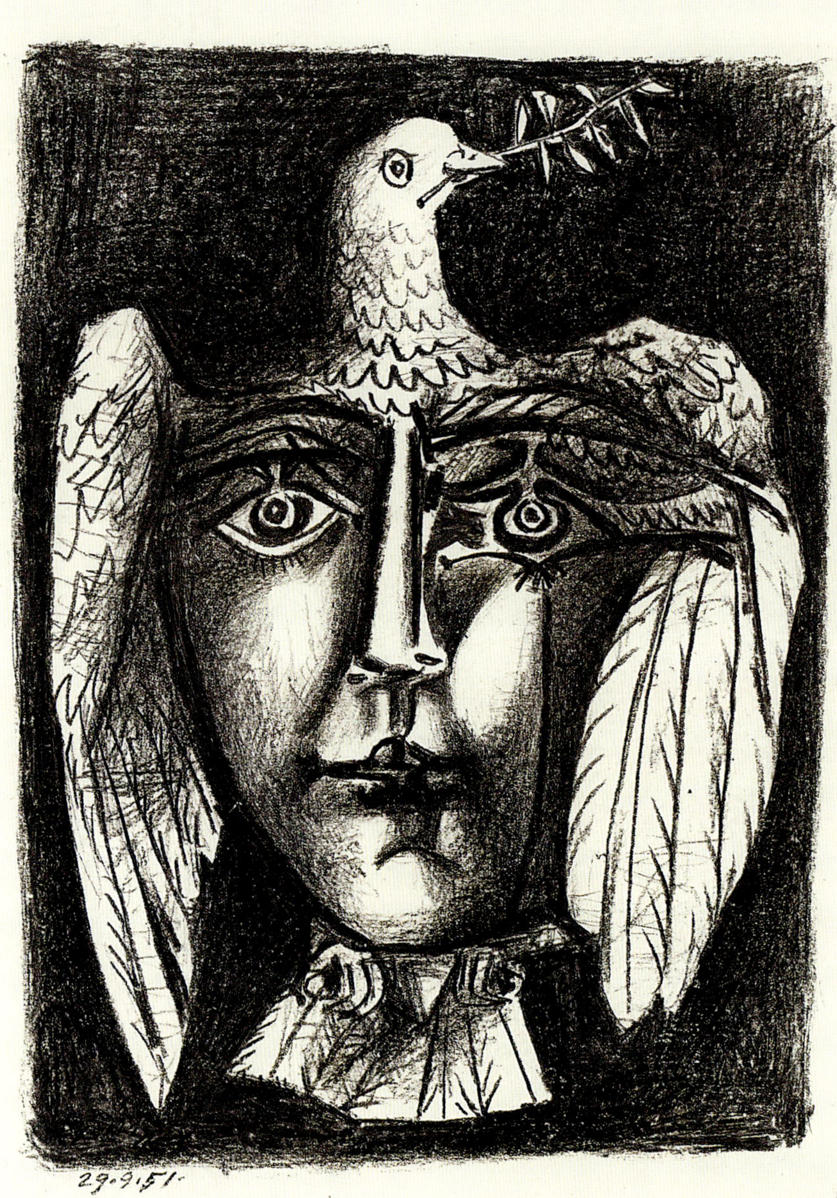

29.9.51.

Contents

Foreword
Olivier Widmaier Picasso

Pablo Picasso and women is a subject as natural as it is fascinating. It is natural in that my grandfather grew up in a family dominated by women, his mother and sisters to be precise, whereas his father, don José, went out to work as a drawing teacher, leaving his son to rule the roost as the adored and indulged little prince in his absence; natural in that Picasso came of age both emotionally and sexually through his interactions with the young women of Barcelona's red-light district, which is where the young art student found his first models and the inspiration for future masterpieces; and natural in that he discovered Paris through and with the many women who found themselves unable to resist the charm and talent of a young Spaniard, who despite being penniless had gifts great enough to conquer the world. What followed was a long journey and a kind of intertwining of love and art, which is what makes the connection between the man and artist and all the women in his life—women as different from each other as the periods in Picasso's oeuvre with which each of them in turn is associated—so fascinating. While his mother, doña María, his sister Lola, and his friend Gertrude Stein belong in a class of their own, his companions Fernande Olivier, Eva Gouel, Olga Khokhlova, Marie-Thérèse Walter, Dora Maar, Françoise Gilot and Jacqueline Roque are as radically unlike each other as the cubist works are unlike the neoclassical portraits or the dismembered nudes to which the genius Picasso was inspired by one or another of the sitters for whom he had such a compulsive need.

As the purview of any study of famous individuals has broadened to include those closest to them, so our interest in the lives of the women with whom the iconic figure of Picasso was most intimate has grown. Besides acquainting us with the women who accompanied the artist through different phases of his life, these exploratory biographies also deepen our understanding of his life and work, if only by placing them in a larger historical, sociological and artistic context. What makes this project, which was initiated by the editor and curator Margrit Bernard and brought to fruition by the authors Marilyn McCully and Markus Müller, so timely and relevant is its reconstruction of the lives of these women in their *totality*. That Picasso looms very large in their very different life stories goes without saying; yet the authors also draw on their own research to shed light on what these women did before and after Picasso, and they certainly do not confine the scope of their discussion to the time Picasso's companions spent at his side. What the authors have done, in other words, is to give these women a voice.

As a producer of documentary films and an author of books about my grandfather, I have studied his life in considerable depth and thanks to my own family ties, above all to my mother, Maya, and grandmother Marie-Thérèse, have acquired an intimate insight into what Picasso was like as a person.

It seems to me that the way Picasso bonded with women is not unlike the way he bonded with his brushes and palette, which is to say absolutely. Women were of existential importance to him: no women, no works; and above all, no emotional ties, neither in the family, nor in love. Women gifted Picasso their presence; and he gifted them immortality. Every one of the women who shared her life with my grandfather possessed an inner force that warrants and rewards further scrutiny.

This book by Margrit Bernard, Marilyn McCully and Markus Müller, all of whom have won acclaim for their conception of Picasso exhibitions and knowledgeable writings of encyclopedic range, is remarkable for its shift of perspective. Like the card catalogues that once served researchers as a tool for recording facts and anecdotes gleaned from the literature, it sets the stage for us to meet the women most closely associated with Picasso, as revealed to us by the latest research findings and the ongoing inquiry into their lives.

There is a saying in French that translates as follows: "Show me your friends and I'll tell you who you are," which in this instance might be adapted to say: "Show us the women and we'll know who Picasso is!"

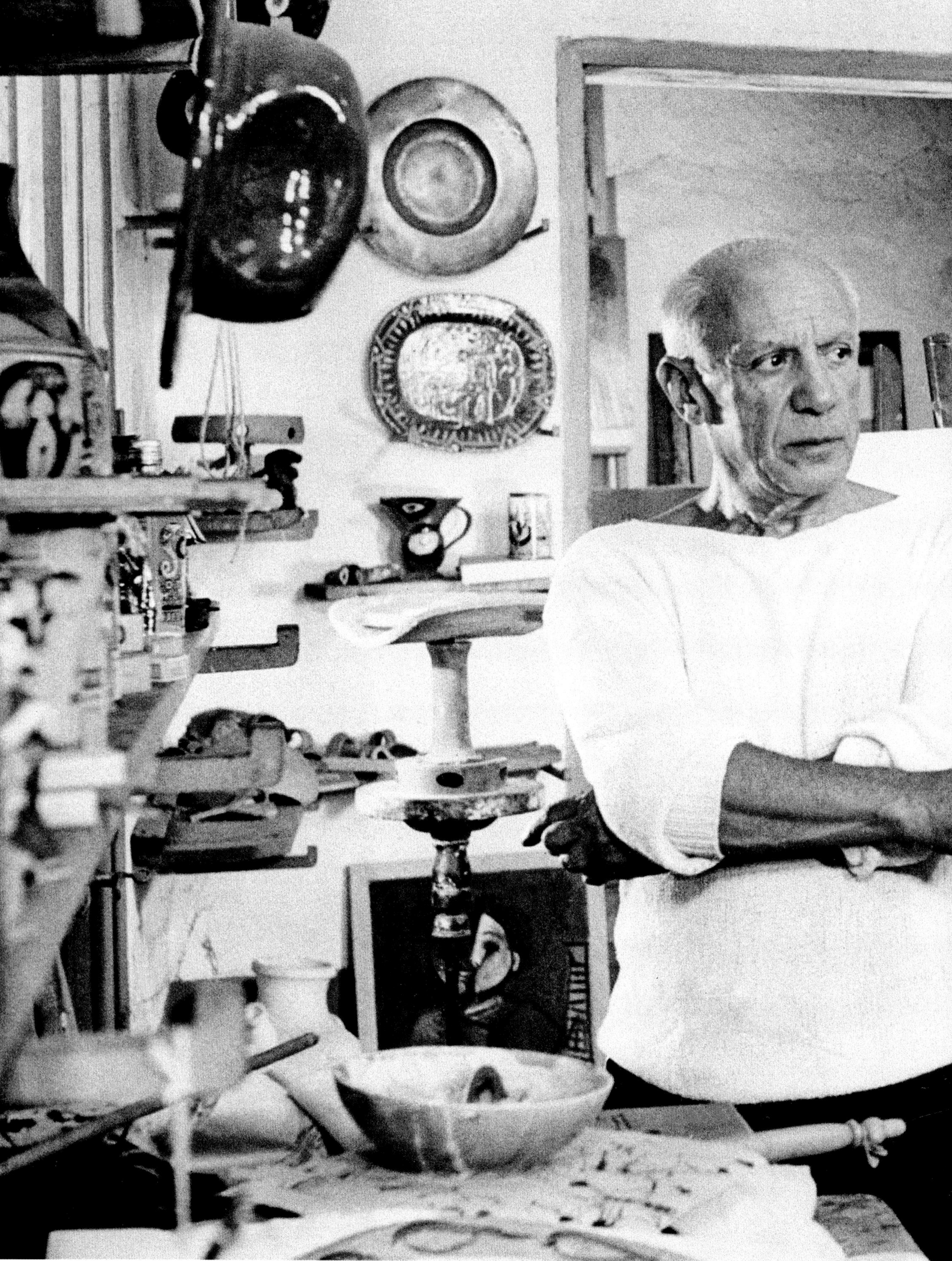

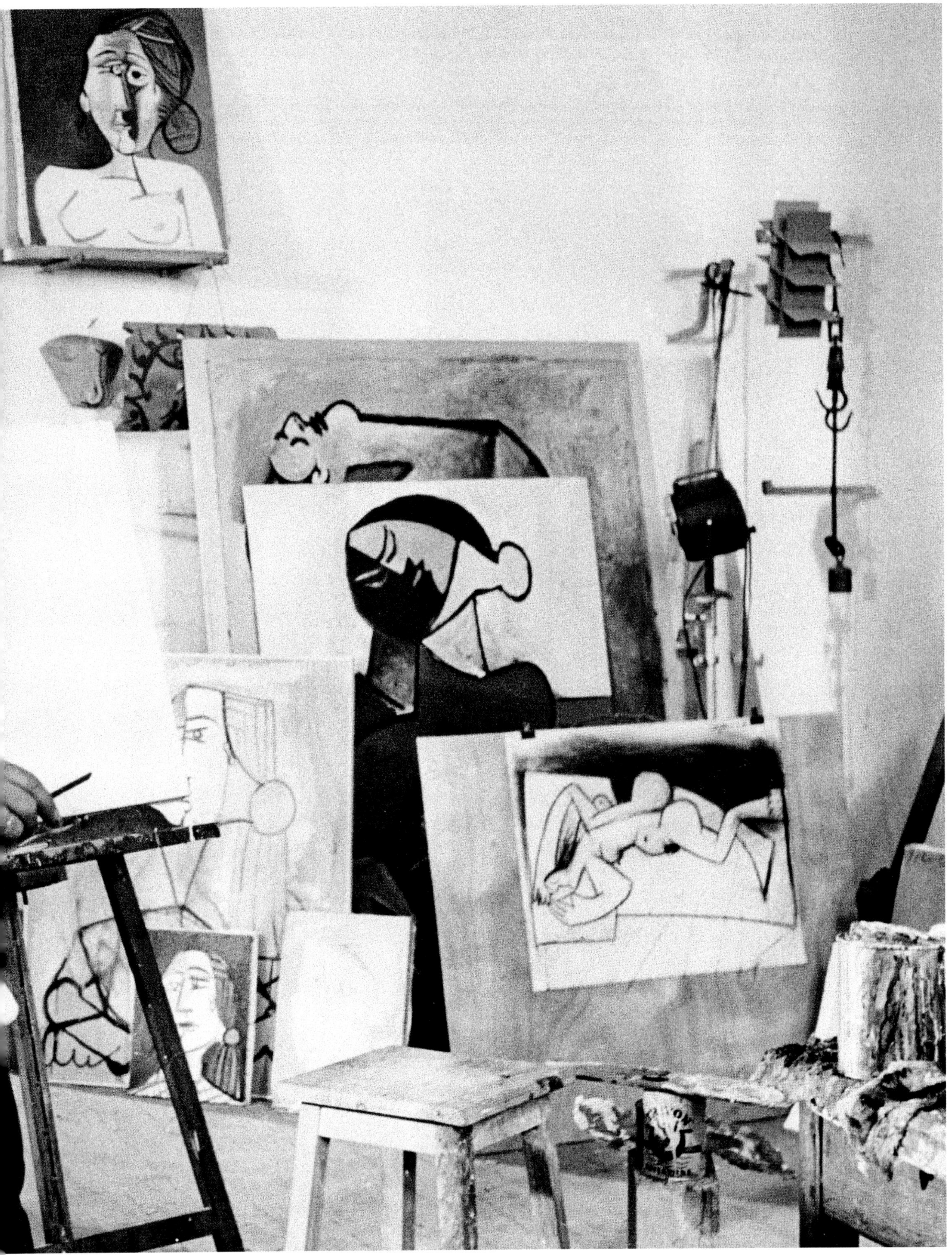

Doña María Picasso López

Marilyn McCully

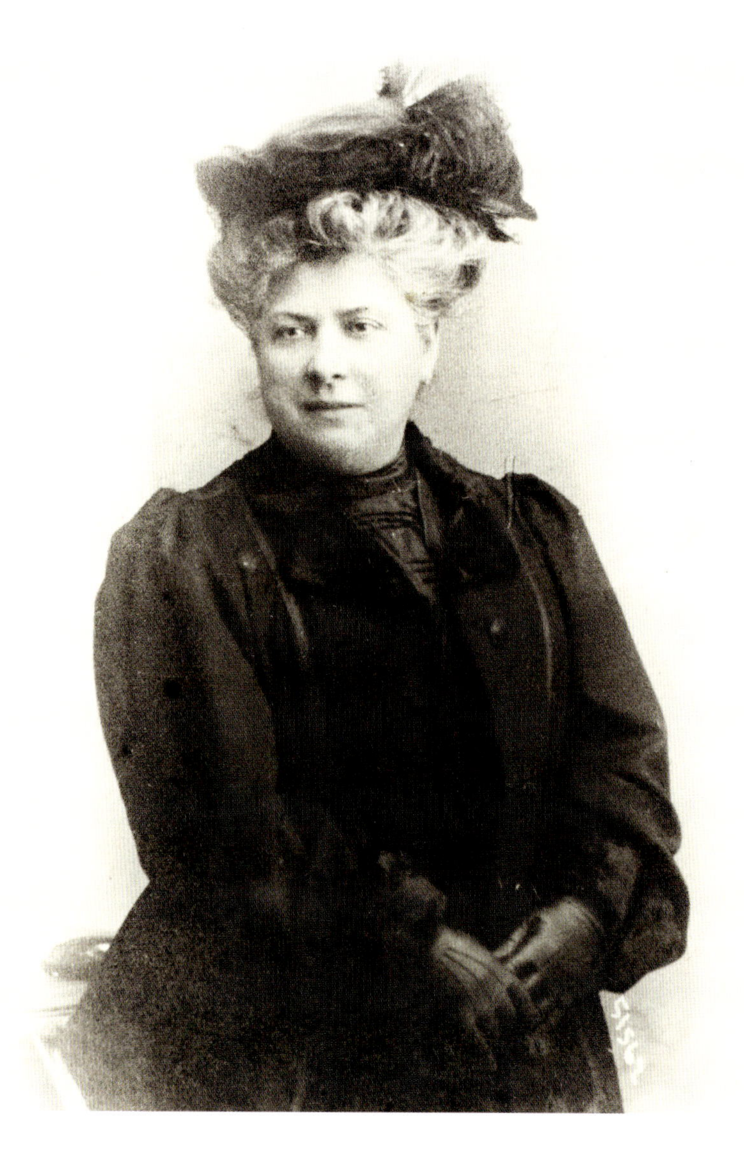

Picasso's Mother: Magnificent, Intelligent, Lively and Tolerant

They tell me that you are writing. About you I believe anything. If some day they were to tell me that you had sung mass, I would believe that too.

> Letter to Picasso from his mother, 1936[1]

Throughout her life, Pablo Picasso's mother, doña María Picasso López, had blind faith in her remarkable son, from the time of the family's earliest days in Málaga, where he was born, to Paris, where he achieved international fame. Although he had left Spain and settled in France as a young man, he would keep in contact with his mother until her death, in 1938, and he made several visits to Barcelona (until the outbreak of the Spanish Civil War) to see her. Their closeness reflected a similarity of vivacious, outgoing personalities as well as a strong physical resemblance. Moreover, they shared a generally optimistic outlook on the opportunities that life offered. For her part, Picasso's mother stayed in contact with her son by writing him at least once or twice a week throughout her life.[2] In her letters, she provides details about the family and domestic affairs, and she also kept him up to date on church festivals and local events. However, her main purpose in writing was to keep him as close to her as possible. She sometimes says that if she had the money, she would take a train to Paris to see him. Doña María also followed coverage in the press of his artistic accomplishments, and, as one of her grandchildren later said, it did not matter what he created; as long as it was by Pablo, she enthusiastically approved (fig. 1).

María Picasso López was born in the working-class district of Málaga known as the Percheles in 1855. She was one of six daughters (two of whom died in infancy) born

1
Doña María Picasso López, c. 1910

Doña María Picasso López

to Inés López Robles and Francisco Picasso Guardeño: of the surviving children, Aurelia was the eldest, followed by María, Eladia and Eliodora. Their father, in part to secure financial security for his family, left for Cuba, where he worked for a number of years, but died of yellow fever before he could return to his native Spain. His widow was left to cope with raising the family on her own. When the shares from a vineyard dwindled to nothing after the devastating outbreak of phylloxera in Spain in the late nineteenth century, they all did what they could to make ends meet. Picasso always remembered that his Aunts Eladia and Eliodora made the braid for railwaymen's caps to earn a little extra money, and he admired both their craft and their invention in the decorative spirals that they created.

When María Picasso López met José Ruiz Blasco, some seventeen years her senior, she was happy to marry and create a home of her own. In typically Andalusian fashion, she brought her mother and two unmarried sisters (Eladia and Eliodora) with her, and the family settled into the bourgeois neighbourhood of the Plaza de la Merced. Pablo (b.1881) and his two sisters, Lola (b.1884) and Conchita (b.1887), would soon join the predominantly female family. For most of the day, Pablo's father occupied himself as an art restorer and spent his free time with his male friends at the local cafés. He would take his son with him to bullfights on Sunday afternoons. Pablo's mother, for her part, looked after the large household. She was also a member of the Hermandad de la Victoria and, reportedly, had a special devotion to the Virgén de la Merced. She had received a good education as a child and had acquired the habit of reading, which she continued in subsequent years.

Doña María's world, which centred on her extended family and the familiarity of Málaga, would be turned upside down when her husband accepted a post at the Escuela de Bellas Artes in the Galician town of A Coruña in north-western Spain. They moved in 1891 (leaving Pablo's grand-mother and two aunts behind) and settled into an apartment near the art school. In some ways, with its different lan-guage – Galego was spoken by many locals – and its cold, rainy climate, the region could not have been more different from Andalusia. While the parents missed life in Málaga, the children, especially Pablo, greeted the move as an oppor-tunity to experience a certain amount of independence. His mother's response was predict-ably protective. Picasso later remembered that when he would play with his young friends in the street, she would climb on top of the water closet and stand on tiptoes, so that she could peer through a small crack and observe their games. While playing in the street was normal for a boy of ten or eleven, she was fully aware that he was quickly achieving maturity as an artist, both as a student in the local school and with his father's instruction. She realized that even from this young age, Pablo would soon break out of the confines of the family circle and make his way on his own.

When they were living in A Coruña, the boy began to draw pretty much all the time. His sketchbooks include quickly recorded Galician scenes as well as portraits or studies of his father, his sister Lola and at least one of Conchita. Of the few sketches that depict his mother, one is a close-up of her at rest, while another por-trays don José comforting her at the time of the shattering event that dramatically changed the lives of the family. Conchita, the youngest of the three children, contracted diphtheria and, in spite of last-minute but failed attempts on the part of the doctor to obtain the necessary serum to cure her, she died at the age of seven in January 1895. A few months later, Picasso's father decided to accept an offer to

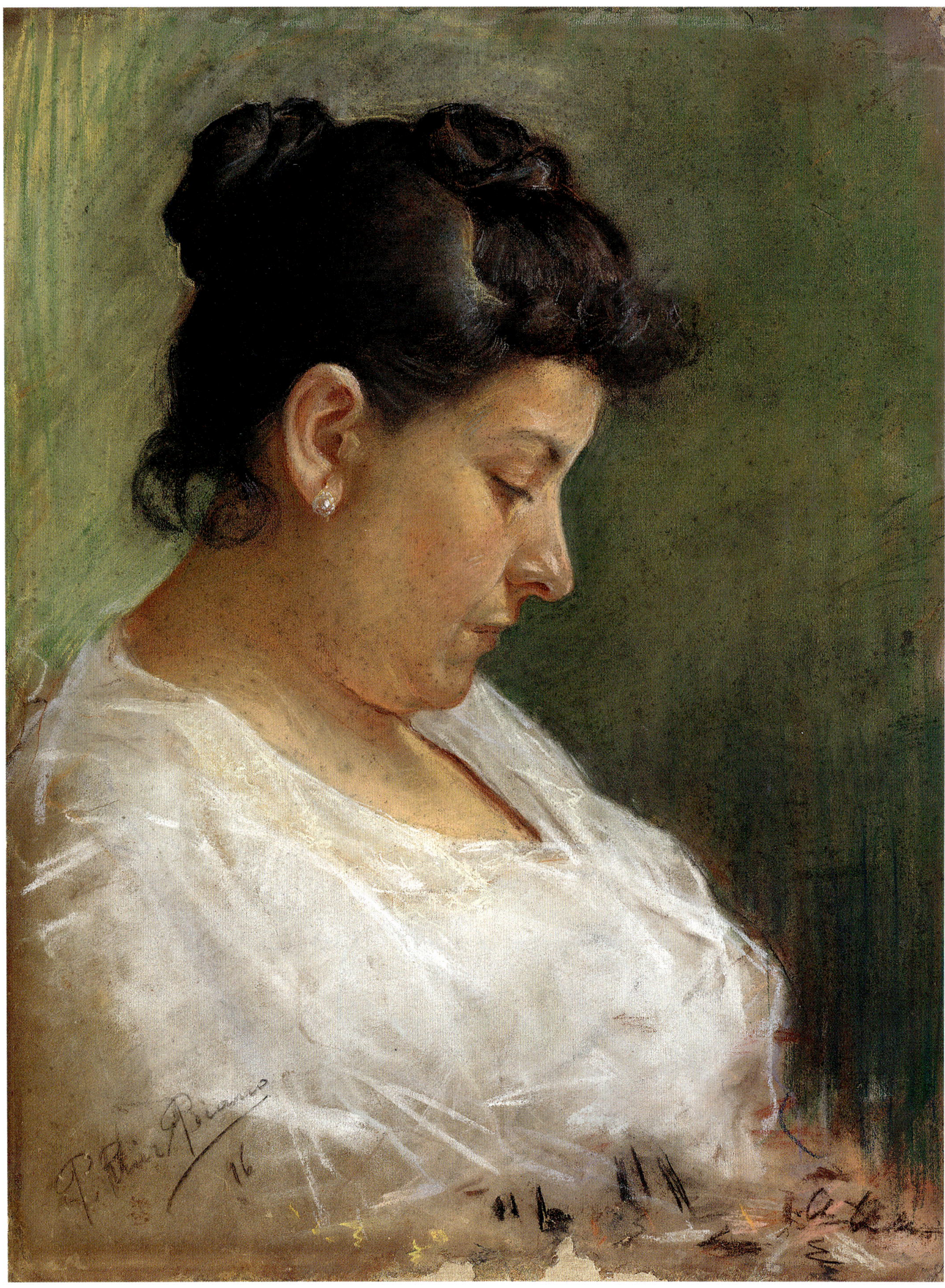

take up a position at La Llotja in Barcelona and leave the distressing memories of A Coruña behind.

The Ruiz Picasso family arrived in Barcelona in September 1895, and after spending some time in lodgings on the calle Cristina, they moved into the apartment on calle de la Merced that would become the family home until the 1920s. It was close enough for don José to walk to the local art school, where he taught and where his son was enrolled as a student. In addition, Picasso's father also rented him a small studio nearby, where he could work on large canvases. Among the quite accomplished paintings and drawings that the fifteen-year-old Pablo did of his family and friends is a pastel portrait of his mother for which she most likely posed (fig. 2). Seen in profile, the young artist focused on her strong features and abundant black hair, which is piled on her head. Her warm skin tones are rendered with touches of flesh-coloured pastels that are blended together, and they contrast the freely applied whites of her blouse. At the lower left is the boy's signature and the date: *P. Ruiz Picasso/96*. Five years later he gave up his patronymic name, *Ruiz*, for his mother's surname, *Picasso*. When doña María began to notice that her son was referred to in newspaper articles in 1901 as just Pablo Picasso, she told him what his father said about dropping the name Ruiz. Don José thought it a shame to lose the distinguished family names of his ancestors (Ruiz Almoguera), but he agreed that if Diego Velázquez had used his second name, Pablo might as well do the same. Thought to be of Genoese origin, the Picassos had established themselves in the nineteenth century in Málaga. According to some accounts, Picasso preferred his mother's surname to Ruiz because it was more unusual; others say that he liked the fact that the name had a double 's', just like Henri Matisse or Nicolas Poussin. In any event, to take his mother's name would prove a lasting, personal tribute to her memory.

The next important step in the young Pablo's artistic education was the decision by the family in 1897 to send him to the Academia de San Fernando in Madrid. While his father recognized his son's extraordinary artistic aptitude, he always hoped that he would become a conventional painter. His mother, on the other hand, convinced her husband to let the boy go his own way. From the beginning, she understood her son well and was determined to help him achieve his independence both as a person and as an artist. 'Why put obstacles in his way? He knows where he is going. He knows what he has to do. Even if [his mother] cannot explain, she understands. Pablo has but one passion, and that no one can change.'[3]

Over the course of the next decade, doña María spent much of her time ensuring that her husband, who was still teaching but also suffering from weak eyesight, was well looked after. Their son was spending more and more time in Paris, although he still asked his father in Barcelona to help prepare canvases or panels for him (such as for the *Old Guitarist*, which was painted on an old wooden tabletop that don José prepared for him in 1903; now in the Art Institute of Chicago). On occasion, he also asked his mother to help him obtain studio props. In the case of the *Portrait of Señora Canals* (1905; Museu Picasso, Barcelona), he asked his mother to send him the typically Spanish mantilla worn by the Italian model Benedetta Bianco. His parents also stored the many paintings and drawings he had done as a youth in their calle de la Merced apartment. Then, early in 1913, don José became ill and, in the spring, died. Picasso came back for the funeral but returned to France immediately afterwards. Lola Ruiz Picasso, now married with a small child, also returned for the funeral from Menorca, where her husband, Juan Bautista Vilató Gómez, had established his medical practice. Nevertheless, the Vilatós moved back to Barcelona, and thereafter life would change again for doña María, as well as for her daughter and her growing family. In good Andalusian fashion, the two households would live together in the mother's Barcelona apartment.

Doña María's grandson Javier Vilató (b. 1921) has left a delightful account of how his grandmother set the lively, somewhat Bohemian tone of the large family living together. He reports that she was 'very short, dark like a gypsy, magnificent, intelligent, lively and tolerant … she liked the theatre, she read a lot, and even became a swimmer, which in those days was considered eccentric. Nothing or no one frightened her.'[4] He goes on to say that although she understood Catalan, they spoke Spanish at home. Among Lola Vilató's children, Javier himself expressed the most interest in art, and he remembered that this was encouraged by his grandmother, who let him use his Uncle Pablo's paints and brushes that were still in the apartment. Moreover, it was she who taught him to stretch canvases. He also mentions that Picasso's Barcelona painter friends continued to come to the apartment to see doña María, even though the artist was living in France.

In 1917 Picasso returned to Spain for the Ballets Russes production of *Parade*. Not only had he designed the sets and costumes for the ballet, but his fiancée, the Russian Olga Khokhlova, was dancing with the company. After a stay in Madrid, where *Parade* was put on for the king, Picasso and Khokhlova travelled to Barcelona. She stayed at the Pension Ranzini on the paseo de Colón, where Picasso spent much of his time and where he also painted and drew her in her room and on the balcony. It was on this visit that he introduced the Russian dancer to his mother and told her of their intentions to marry. She apparently responded: 'You poor girl, you don't know what you're letting yourself in for. If I were a

17

friend I would tell you not to do it under any conditions. I don't believe any woman could be happy with my son. He's available for himself but for no one else.'[5] Neither Khokhlova nor Picasso heeded her warning, and they married the following year. His mother would become good friends with his wife over the years, especially after the birth of Paulo in February 1921, and she would make every effort to see her grandson thereafter. Her first trip to France, which she made on her own, was in the late summer of that year. She joined the couple and their baby in Fontainebleau, where the artist had rented a spacious villa with a garden (fig. 3).

The next time they spent a holiday together was on the Côte d'Azur in 1923, when they all stayed in the Hôtel du Cap in Antibes. Picasso took four rooms in the hotel: one for him and his wife; one for their son, Paulo, and his nurse; one for his mother and one presumably as a studio. They had many friends already in Antibes, including the Americans Gerald and Sara Murphy, with whom the Picassos were photographed (fig. 4). Visits were also made by other friends, including the Ballets Russes impresario Serge Diaghilev and the American writer and col-

**3
Olga holding
Paul, doña
María and
Pablo Picasso,
Fontainebleau,
1 September
1921**
Courtesy Archives
Olga Ruiz-Picasso,
Fundación Almine y
Bernard Ruiz-Picasso
para el Arte, Madrid

**4
Picasso (front
row centre)
and his mother
(at right), with
friends on the
beach at La
Garoupe, 1923**
Gerald and Sarah Murphy
Papers, Yale Collection
of American Literature.
Beinecke Rare Book and
Manuscript Library, Yale
University

lector Gertrude Stein and her partner, Alice B. Toklas. Stein recalled meeting doña María:

> It was once more summer and this time we went to the Côte d'Azur and joined the Picassos at Antibes. It was there I first saw Picasso's mother. Picasso looks extraordinarily like her. Gertrude Stein and Madame Picasso had difficulty in talking not having a common language but they talked enough to amuse themselves. They were talking about Picasso when Gertrude Stein first knew him. He was re-markably beautiful then, said Gertrude Stein, he was illuminated as if he wore a halo. Oh, said Madame Picasso, if you thought him beautiful then I assure you it was nothing compared to his looks when he was a boy. He was an angel

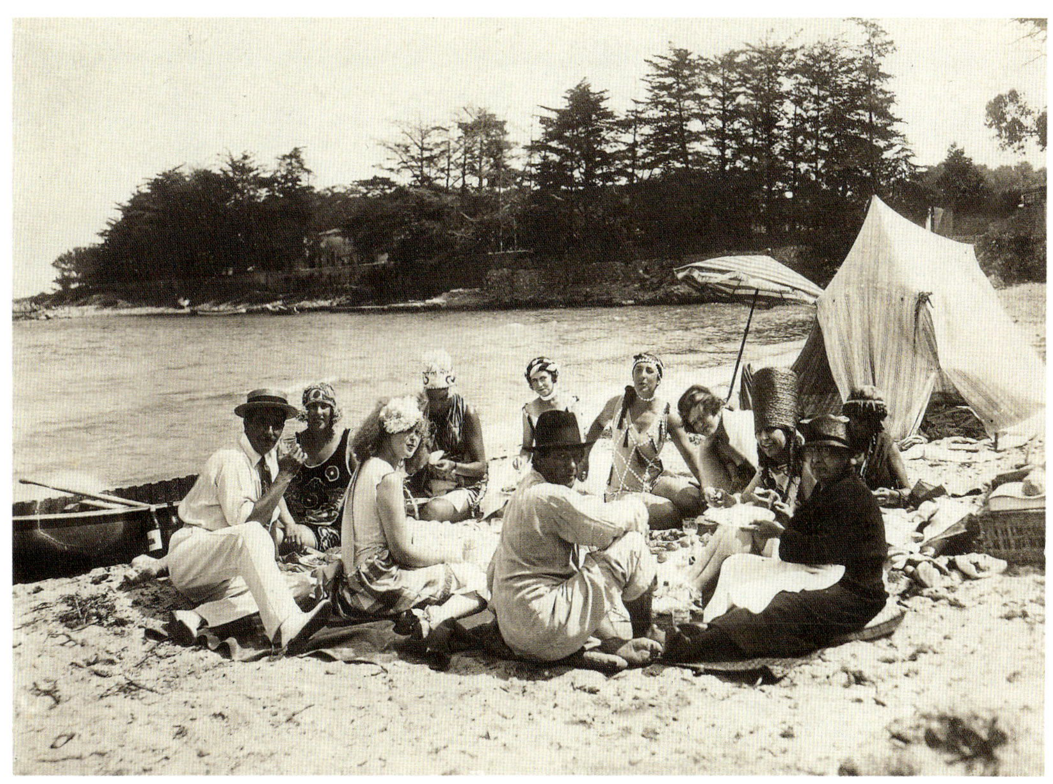

and a devil in beauty, no one could cease looking at him. And now, said Picasso a little resentfully. Ah now, said they together, ah now there is no such beauty left. But, added his mother, you are very sweet and as a son very perfect. So he had to be satisfied with that.[6]

In addition to beach expeditions to La Garoupe and get-togethers with Stein and Toklas, Picasso apparently took his mother (and probably his wife) to Monte Carlo, where he played at roulette. The story goes that he put his money on many different numbers at the same time and lost all that he had gambled.

After their stay in Antibes, doña María accompanied the Picasso family back to Paris to spend some time in their apartment on the rue la Boétie. One day she was spotted on the street by Clive Bell, an English writer who was a great fan of the artist. He remarked that he met her in the company of Olga Picasso, who was, as he remembered, 'as exquisite as ever'. Picasso's mother, on the other hand, he described as 'shorter than Olga, comic looking and very shy'.[7] The two women were apparently on a shopping trip together.

Practically all of the work Picasso did at the Hôtel du Cap was on paper, so the portrait of his mother (fig. 5) that dates from 1923 was likely carried out in his Paris studio rather than in Antibes. The painting, which is an oil on canvas, has, in certain respects, quite striking qualities of drawing. The features of his mother's face, seen in three-quarter view, are delineated as if executed in ink rather than oils. Our attention is focused on her gaze, which is directed beyond the picture space at the left, and also on her wavy hair. As in the earlier portrait (1896), her abundant hair – now grey rather than black – is piled on her head. Picasso contrasts the light seeming to emanate from around her head with the dark

5
Pablo Picasso, *Portrait of María Picasso López*, 1923

Musée Réattu, Arles, gift of Jacqueline Picasso

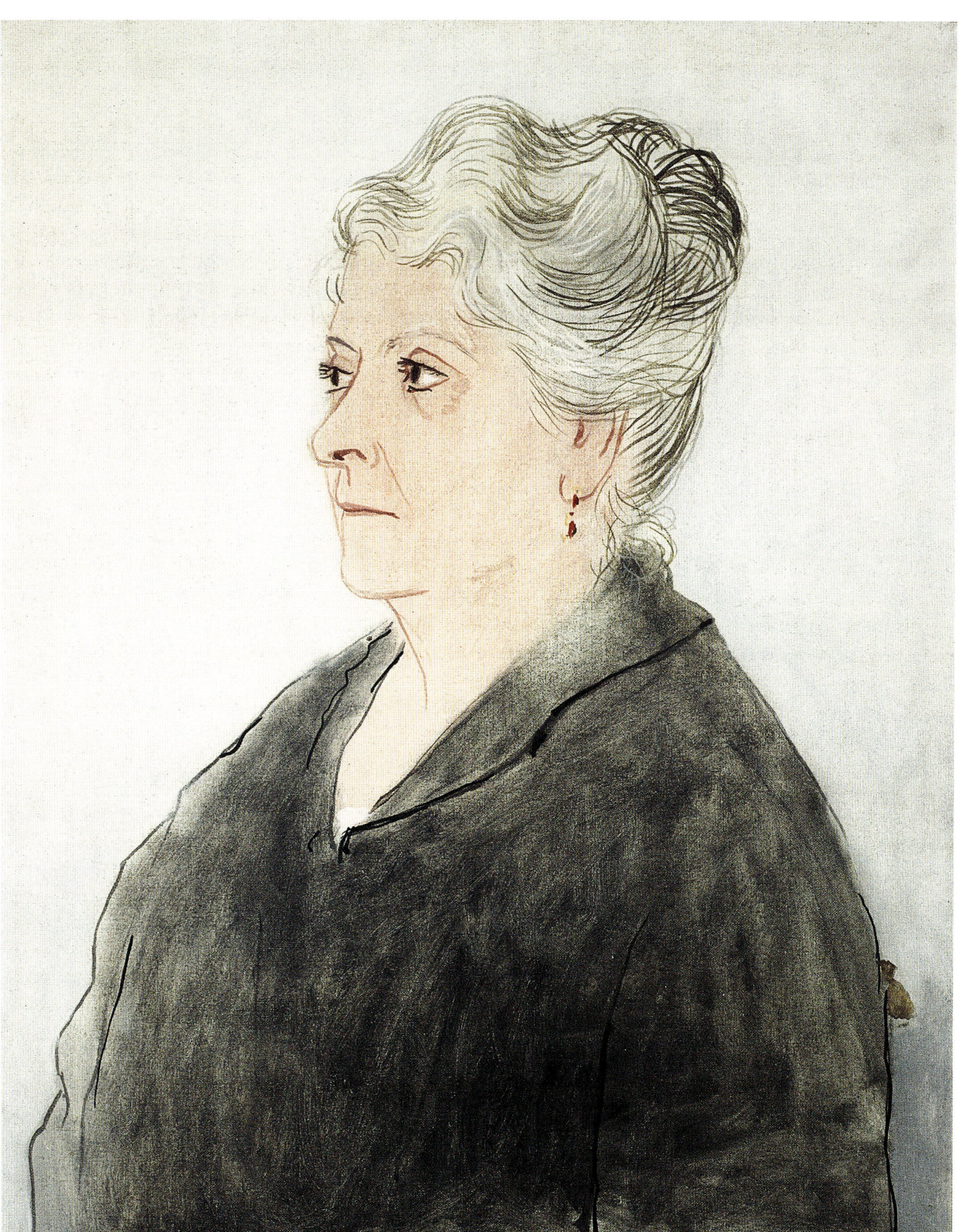

tones of her dress. There is no particular articulation of the garment apart from a collar and a touch of white below her neck, but these simple details lead the viewer back to the face of the sitter.

Three years later, Picasso arrived with his family in Barcelona in the artist's chauffeur-driven Hispano Suiza. On this occasion they had travelled from the Côte d'Azur (via Céret) to the Catalan capital and, this time, they stayed at the Ritz. Picasso's sister Lola Vilató was in the process of moving to a new apartment on the paseo de Colón, on the waterfront. All of the family moved into the spacious surroundings, including doña María, the grandchildren and, of course, his sister and her husband, Juan Bautista

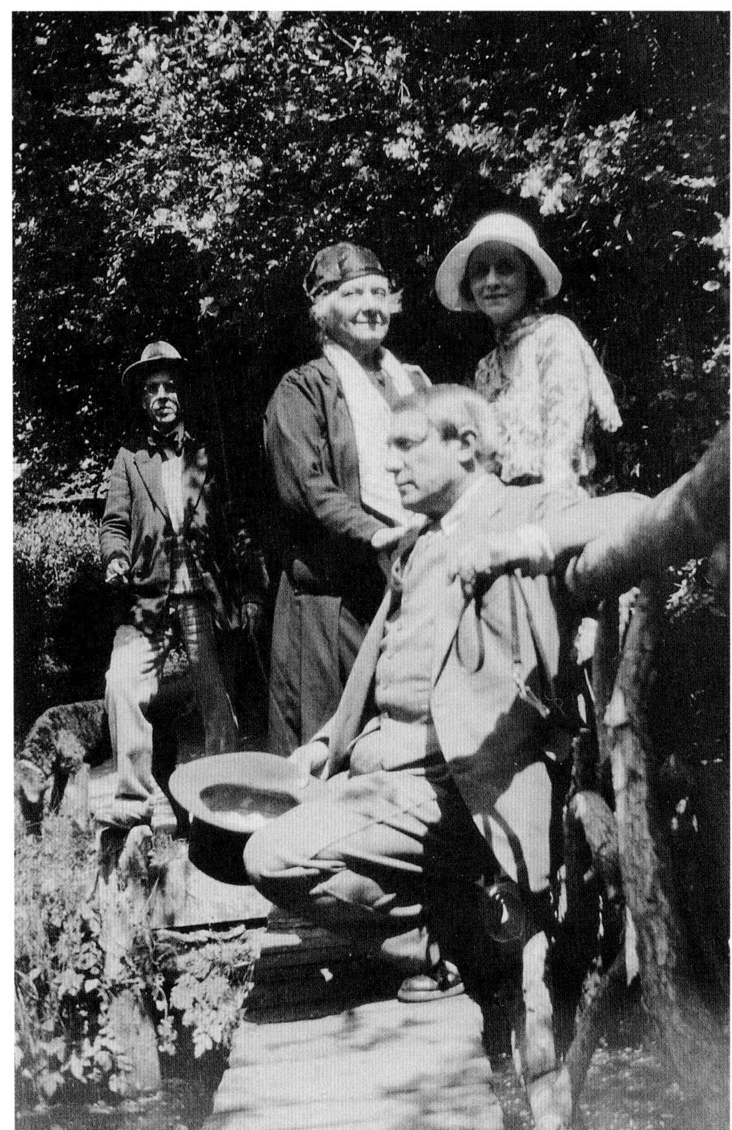

Vilató. Their son Javier was the same age as Pablo and Olga's son, Paulo, so they probably played together. As part of the move, they took all of Picasso's youthful work with them, along with the paintings he had done in Barcelona in 1917. He had been unable to ship them across the French border because of the war, so these works had stayed behind.

The fact that so many youthful works by Picasso remained in the hands of the family in Barcelona would lead to a huge scandal in 1930, in which his mother was involved. Early works began to appear on the market in France, without the knowledge of the artist or his dealers. It turned out that two unscrupulous men had gained entry to the paseo de Colón apartment, when doña María was there alone. They told her they were great friends of her son's and that they were writing a study of his early work. She allowed them to take a basket of things that had been stored in the attic. Picasso later wrote to the state prosecutor, 'Taking advantage of my mother's great age and credulity, they persuaded her to entrust them with my work … and handed over 1,500 pesetas by way of receipt.'[8] When the artist discovered what had happened, he enlisted the help of his lawyers and some plain-clothes detectives and went round various Parisian galleries in an effort to recover the stolen drawings and paintings. He managed to get back about three-quarters of the works that had been extorted. News of the raids on the galleries made headlines in the press, and the scandal was soon called 'L'affaire Picasso'. In part to suggest that it had all been a publicity stunt on the part of the artist, *Le Matin* published a letter from Picasso's mother saying: 'how could I possibly have wanted to harm the person I love the most and to whom I owe the most.'[9] As it turned out, doña María and her son-in-law, Dr Vilató, had to make trips to Paris (in 1930 and 1932) to make statements to a judge (fig. 6). The case was finally settled in Picasso's favour in 1938.

Picasso and his family made two more visits to Barcelona, in 1933 and 1934. For the first of these, they once again travelled from the Côte d'Azur in the Hispano Suiza, arriving at the end of August. Unbeknownst to his

6
Juan Bautista Vilató, doña María, Pablo (seated) and Olga Picasso, Clos Normand, Martin-Eglise, 1930
Courtesy Archives Olga Ruiz-Picasso, Fundación Almine y Bernard Ruiz-Picasso para el Arte, Madrid

wife (or to the press, who as-
siduously followed the artist
around the city), Picasso had
arranged for his mistress
Marie-Thérèse Walter to be
installed in a local hotel.
Whether or not he presented
her to his mother, we do not
know for sure. The second,
and last, visit to Barcelona took
place in the following year. The
family had decided to vacation
in the north of Spain, and they
travelled around – again in
the chauffeur-driven Hispano
Suiza – to San Sebastián,
Madrid, Toledo and other cities,
arriving in Barcelona around the
first of September. Picasso's
visit was mentioned in the
press, but he stayed for only
a few days. His feelings about

the political situation at this
time and how it might affect his
mother and the Vilató family
must have been of growing
concern.

Two years later, in 1936,
Lola Vilató moved the family for
the last time to an apartment
on the paseo de Gracia, and
she hung the walls with some of
the youthful works by Picasso
that they took with them. The
other drawings and paintings
that had been left by the artist
so many years before were
also stored in the apartment.
A Picasso exhibition was held
in Barcelona in January of that
year, organized by the group
known as ADLAN (Amics de
l'Art Nou), although no early
works from the family's collection were included. Picasso's
mother and sister and Dr Jacint
Reventós, a close friend of
the artist's from his youth in
Barcelona.

The Spanish Civil War
broke out in the summer of
1936. Picasso's mother wrote
her son several distressing
letters about what she had
witnessed first-hand:

> We are doing better in
> that the firing has
> stopped, and we only
> hear a few shots from
> time to time: but the fires
> are still burning and, as

far as I know, there are still sixteen of them, one opposite our balcony. [She goes on to describe how many nuns have been randomly killed], but the newspapers don't say anything about all of this. Some troops have left for Zaragoza, flanked by trucks and medical teams – let's see how it goes – youths in shirtsleeves, some of them in uniform, others just with military jackets, standing in the trucks and packed together against each other, just as they were after four days of intense fighting. How much blood spilt (Barcelona is in mourning)! How sad to see so much destruction! How many beautiful things destroyed by fire that have been thrown down from the balconies! I could tell you about massacres that go beyond horror, but I am afraid my letter might be read by certain persons. Who would have believed it could have come to this? A little while back I counted the fires I had seen, and there were more than sixty. Our health is good, and we think of you all the time.[10]

No matter how she longed to be with Pablo, she would never see her son again. Some thirteen days before Franco's troops entered Barcelona, doña María died, in January 1938. Although the artist did not return for her funeral, he felt her loss profoundly.

25

Lola Ruiz Picasso

Marilyn McCully

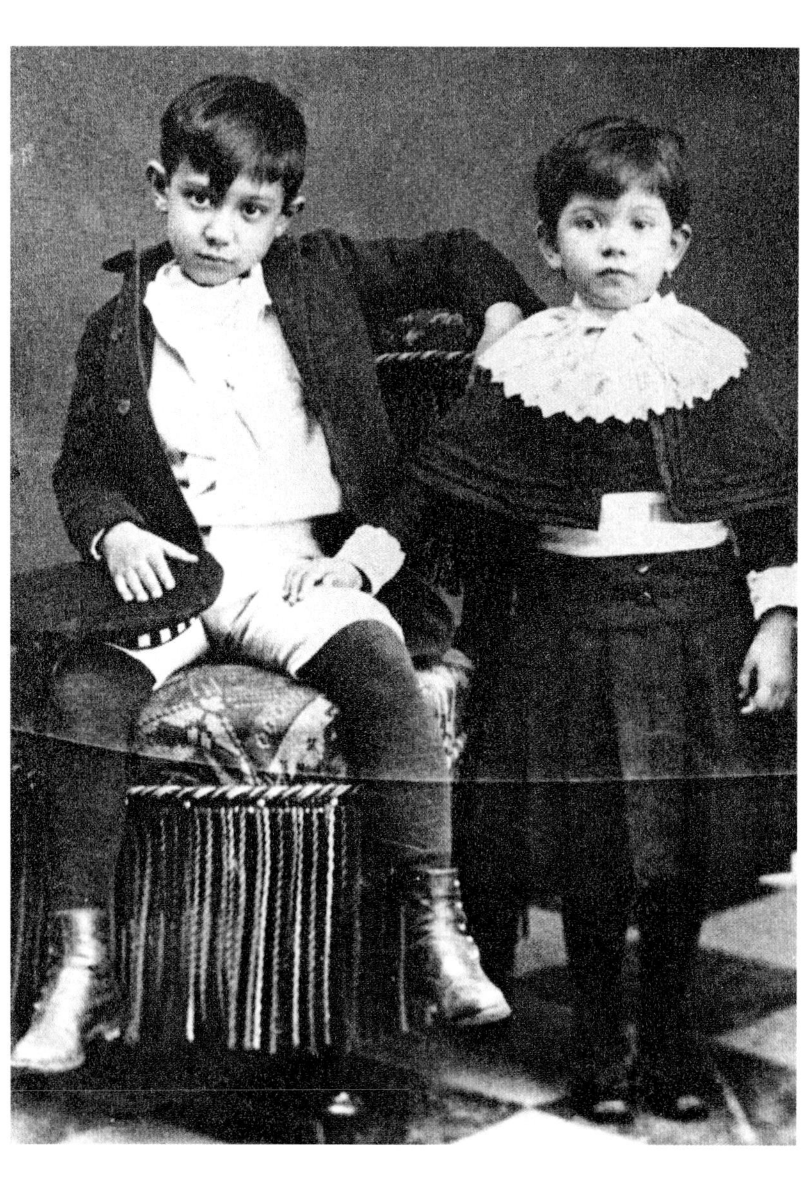

Picasso's Sister: The Little Earthquake

The arrival of a second child in the Ruiz Picasso family in December 1884 could not have been more dramatic. Málaga had suffered an earthquake on Christmas evening, and beyond the initial impact, tremors lasted for several days. Numerous people were killed or seriously injured, while many of the buildings in the town, including the cathedral and the hospital, suffered damage. When the time came for the baby to arrive, Picasso's father collected his wife and three-year-old son, Pablo, and rushed them to a safe building, where doña María gave birth to a girl. In typically Andalusian fashion, she was given a string of names: María Dolores Joaquina Juana Josefa Teodora de la Santísima Trinidad Ruiz Picasso. She would always be known simply as Lola, but the family sometimes affectionately called her 'La Terremótica' ('the little earthquake'), partly because of the circumstances of her birth, but also because of her restless and inquisitive nature.

The relationship between Lola and Pablo was very affectionate. A studio photograph (fig. 7) shows them posing together, the seven-year-old Pablo seated and four-year-old Lola standing next to him. On one copy of this photo, Picasso wrote on the back (as if he were making colour notations for a painting): 'Lola's costume, black, belt blue, collar white. Me, suit white, overcoat navy blue, beret blue.' Lola's outfit has subsequently been identified as her Sacred Heart school uniform. She attended the school, which was run by French nuns, between 1889 and 1891.

Another daughter was born in 1887, and both Pablo and Lola were happy with the presence of a new sister, who was named Josefa Aurelia Salvadora Angela Simona de la Santísima Trinidad but always known as Concha or Conchita.

Pablo Picasso at the age of seven, with his four-year-old sister Lola, c. 1888

Musée national Picasso, Paris (APPH 15359)

Unlike the older two siblings, who resembled their mother's side of the family – dark with piercing black eyes – Conchita looked more like her father: blonde, delicate and slim. When the family moved to A Coruña, in 1891, Pablo attended the art institute, where his father was a professor, and Lola and Conchita presumably attended the regular school that was housed in the same building. One of Pablo's drawings (dated 1895) shows Lola taking Conchita by the hand on their way to school. Their mother took a keen interest in their cultural education and sent them to children's theatrical performances as well as introducing them to music. School records show that in 1894 Lola was enrolled in piano classes at the Escuela de Bellas Artes. Once Pablo started what would become a lifelong habit of drawing, his first models were family members. Most of his drawings and some of his paintings were either of his father or of Lola; only a couple portray Conchita. There are a number of drawings of Lola that were done in sketchbooks, and they show her at play, sometimes with a doll, or doing embroidery or other domestic tasks.

Although Lola and Pablo were settled and happy in A Coruña, at the end of 1894 a tragedy struck the family, which would have consequences for their future. Conchita became seriously ill with diphtheria – an outbreak had occurred in the town – and her parents tried in vain to get help. Their friend doctor Ramón Pérez Costales ordered serum from abroad, but it arrived too late to save her life. Conchita died at home at the age of only seven, on 10 January 1895. The family was distraught, and her death made a lasting impact on all of them, including Pablo, who still remembered her fondly at the end of his life. When an opportunity came up for his father to leave A Coruña for a different teaching post in Catalonia, he wanted nothing more than to depart from the place that was so full of memories of grief and

8
Pablo Picasso,
***Girl Seated with a Doll (Lola with a Doll)*, 1896–97**
Fundación Almine y Bernard Ruiz-Picasso para el Arte, Madrid

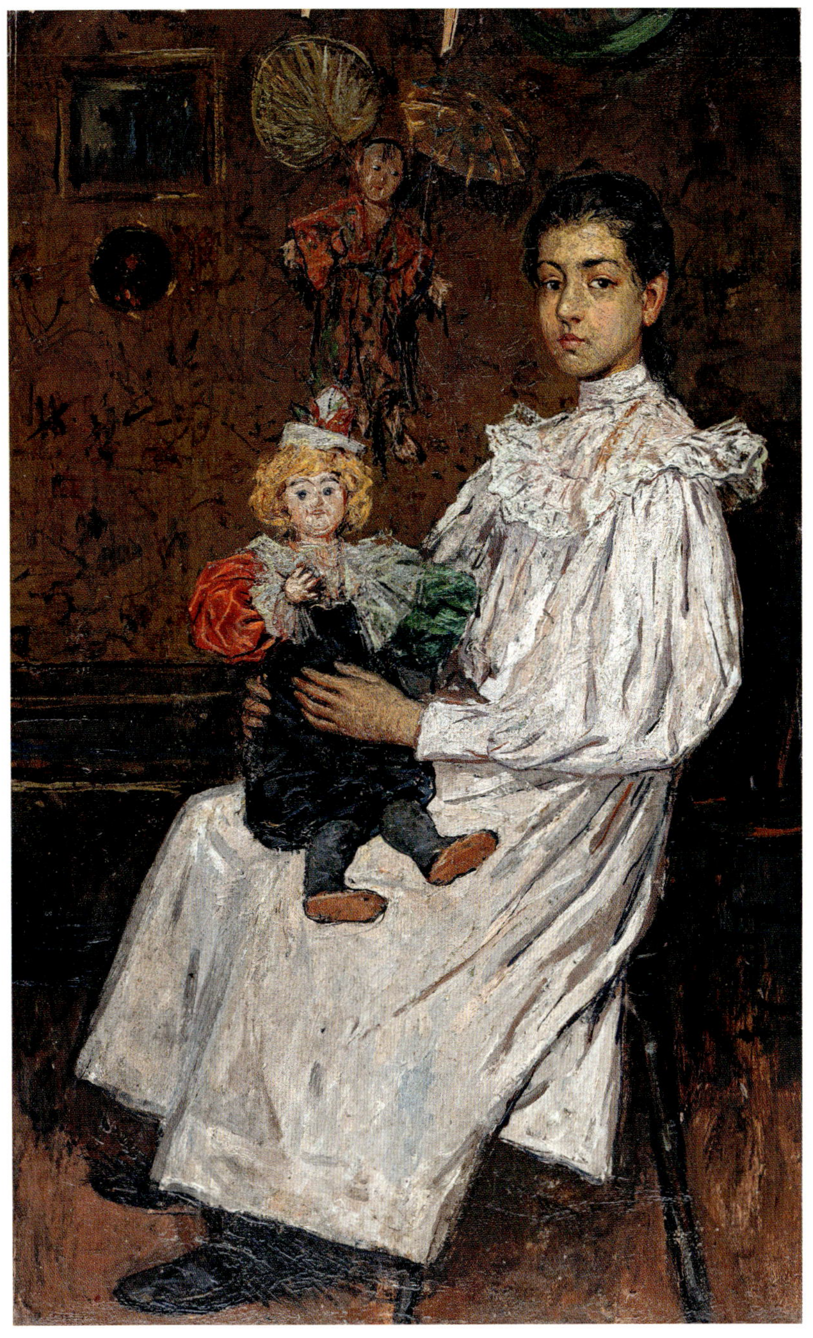

oil on a wooden panel (fig. 8), *Girl Seated with a Doll*, and was painted in Barcelona in 1896–97, most likely in the studio that his father had rented for him. Given the position of the sitter gazing directly at the viewer, it is likely that Lola posed for her brother. She wears a long white dress with a ruffled top, which contrasts with the gaily coloured outfit of the doll on her lap. Behind her, hanging on the wall is another doll, but this one is Japanese and dressed in a kimono. A large oriental fan and a parasol also hang above on the dark wall in the background. The size of the two dolls and the lavish way in which each is costumed suggests that they are rather expensive imported toys, possibly studio props. Pablo's attention both to the details of the sitter and the space around her are remarkable. Of this period of Picasso's painting, Gertrude Stein was later to write that 'He made when he was fifteen years old oil portraits of [his younger sister], very finished and painted like a born painter.'[1]

Lola sometimes modelled for some of Pablo's early set-pieces, such as *First Communion* (1896, Museu Picasso, Barcelona) – that is, compositions that were

sadness. After completing the school term, the Ruiz Picasso family made a summer visit to Málaga, followed by a permanent move to Barcelona, where don José became an art professor.

Picasso's first large-scale portrait of Lola was an

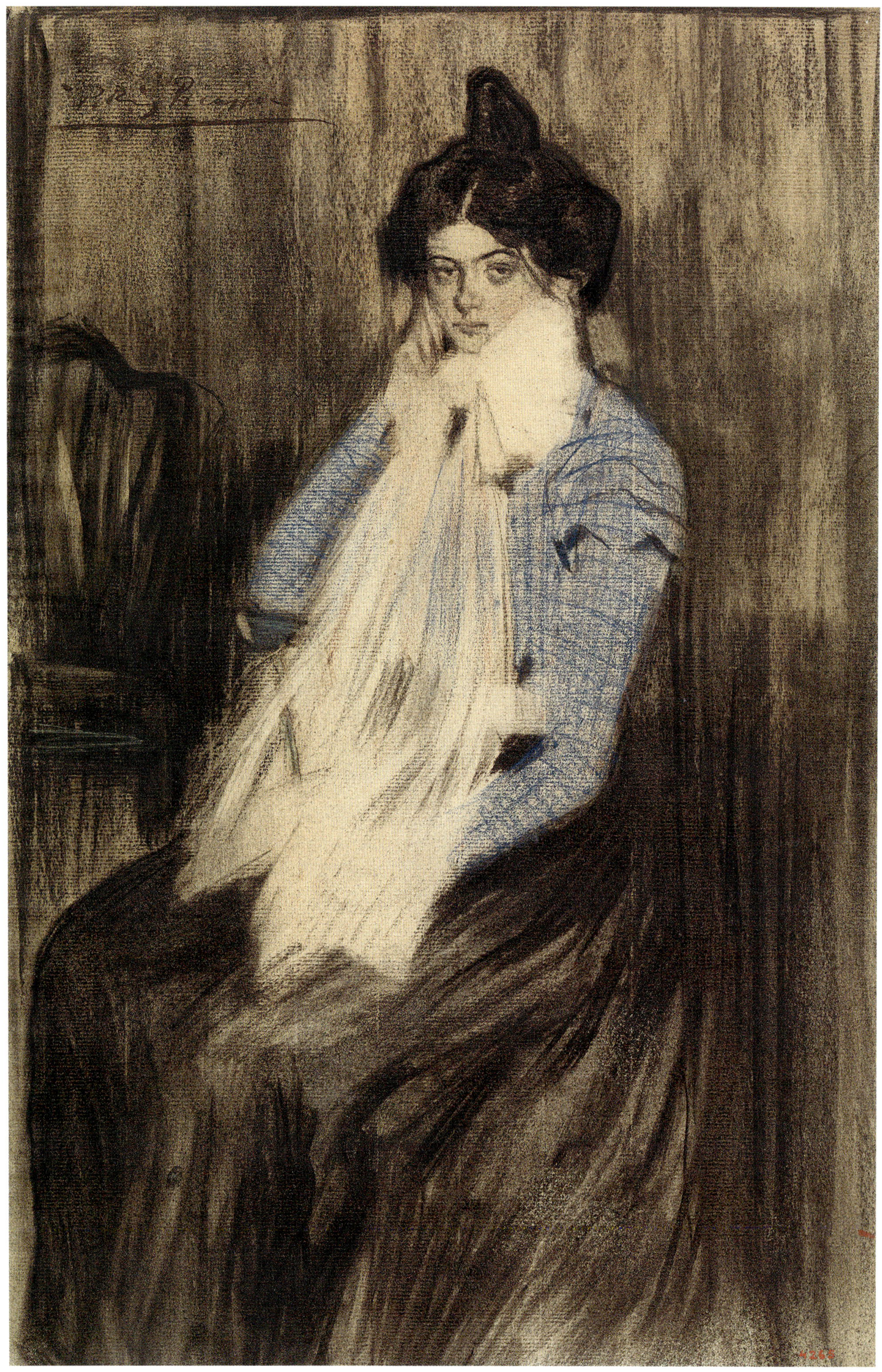

dictated by his father and intended for public exhibition. In this case, the painting was shown at the annual Exposición de Bellas Artes é Industrias Artisticas in the spring of 1896. More often than not, however, Lola sat for portraits, and these paintings and drawings reflected the artist's stylistic concerns at the end of the century. A pastel portrait, done around 1899, for example (fig. 9), reflects Picasso's interest in *modernista* graphic techniques. Repeated strokes of charcoal define the background and the skirt of the seated figure, while her voluminous scarf is left untouched, leaving the white of the paper to define the cloth. The blue pastel used for her dress provides the only colour in the composition. It is interesting to note that Lola herself made pastel and charcoal drawings around this time, and that some of them portray well-dressed young women (like herself), often wearing typical turn-of-the century attire.

Picasso's close-up oil portrait of Lola formerly in the collection of Mr and Mrs Paul Mellon is probably the last she posed for. It may have been painted in the spring of 1901, when, travelling from Madrid, he stopped in Barcelona on his way to Paris. There, he worked furiously to have enough works for his first major exhibition at Ambroise Vollard's gallery in the French capital, which opened in June. For many of the new works in the show he used the signature *Picasso* (as he did in Lola's portrait) rather than *Ruiz Picasso*. The *Picasso* signature suggests that this portrait of Lola may have been painted after the exhibition and after he returned to Barcelona early in 1902.

Once Picasso settled permanently in France (in 1904), his sister, now aged twenty, kept in touch with him by writing, but she was usually disappointed not to receive replies. In 1907, for example, she wrote in a letter addressed to his Bateau-Lavoir studio:

9
Pablo Picasso,
Lola, the Artist's
***Sister**, c. 1899*
Museu Picasso, Barcelona
(MPB 4.265)

We are shocked because it has been more than a month and a half since we have heard from you. We have written four letters without any response. If you don't answer this one, we will conclude that something has happened to you and we will have to write someone else in Paris to find out what has happened.[2]

She also wrote to her brother when, in 1908, their Uncle Salvador Ruiz Blasco was dying, and asked him to come back to accompany their father to Málaga to see him. Needless to say, Picasso, who was much too preoccupied with his work and his personal life, did not return.

Lola Ruiz Picasso met her future husband, Juan Bautista Vilató Gómez, in Barcelona, when he was working as a medical officer at the Port, and they married in August 1909. It happened that the artist was also in Spain that summer, in Horta de Sant Joan. His mother and sister both wrote him repeatedly, asking him to come for the wedding, but he was completely absorbed with the paintings that he was doing – and Fernande Olivier was also with him, and she was seriously ill. Olivier explained to Gertrude Stein in a letter that Pablo 'managed quite easily to avoid the chore of attending the ceremony.'[3] Exasperated by his unwillingness to come, his mother told him he should at least send his sister some money to cover the cost of the celebration. This he did, and his sister wrote him thanking him for the cheque, but she still urged him to be present at her marriage. Picasso and Fernande Olivier did go to Barcelona at the end of the month, and presumably the late visit to his sister and her new husband, as well as to his parents, went some way to make up for his absence at the wedding.

In the following year, the Vilatós' first child was born, and in the autumn they moved

10
The Artist's Sister Lola, 1899–1900
The Cleveland Museum of Art, gift of Mr. and Mrs. David S. Ingalls (1966.377)

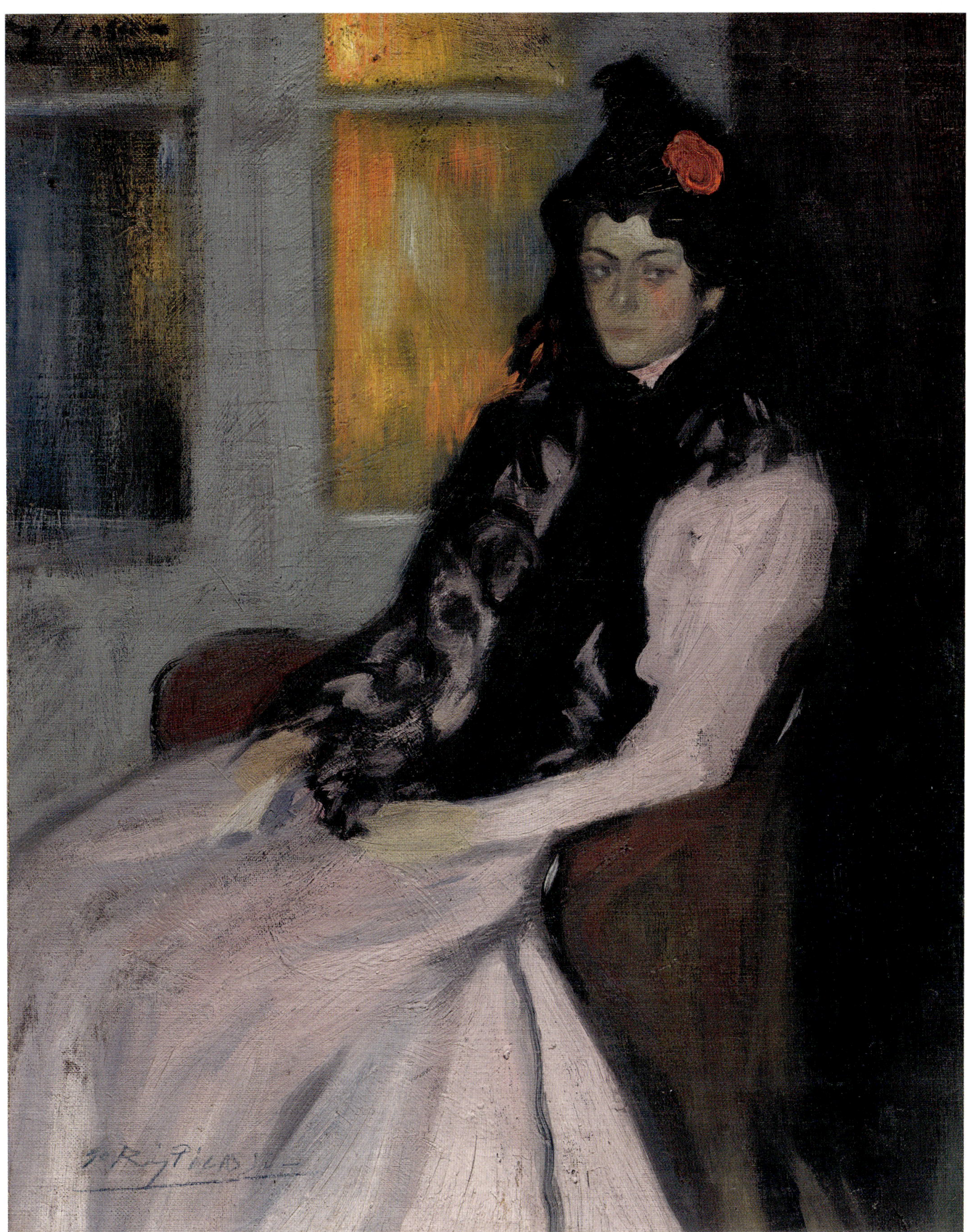

with their baby to Menorca, where Dr Vilató had been offered a post on the island. They would remain there until 1913, when Lola's father became ill and died. Shortly afterwards, they came back to Barcelona and moved in with doña María in the family apartment on the calle de la Merced. The couple would have six more children (a daughter born in 1920 died in infancy), and while Lola Vilató took on some of the responsibilities of domestic life, her mother was principally in charge.

Javier Vilató (b. 1921) recalled that his mother, unlike his grandmother, was happy living in Barcelona, although neither of them learned to speak Catalan. He said that his mother had been well educated and liked to draw, but she was not a reader like her own mother. She also had a circle of friends outside the family. At home, however, it seems the family lived more like Andalusians than Catalans (even though Juan Bautista Vilató was Catalan). Their son said that they were like a gypsy tribe and all of them were very close. 'At home we always spoke Spanish, and we had traditional Andalusian meals, including ajo blanco and gazpacho, although everything was always combined with Catalan culture.'[4]

When Picasso visited Barcelona in 1917, he stayed with the family on the calle de la Merced. He, his mother and sister, with two of her children, were photographed by Dr Vilató on the rooftop (fig. 12). It was on this occasion that the artist presented Olga Khokhlova to his family and told his mother that they intended to marry. His Russian fiancée stayed in the Pension Ranzini on the paseo de Colón, and Picasso spent most of his time either with her there or visiting old friends. Even though Khokhlova had decided to give up dancing, she had visa problems, so they stayed in Barcelona through the autumn. Picasso continued

11
Lola Ruiz Picasso at the age of nineteen, c. 1904
Private collection, Paris

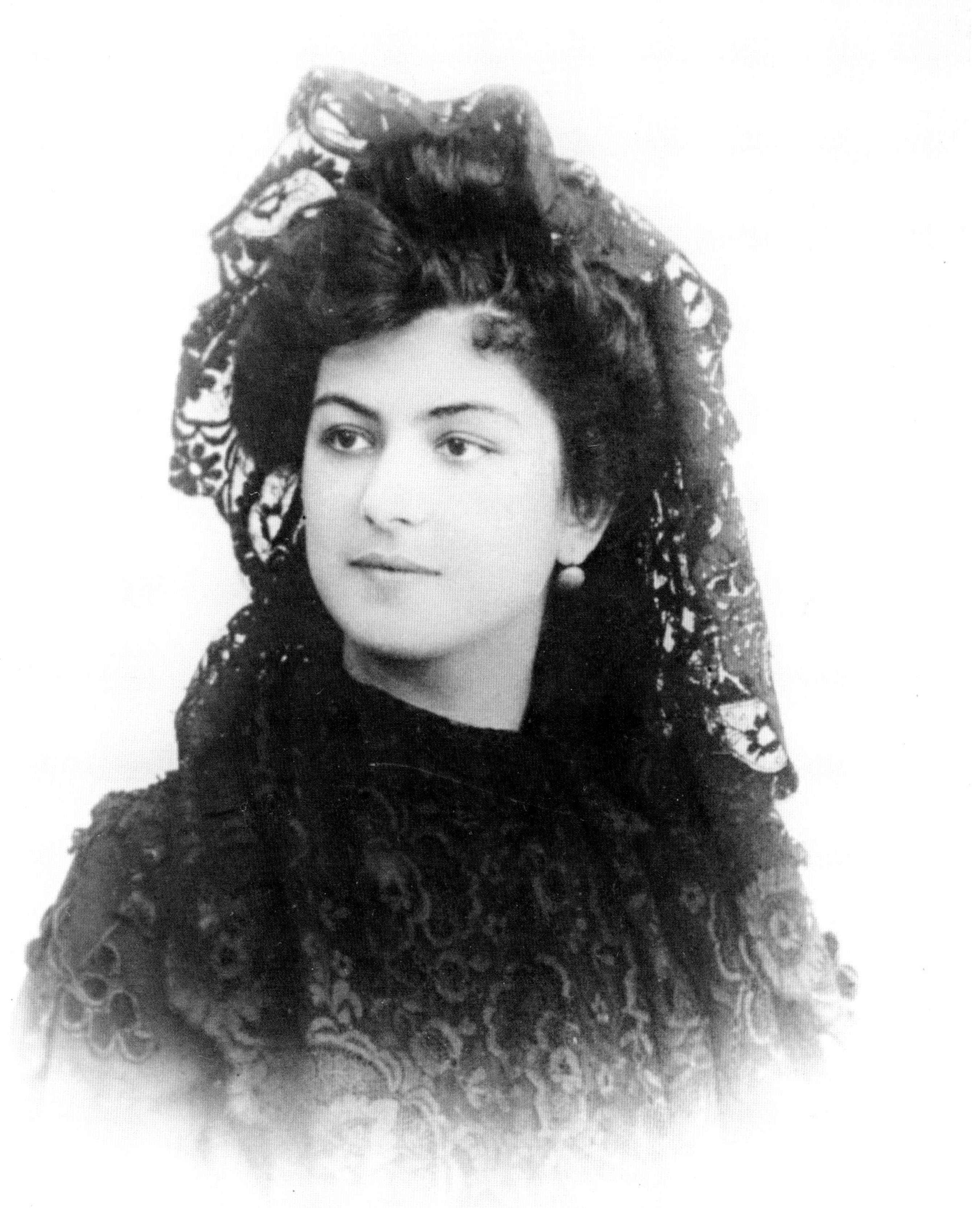

to paint, and the couple were also in touch with members of the Ballets Russes, when the company (with whom Khokhlova had formerly been a dancer) came to Barcelona for a season at the Liceo theatre. On 10 November, *Parade* was premiered, with sets and costumes by Picasso. At the performance, the Vilatós introduced Picasso to a young friend of theirs, who turned out to be Joan Miró. The young painter was apparently disappointed that the older artist did not ask to see his work.

Before Picasso and his fiancée left Barcelona, he discovered that he was unable to send back the paintings he had done during the previous months. He explained to Gertrude Stein that he had to leave everything behind. 'I

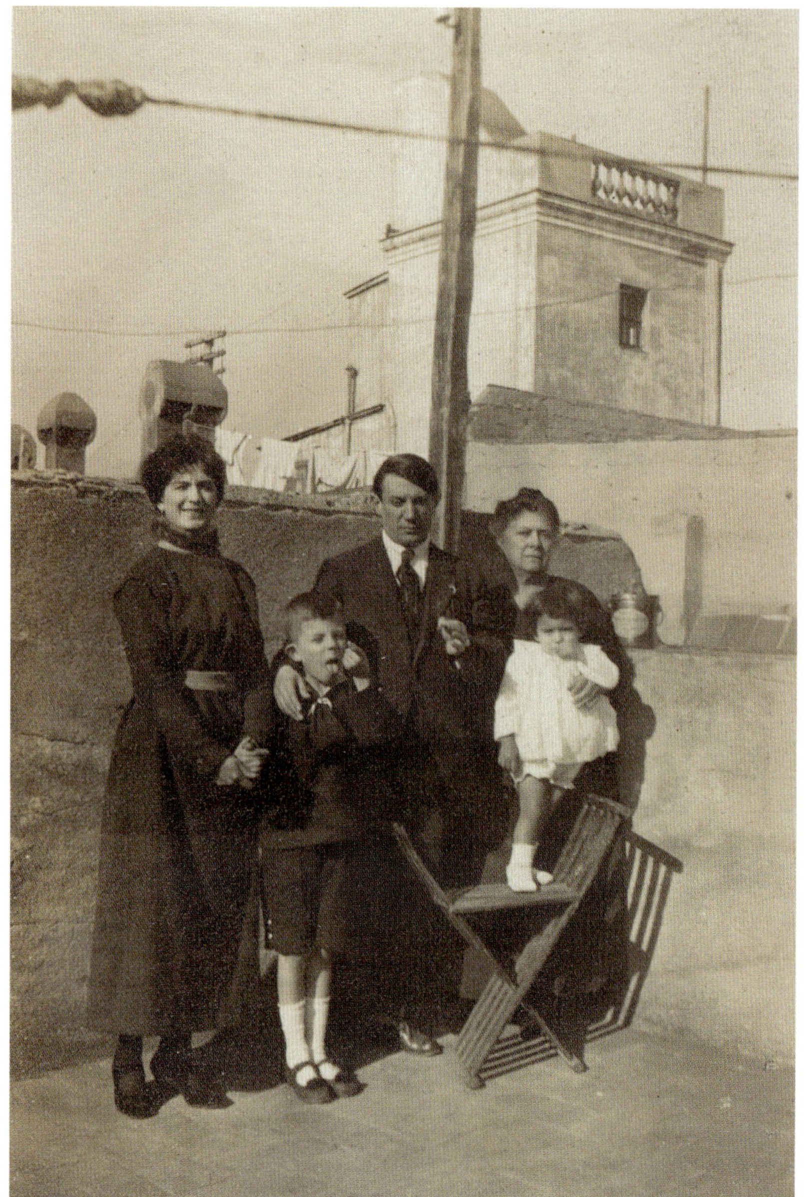

didn't work badly in Spain, but I wasn't allowed to bring my paintings, which [during wartime] were considered as luxury objects.'[5] These works, many of them oils on canvas, some of them done on a large-scale, included still life paintings, a view of the port, and portraits of entertainers. Without the necessary papers to send them across the border to France, he had to leave them with the family to be stored (along with works from his youth) in the apartment on the calle de la Merced. It would be his sister's responsibility to look after them, and she took all of the works that she had stored with her when they moved in 1926 to the paseo de Colón.

On a visit to Barcelona with his wife and son in the late summer of 1933, Picasso introduced his sister to his French mistress, Marie-Thérèse Walter, whom he had installed in a local hotel (presumably without the knowledge of his wife). According to Marie-Thérèse Walter's grandson, the secret visit was made partly so that the artist could show her the works of his youth, but the private nature of the meeting also reflects the continuing confidence that he and his sister shared in each other.

Apart from a group of drawings that were unlawfully acquired from Picasso's mother when she was alone in the apartment in 1930, the rest of his drawings and paintings remained with his sister, and many of them would adorn the walls of the apartment on the

paseo de Gracia, where the family finally moved in 1936, not long before the death of their mother, in 1938. The Vilatós would survive the Spanish Civil War, although two of their sons (Fin and Javier) fought for the Republicans and had to leave Spain and seek refuge in France, where they were helped by their Uncle Pablo. He and his sister, however, would not see each other again (his last visit to Barcelona had been in 1934). Dr Vilató died in 1947, and his widow remained in the paseo de Gracia apartment with several of her children.

When in 1954 the Austrian photographer Inge Morath was asked to photograph doña Lola for the French art magazine *L'Œil*, she took on the assignment with great pleasure. This

12
Lola and Juan Vilató, Pablo Picasso, doña María and Fin Vilató, 1917
Musée national Picasso, Paris (APPH 6049)

would be the first time that Picasso's sister had agreed to pose in the apartment. Morath remembered that in her 'shaky Spanish' she telephoned and whoever answered said, 'Come at midnight.' After spending a nervous evening, unable to eat, Morath arrived. She recalled that the apartment was large and dark, and she was met by Picasso's nephews Pablo and Jaime along with their sister Lolita Vilató. Together:

> They carefully escorted in their mother. Lola Ruiz Vilató had been crippled for many years by an attack of Maltese fever [which she had contracted during the Civil War]. Her body was weak from disuse, but

she had a proud head, with features resembling those of Tío Pablo. … They seated her in a chair in the corner of a small salon adjacent to the corridor which was dominated by Picasso's huge painting of a First Communion in which Lola posed as a little girl for her brother.[6]

'I didn't want to pose,' she said, 'but he insisted. In the painting, those are not my clothes; we borrowed a first communion dress from a friend.'[7] She went on to point out that her father served as the model for the doctor in another painting, *Science and Charity*, which could just be made out in the semi-darkness of the apartment. Lolita Vilató added that a portrait drawing Picasso made of his father, José Ruiz Blasco, could be found hanging on the wall in her bedroom. So that the photographer could see everything, Picasso's sister insisted that her children take Morath for a tour of the apartment, so that she could photograph some of the many works by Picasso that they had displayed. All of the works in her home would eventually be given by Picasso to the Museu Picasso, Barcelona.

13
Lola Vilató
photographed
by Inge Morath,
Barcelona, 1954

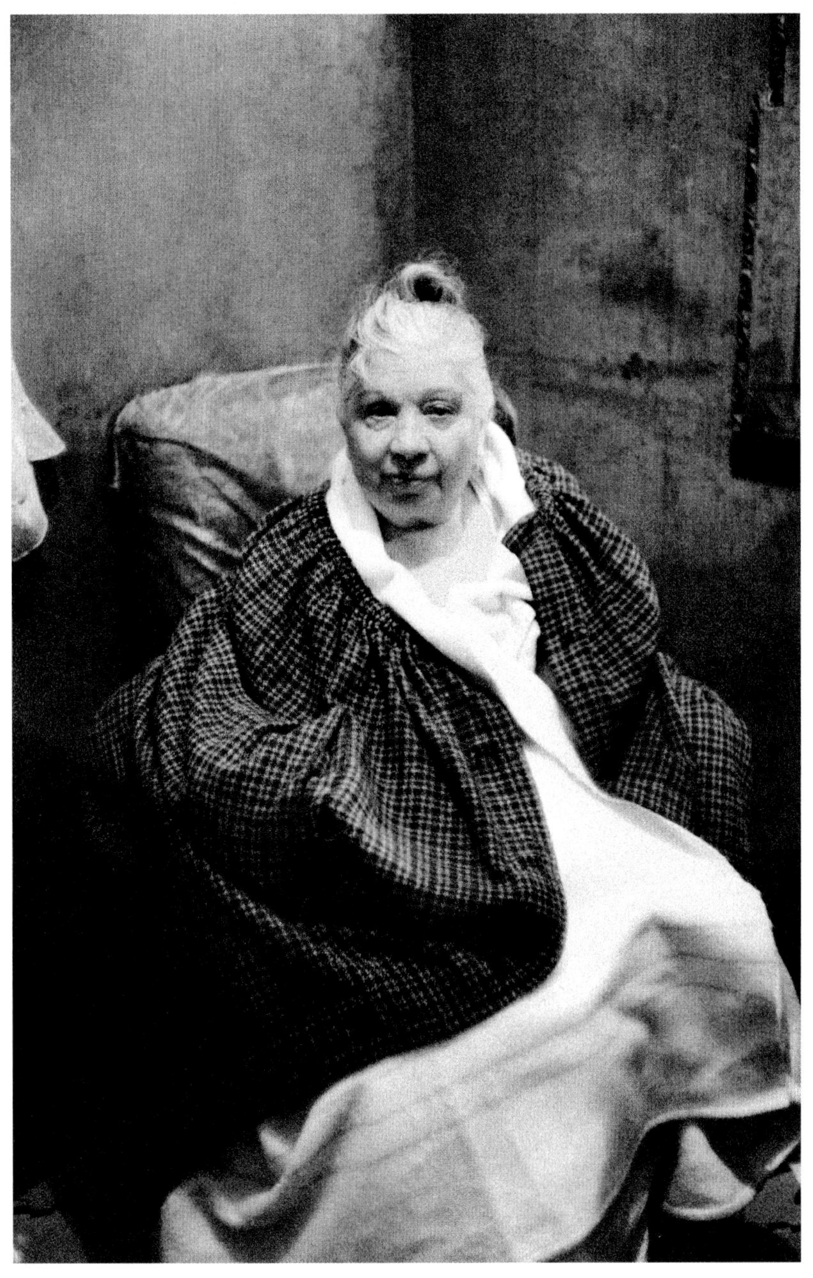

I got up my courage to ask for a shawl or cloth to cover her thin shoulders. We all scurried around, one of us finally taking a curtain from the kitchen window and draping it around Doña Lola. Then she said, 'And now, how do you want me to look?' I said, 'As you would look at Pablo.' And she did, with a solemn gaze, sitting very erect. (fig. 13)[8]

Morath goes on to relate that Lolita Vilató played the piano and danced flamenco, while one of her brothers played the guitar:

> Doña Lola obviously loved the night. As time passed she started to feel more at ease and

Picasso's sister Lola died in 1958, four years after this memorable visit.

Fernande Olivier

Marilyn McCully

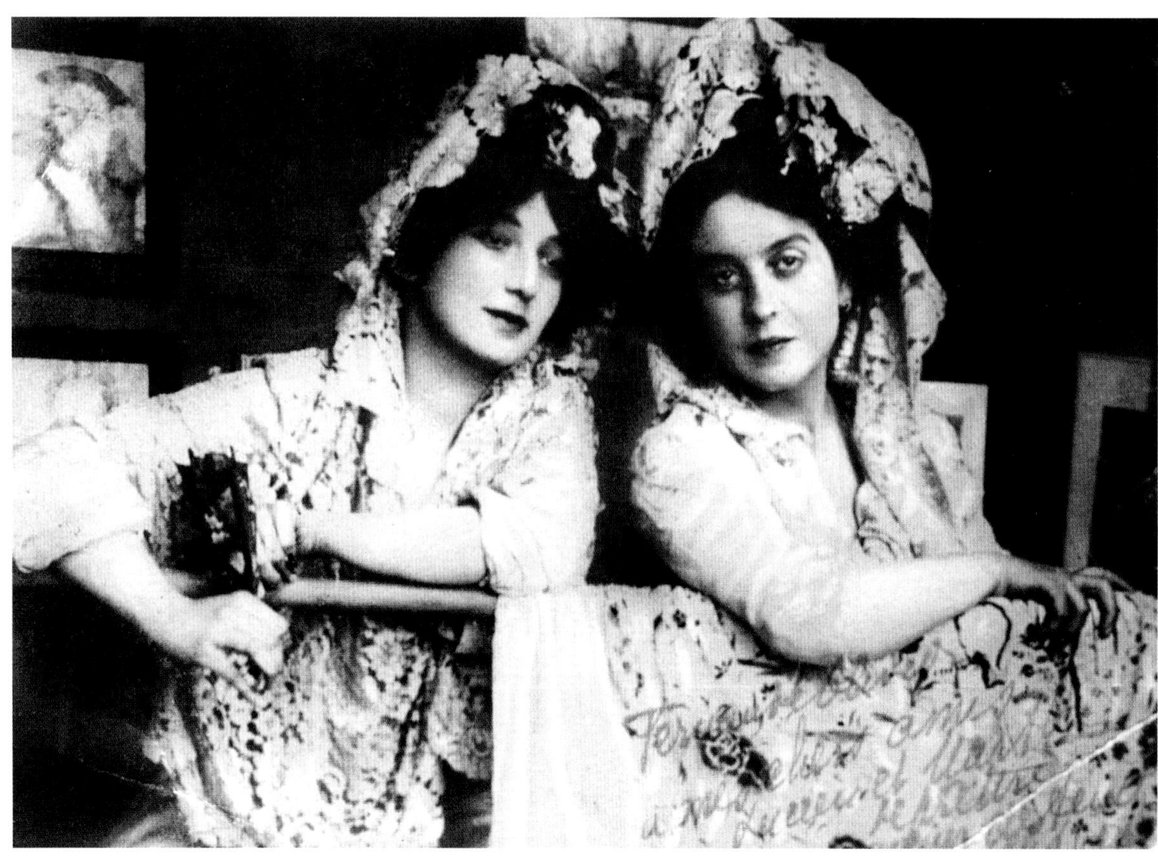

Artist's Model, Muse and Chronicler

The journal that Fernande Olivier kept for many years, posthumously published as *Souvenirs intimes* in 1988,[1] includes the story of her life before she met Pablo Picasso as well as that in the years they spent together. Her lively account of her youth reads at times like a novelette, but many details, including citations of specific names and events, confirm her story to be essentially authentic. Her real name was Amélie Lang, and she was the illegitimate daughter of a certain Clara Lang, who signed an act of recognition after the child's birth, in 1881, but her father's identity is something of a mystery. He was probably called Bellevallée, a surname that she later, on occasion, adopted. The girl was raised by an aunt (thought to be the half-sister of her father), who resented and mistreated her, and an uncle who was a *fleuriste* (manufacturer of feather and flower ornaments) on the rue Réaumur in Paris.

Although melodramatic in tone, Fernande Olivier's record of her life (as Amélie) before she met Picasso provides a startlingly frank and close look at the experiences of a young woman making her way in Paris in the late nineteenth to early twentieth century. As a teenager she worked happily for a time as an accountant in her uncle's shop, but home life with her dominating aunt was without love or emotional support. When she was eighteen, she was forced by her aunt into marriage to a man who raped and beat her. After a miscarriage and repeated beatings, she ran away in April 1900, never to see her husband again. It was at this time that she changed her name from Amélie Lang to Fernande Olivier.

Fernande Olivier

In her journal, she reveals that soon after her flight from the abusive marriage, she moved in with a sculptor whom she calls Laurent Debienne (Gaston de Labaume), and, in order to support herself, became an artist's model. She was confident in her chosen profession, at which she apparently excelled for her patience and ability to sit for long periods of time. Her descriptions in her journals of the different studios in which she worked and the demands of the painters and sculptors whom she encountered provide a valuable view of the world of artists, models and patrons at this period. After a few months in Montparnasse, she and Debienne moved to Montmartre, where they settled into the warren of studios known as the Bateau-Lavoir. In addition to sitting for Debienne

(which was how she paid her part of their living costs), Fernande Olivier found work as a model for the painters who lived on the nearby boulevard de Clichy, for examination students at the Ecole des Beaux-Arts, and also for academicians, including the artist Fernand Cormon, who took an interest in her future. He introduced her to the sculptor François Sicard, for whom she posed for several studies and maquettes, notably a series for a statue designed for a port in Algeria, which depicted a woman, easily recognizable as Olivier, in peasant dress with her arms outstretched, holding a large raffia basket (fig. 15). Cormon also gave her some fatherly advice: 'Marry a young man who's rich. Think of your future. Don't let yourself get sucked into this Bohemia.' Nonetheless, she ignored his warnings: within a short period of time, through her many friendships and especially her relationship with Picasso, she would soon establish her own identity as 'la belle Fernande' at the heart of an emerging avant-garde.

In 1904 she left Debienne and moved into a neighbouring studio in the Bateau-Lavoir, which was occupied by her friend and fellow model

15
Algerian Woman with a Basket of Fruits. In 1905 Fernande Olivier posed as the model for this figure for François Sicard's monument to Jérôme Bertagna at the port of Bône (now Annaba) in Algeria.

Musée des Beaux Arts, Tours

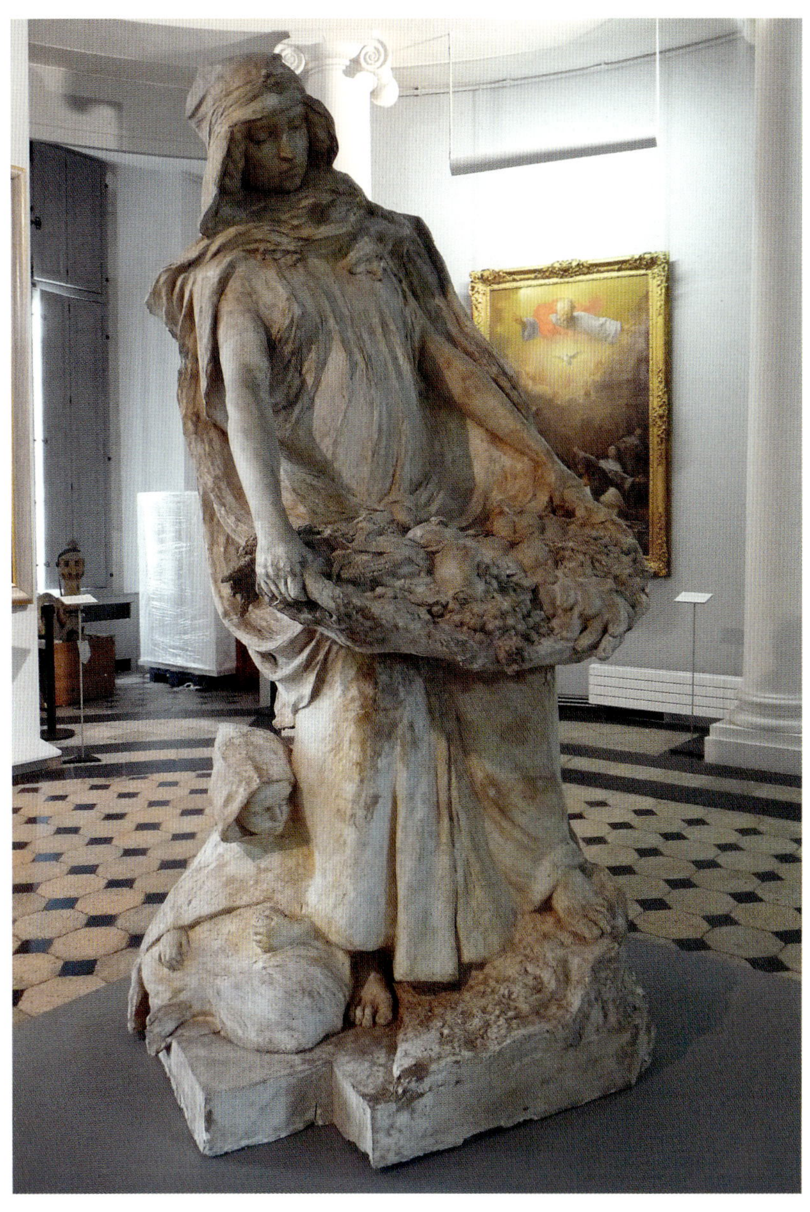

Benedetta Bianco, who lived there with the Catalan artist Ricard Canals. The Italian had famously posed for Edgar Degas, whom she introduced to Olivier, who in turn noted in her journal that she wouldn't be his type as a model and that he was 'a strange old man'. The two women did pose together for Canals as Spanish *majas* at a bullfight, which he recorded both in a photograph (fig. 14) and in a painting that he sold to a Catalan banker who lived in Paris. Among the mostly Spanish artists who regularly met up in the Canals studio was another Catalan, the painter Joaquim Sunyer, for whom the two friends again modelled together.

Although Sunyer became Fernande Olivier's lover, it was Picasso, who also lived in the Bateau-Lavoir, who pursued her most fiercely. She describes her first visit to his studio, in the summer of 1904: '[It] is full of large unfinished canvases – he must work so hard, but what a mess! Dear God! His paintings are astonishing. I find something morbid in them, which is quite disturbing, but I also feel drawn to them.' Over the ensuing months Picasso repeatedly asked her to move in with him, but it would not be until the

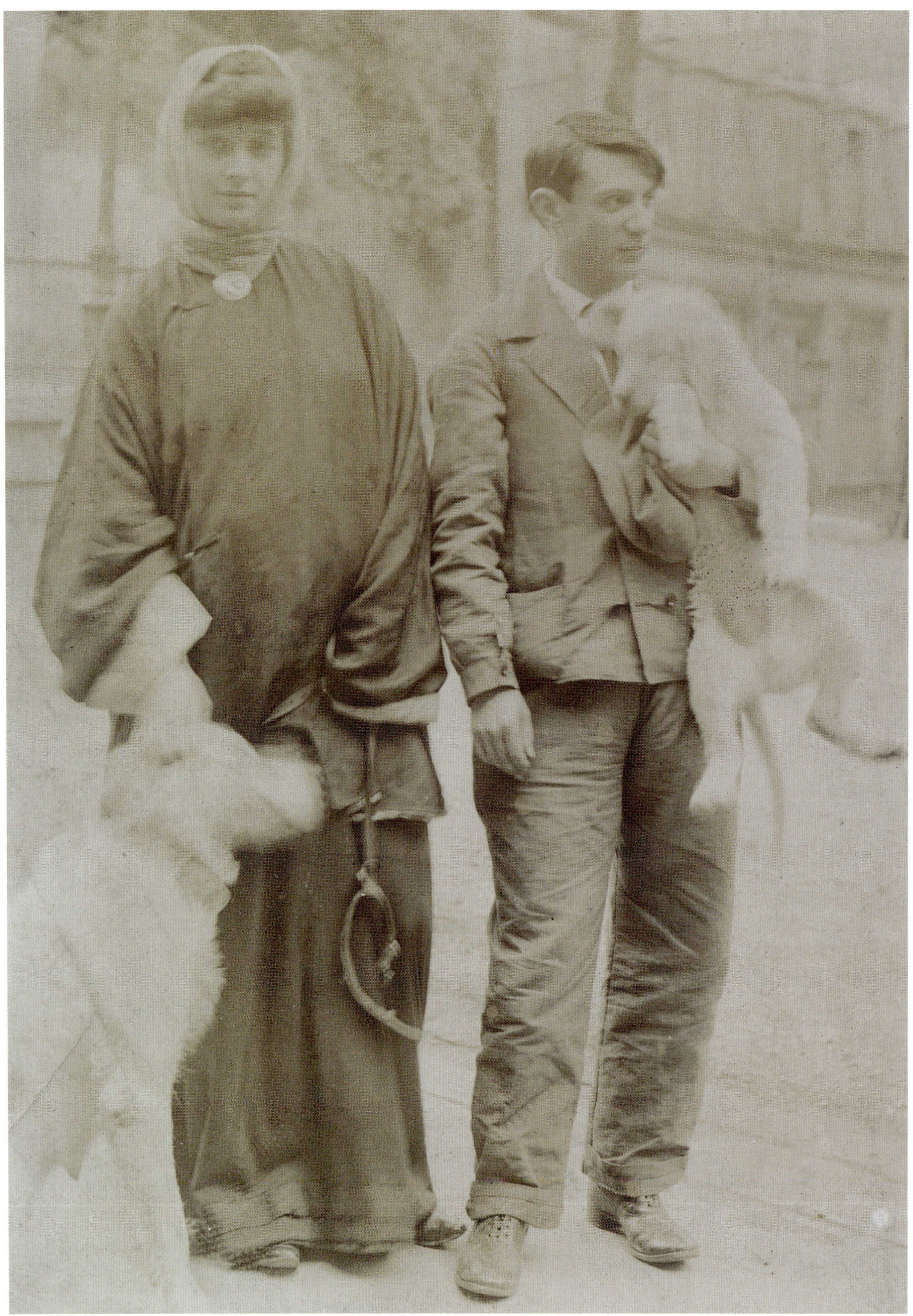

following year that they began to share their lives – though not as man and wife, as Picasso would have liked, since she was still married (fig. 16).

Fernande Olivier's role in the so-called *bande à Picasso* – the group of writers, artists and models who frequently met up in the artist's Bateau-Lavoir studio – would be, like a wife, a stable and supportive influence. Once she moved in, Picasso insisted that she give up modelling for other artists, including Sicard, who complained that he had not yet finished his Algerian monument. Although she did not often actually pose for Picasso, she recounts that he made portrait drawings of her as she slept. Apart from a little housekeeping and cooking, she occupied herself by doing some of her own painting – one of her portraits was mistaken by a collector to be by Picasso himself – and she liked to read. This allowed her to establish friendships with a number of the regulars, including the poets Max Jacob and Guillaume Apollinaire, who dropped by the studio almost on a daily basis. She remembered that Picasso, who became totally preoccupied when he was working, could unwind in their company: 'He was lucky to have friends who were so different from him,' she said. One thing they shared, she goes on to remark, was a sharp brand of cruelty in their humour.

Olivier reports that Picasso was obsessively jealous towards her, which sometimes led to arguments. He essentially forbade her to wander around Montmartre without him, especially if she dared go to neighbourhood bars or cafés, and he took to doing the food shopping himself so that she could prepare their meals in the studio. They did, however, like to go to open-air markets together on Sunday mornings, where they found items of clothing as well as assorted objects and furniture. The bric-a-brac that they accumulated would come in handy when the artist later began to make assemblages and collages. She observed that Picasso especially enjoyed the working-

16
**Fernande Olivier
and Picasso
in Montmartre
with their dogs,
Frika and Gat,
1906**
Musée national Picasso,
Paris, Picasso archives

class 'hubbub' of the market, since it again took him away from the isolation and intensity of his creative life.

In her memoirs, Fernande Olivier not only provides lively portrait sketches of the different people who came to the Bateau-Lavoir, including dealers and other prospective buyers of Picasso's work; she also made important comments about his artistic practice. The value of her observations lies in their detail, and from them we can date works in progress as well as get a good idea about how Picasso used his materials and how he proceeded to work either on canvas or paper. On her first visit to his studio, in 1904, for example, she described the apparent chaos, with 'a wicker chair, some easels, canvases of every size, tubes of paint scattered all over the floor, paintbrushes, containers with turpentine [and] a bath of etching acid.' The latter was used for Picasso's first major etching known as *The Frugal Repast*, whose principal figures (an emaciated man and woman) impressed her when she saw it for their 'intense feeling of misery and alcoholism [realized] with terrifying realism'.

Once she was installed in the Bateau-Lavoir studio in 1905, Olivier remarked that the paintings Picasso was doing were quite different from the previous year, and that he was actually painting over many of his earlier canvases. The practice of covering over existing compositions, especially those he had executed during the Blue period (late 1901–early 1904), has been the subject of much recent technical analysis and interpretation by conservators and art historians alike. She also remarks that Picasso sometimes hired models, including on one occasion, a street urchin who was infested with fleas. Olivier intervened and washed the girl but refused to let her return, unless she was clean. 'Pablo's Joan of Arc [for which the girl was supposed to pose] never got any further.'

The dealer Ambrose Vollard, who had given Picasso his first major Paris show in 1901, came to the studio in 1906 and bought some twenty paintings for 2,000 francs. This windfall allowed the couple to travel to Catalonia for the summer, where they first stopped in Barcelona so that Picasso could introduce his companion to his family and close friends. 'Pablo is quite different in Spain,' she remembered, 'he's more cheerful, not so wild, more sparkling and animated … he glows with happiness, so unlike the kind of person he is in Paris.' The sense of euphoria that she describes is reflected in the memorable images of Fernande Olivier that the artist did in Gósol, the Pyrenean village where they stayed until the end of the summer. In these works, Picasso celebrated her beauty and focused on her abundant red hair, almond-shaped eyes and curvaceous body (fig. 17). She may have only posed for a few of them, if she did at all, but it was her close presence that inspired them. Picasso typically absorbed the features of those nearest to him, especially his women, when he referred to them in his work. According to her, they were happy in Gósol, so far away from the jealousies and anxieties of Paris, and nothing 'cast a shadow on [their] relationship'. They were sorry to have to leave abruptly, after there was an outbreak of typhoid in the village.

The relationship between Picasso and Olivier became less harmonious once they were back in Paris, and this led to a separation in the late summer of 1907. The fact that she does not discuss in her journals the artist's work during this period, notably his celebrated painting *Les Demoiselles d'Avignon*, suggests that the tensions that caused the temporary break-up had completely distracted her. She found a place to live not far from the Bateau-Lavoir, and even contemplated a reconciliation with her aunt, but when she

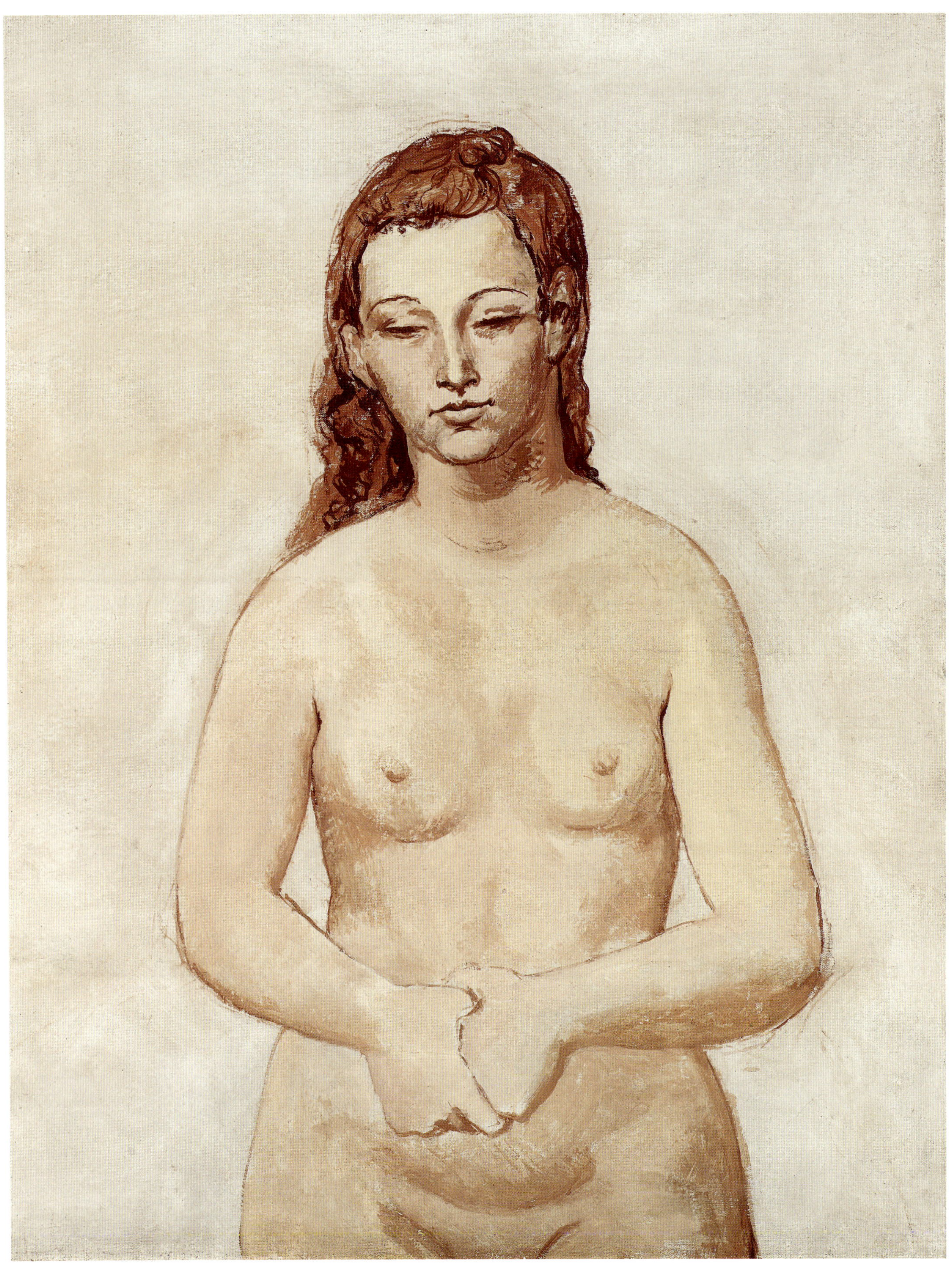

learned that her uncle had died two years earlier, she decided against resuming contact. It was at this time that she began, if only briefly, to sign her letters Fernande Belvalet or Belvallé.

The couple's separation did not last, and she moved back in with Picasso during the winter of 1907–08. Their circle of friends widened to include other artists and writers, and they began to go to parties, especially in the homes of both Guillaume Apollinaire and Max Jacob. For a different type of amusement, Picasso even took up boxing with the painters André Derain and Georges Braque. With time, however, Olivier remembered that 'Picasso's group seemed to grow more subdued, and as the intervals between the bouts of wild socializing grew longer, our existence became more and more reclusive. Work was the only thing that really mattered'. Nevertheless, there were occasionally some dramas in the Bateau-Lavoir that upset the rhythms of their daily lives. On one evening a neighbour, a young German painter called Karl-Heinz Wiegels, committed suicide after taking opium, hashish and ether. 'The studio where he had died became a place of terror for us, and the poor man appeared to us everywhere, hanging as he had been the last time we ever saw him.'

Wiegels's tragic suicide in 1908 left Picasso in a state of nervous depression, unable to work. As a result, Olivier took it upon herself to find a place outside Paris in the countryside, where they could spend what she hoped would be an idyllic summer. La Rue des Bois, the small village where they stayed on a farm, was located on the edge of the Forest of Halatte and not far from the Oise river. She knew the area well from her childhood, when she used to spend holidays with relatives not far away in Méru. A succession of friends came to stay, including the Dutch writer Fritz Vanderpyl and his girlfriend, Amélie; Derain and his wife, Alice; in addition to Apollinaire and Max Jacob. When the summer was

17
Pablo Picasso,
Nude with Clasped Hands (Fernande),
Gósol, 1906
Art Gallery of Ontario, Toronto, gift of Sam and Ayala Zacks, 1970

49

Fernande Olivier

over, Fernande Olivier wanted to rent a large house in the area, where they could remain over the coming months, but she was unable to convince Picasso. 'He wasn't prepared to settle down in this remote corner. It was too damp and green, and too far from Paris.'

Among her closest friends during this period were Gertrude Stein and her partner, Alice Toklas, to whom she gave French lessons. She had got to know Stein well when the writer posed for Picasso's celebrated portrait of her in the spring of 1906 (fig. 23), which Picasso would famously finish after he and Olivier had returned from Gósol. The letters that she wrote Stein and Toklas from Horta de Ebro during the summer of 1909 would represent a first attempt on her part to write an account with the idea of publication, something which she and Stein had discussed. She suggested that her long letters would provide a basis for such a project. Her evocative descriptions of life in the village are mixed with personal complaints, since she was seriously unwell that summer, and valuable observations about Picasso's plans to paint some of the locals, one of whom was the schoolmistress, whose features can be discerned in at least one of his Horta portraits. While she was there, Olivier managed to learn enough Catalan to get by, but she was treated as something of a curiosity because of her Parisian style: her veiled hats, for instance, were thought to protect her from mosquitoes. She also says that since Picasso had a camera with him, the villagers thought they were photographers and willingly posed. On the Feast of Saints Peter and Paul (29 June), his girlfriend arranged to celebrate Pablo's name day by dancing for him to the strains of the pianola in the village. Although the letters are primarily filled with her own observations and experiences, she also remarks that Picasso was again working intensively and that he used the room in the baker's house as a studio.

**18
Paintings of Fernande Olivier in Picasso's studio in Horta, summer 1909, photographed by the artist**
Musée national Picasso, Paris (MP 1998-110)

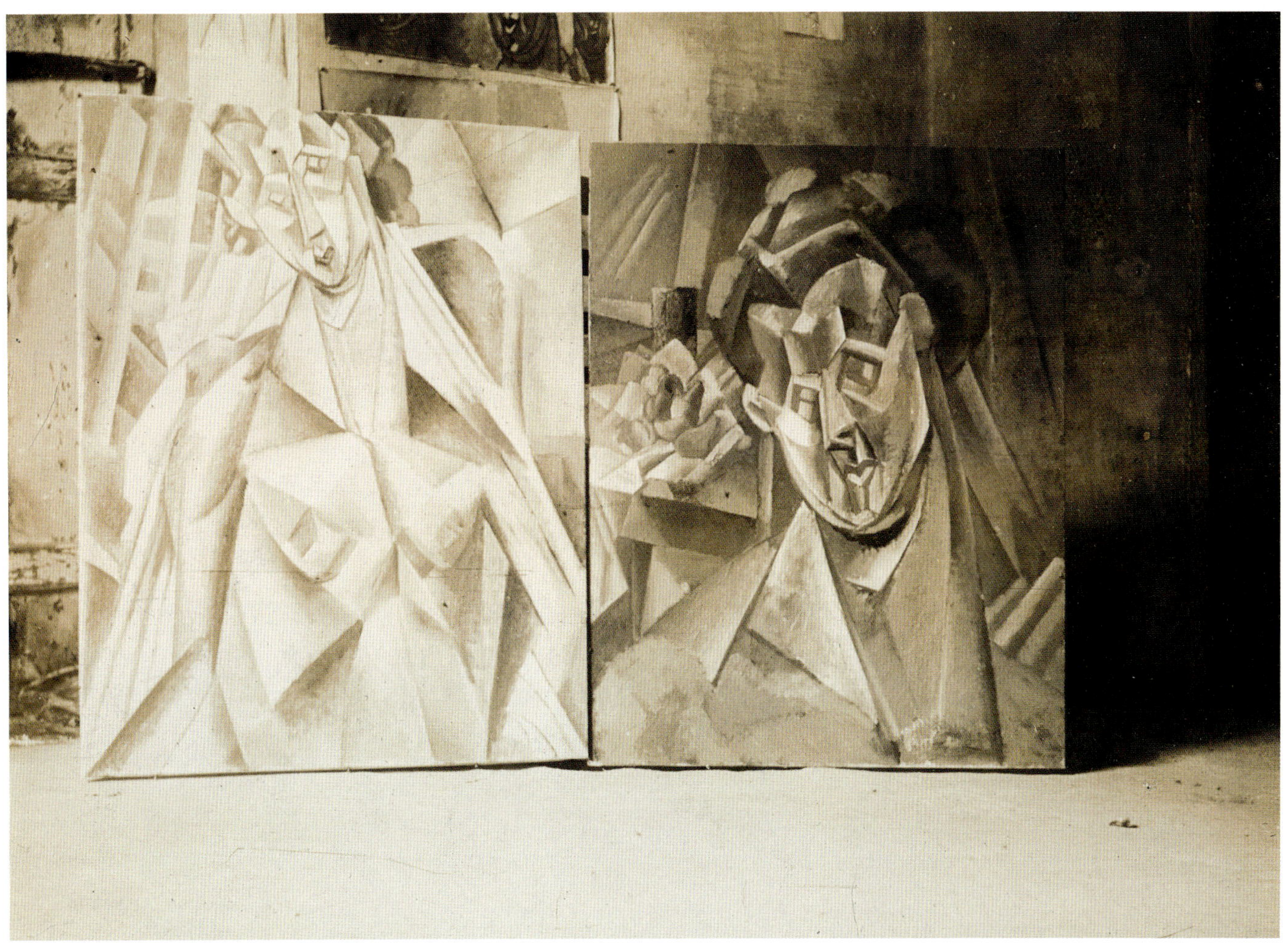

The photographs that he made of the interior reveal that the oil paintings he did in Horta ushered in a new stage in his artistic development, one which would constitute a decisive step leading to cubism. Picasso's compositions were inspired partly by the village and its houses, which were shaped almost like cubes, but most of all they reveal once more the features of Fernande Olivier, sometimes mixing her image with the characteristic twist of the dominating Santa Barbara mountain nearby (figs. 18 and 20.)

When the couple returned to Paris, they decided to move to a larger apartment, which would allow the artist studio space that was separate from their living quarters. They filled the apartment on the boulevard de Clichy with assorted furniture, including a proper bed, and they also employed a maid. The move, intentionally or not, provoked something of a break-up of *la bande à Picasso*, and their

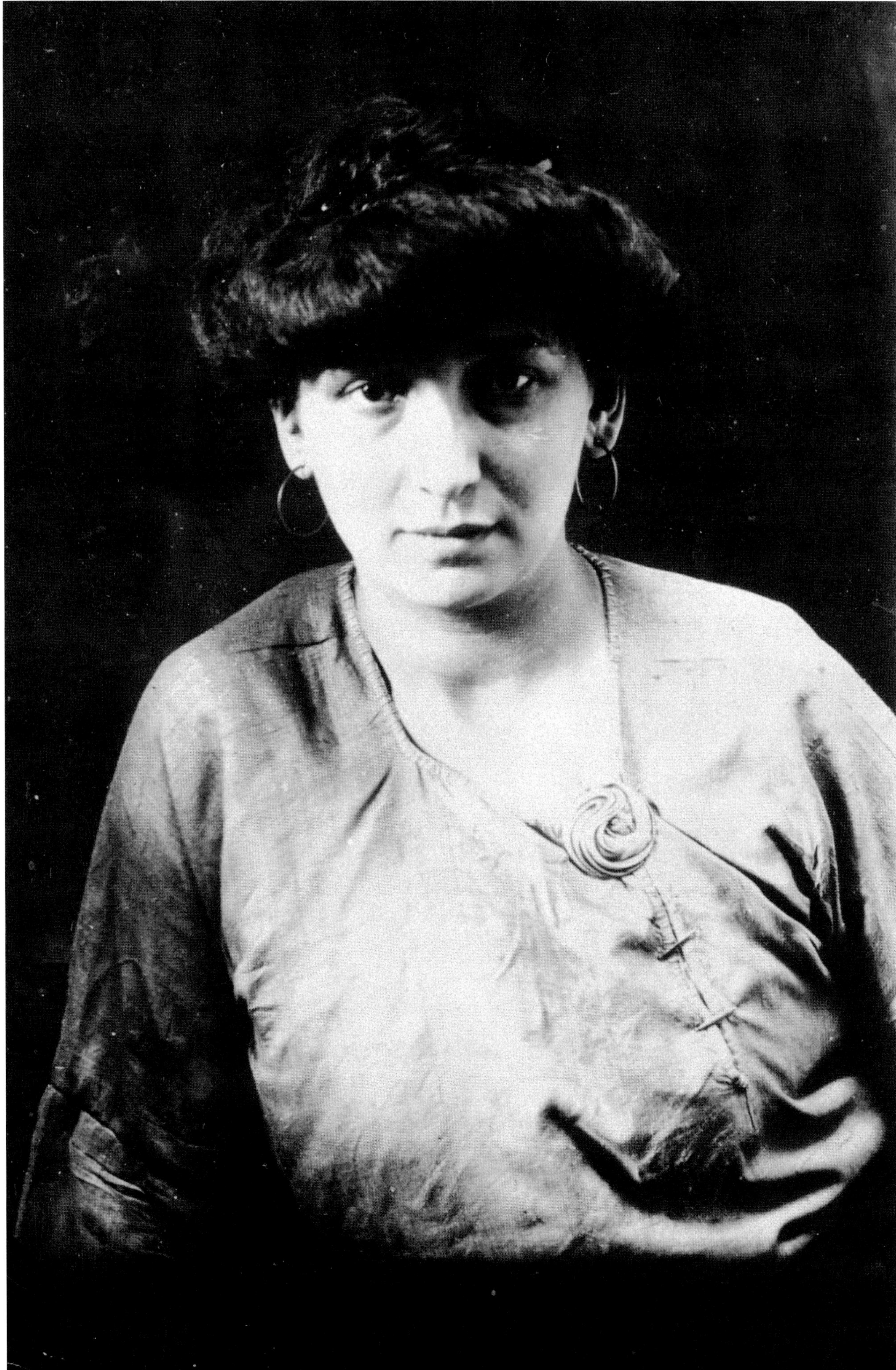

friends no longer came to the studio every day. As a consequence, Picasso and Olivier began to go out more frequently. On Saturday evenings, for instance, they often went to the Steins' apartment, where they met a new group of artists, bohemians and professional people, 'mostly foreigners', she remembered. She recounts that on one occasion Picasso noticed with anger that two of his paintings in the Steins' collection had been varnished by Gertrude Stein and her brother Leo without his permission. From this anecdote we learn something important about the artist's attitude to the qualities of the untouched surfaces of his canvases; restorers have subsequently been careful not to apply varnish to Picasso's cubist paintings. The sales that Picasso made to the Steins, however, allowed him the luxury of renting a small space at the back of a garden in Montmartre, where he could prepare his own canvases and leave them stretched out to dry. He also kept a room in the Bateau-Lavoir, where he could store the paintings and drawings that were accumulating in his boulevard de Clichy studio.

Fernande Olivier's descriptions of the contents of Picasso's studio reveal new interests, some of which would be reflected in his work. She said that along with tapestries and musical instruments, he had a little painting of a woman by Camille Corot and that he had begun to collect African wood carvings. 'Picasso became fanatical about [Negro art] and acquired statues, masks and fetishes from all over. … The hunt for African works became a real pleasure for him.' He was particularly fond of a Mukuyi mask from Gabon of a woman whose face was painted white, which can be seen hanging on the wall in a number of photographs of the studio, including one taken in 1910 in which Picasso's friend and future dealer Daniel-Henry Kahnweiler appears. The artist would sign a contract with Kahnweiler in 1912,

**19
Fernande
Olivier at
Bateau-Lavoir,
1908**

Musée national Picasso,
Paris (FPPH 147)

and over the course of the next few years, the dealer would be responsible for creating a successful market for Picasso's cubist work, especially in Germany.

Towards the end of their relationship, Olivier recounts that in spite of Picasso's improving financial situation, the artist was not as happy as he had been in the past when they lived together in the Bateau-Lavoir. More than ever, he threw himself into his work, leaving her for much of the time to her own devices. When, in 1912, the young Italian painter Ubaldo Oppi managed an introduction to Picasso, the consequences of their meeting were to have a direct impact on Fernande Olivier's future. She and Oppi started an affair (which apparently was quite

brief), while, at the same time, Picasso took up with Eva Gouel (Marcelle Humbert), the girlfriend of another painter by the name of Louis Marcoussis. In the spring Picasso wrote Kahnweiler: 'Fernande has gone off with a Futurist. I'm going to get out of Paris for a bit.' He and Eva Gouel went together to the south, and he proclaimed that she was now his great love. 'If you see Fernande,' he wrote his dealer, 'tell her that she can expect nothing from me, and I should be quite happy never to see her again.'

To make ends meet after her final break-up with Picasso, Olivier found work giving French lessons and, occasionally, poetry readings at the Lapin Agile cabaret in Montmartre (fig. 21). She had a beautiful voice and was known for her careful enunciation when she recited – plus, she was friendly with many of the poets of the day. Her financial situation was, nevertheless, precarious, and she came up with an idea that she thought might bring in more money: she would become an author. Since she had always kept a journal and had, at times, aspired to become a published writer, she embarked in the late 1920s on a memoir of her life with

**20
Pablo Picasso,
*Portrait of
Fernande
Olivier*, Horta
de Sant Joan,
summer 1909**
Städel Museum, Frankfurt
am Main (2110)

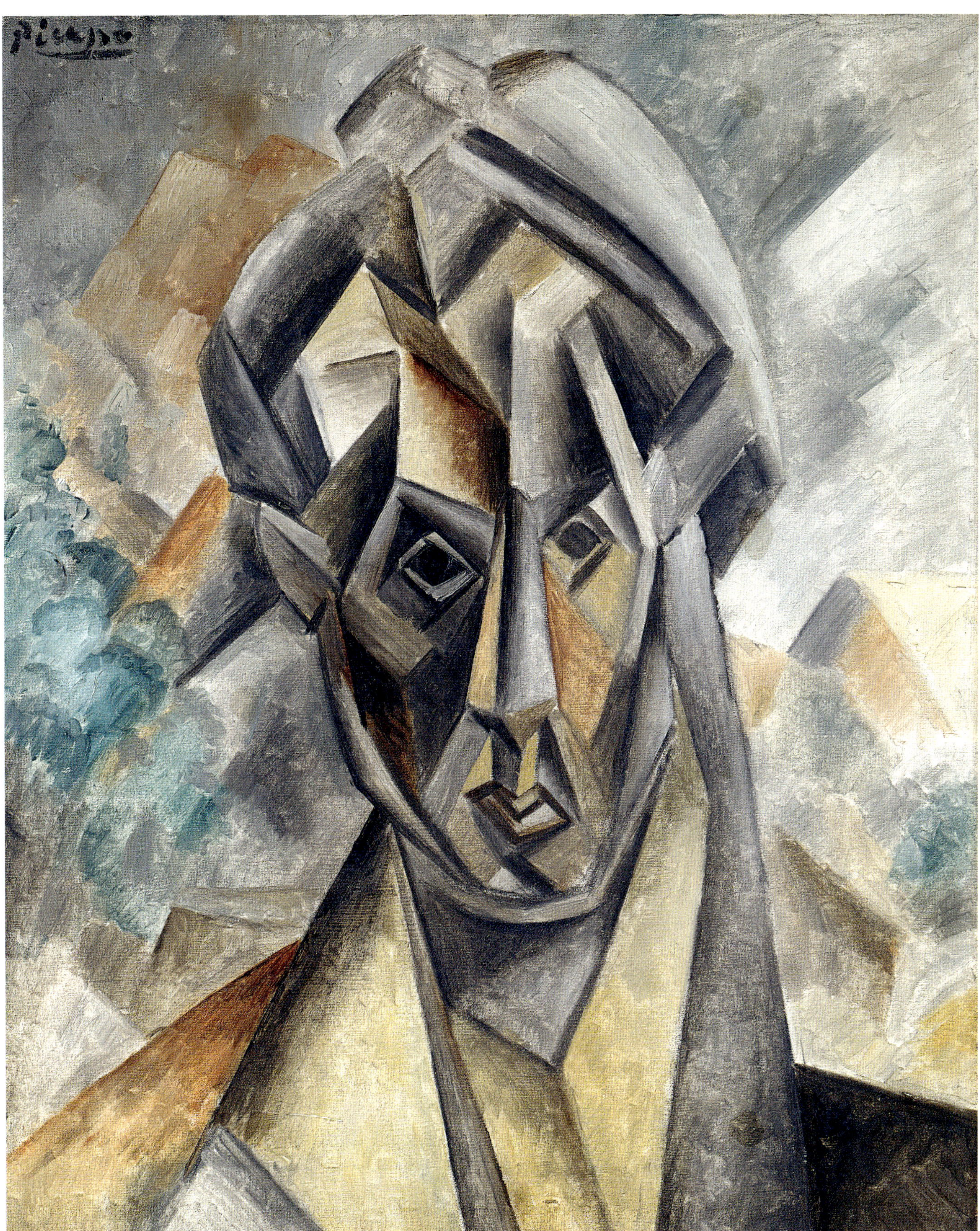

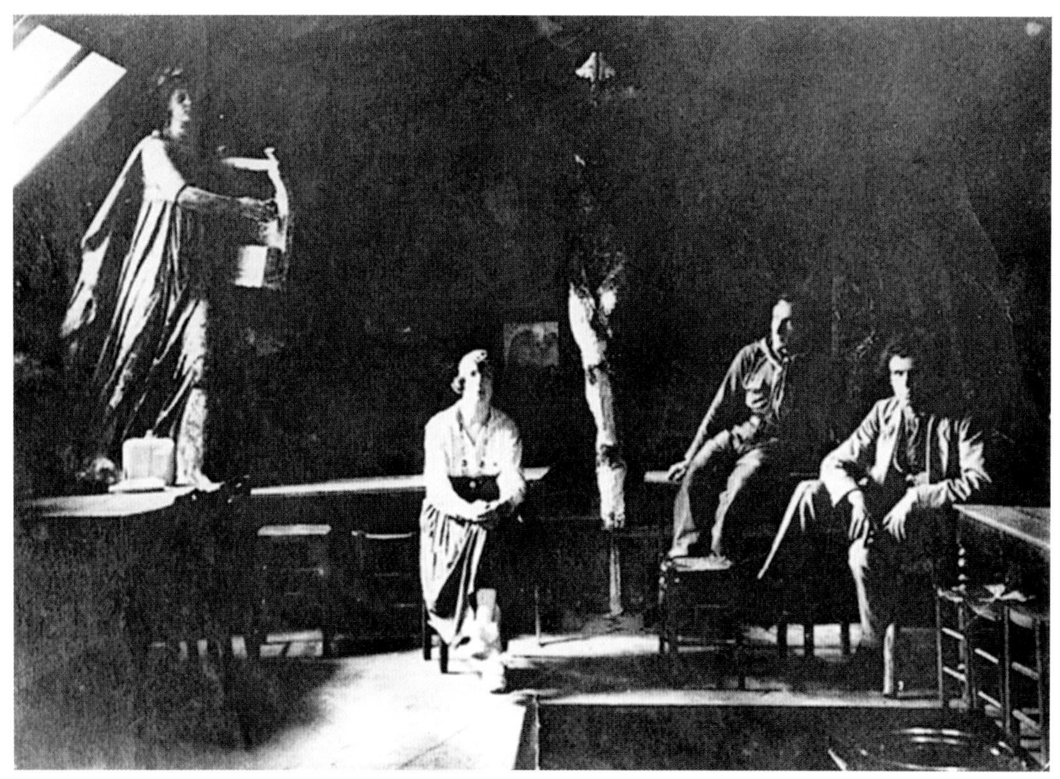

Picasso. A conversation with Gertrude Stein set the project in motion, and the first instalments of her story were serialized in the newspaper *Le Soir* (in 1930). After reading them, the eminent writer Paul Léautaud invited Olivier to discuss the possibility of not only publishing additional chapters in the *Mercure de France* but also to consider turning them into a book. When, in 1931, she asked Stein to help her find an American publisher, Stein referred her to her own agent, who expressed interest. He suggested that Stein might contribute a preface, but she declined. Instead, to Olivier's great dismay, Gertrude Stein came out with her own memoir in 1933, titled *The Auto-biography of Alice B. Toklas*. Olivier was incensed and wrote to the American agent, who had arranged the publication of Stein's book rather than her own, claiming that Stein's 'memoir' had been inspired by her 'souvenirs', and insisted her manuscript be returned to her.

Although Fernande Olivier intended for her memoir to be called 'Neuf ans chez Picasso' (Nine years with Picasso), the book in an edited form, with a preface by Léautaud, finally appeared in 1933 as *Picasso et ses amis.*[2] Picasso himself initially objected to the publication of the book, primarily be-

cause he believed it represented an invasion of his privacy,
but he was later to remark that
Olivier's account of the *bande
à Picasso* and the Bateau-
Lavoir was accurate. The
direct way in which the book is
written and the wide range of
personalities and events that
are described are remarkable.
For all students of Picasso's
life and work, and the history
of the avant-garde in the early
years of the twentieth century,
the book is still read with keen
interest and is widely relied
upon as a factual account.
Fernande Olivier's second
manuscript, *Souvenirs intimes*,
which was based on her journal
and probably written in book
form in the 1950s, would not
see the light of day until after
her death. However, her reputation as a reliable witness to
this period was secured. She
was invited, for instance, to
take part as one of a select
group of writers, artists and
intellectuals in a documentary
film (1959) about the life and
work of her close friend the
poet Max Jacob, directed by
Jean-Marie Drot.[3]

Beginning in 1918, Olivier
settled down once again, this
time living with the actor Roger
Karl, and they stayed together
until the early 1940s, at which
time they separated, and she

moved into a tiny apartment on
her own. Without any real
means of supporting herself
during the war, she wrote
Picasso in 1943 asking for
help. He eventually responded
by providing her a pension for
the rest of her life. 'La belle
Fernande' died, in 1966, at the
age of eighty-four.

21
**Fernande Olivier
in the Lapin
Agile, at the
time she gave
poetry readings
there, c. 1914**

Gertrude Stein

Markus Müller

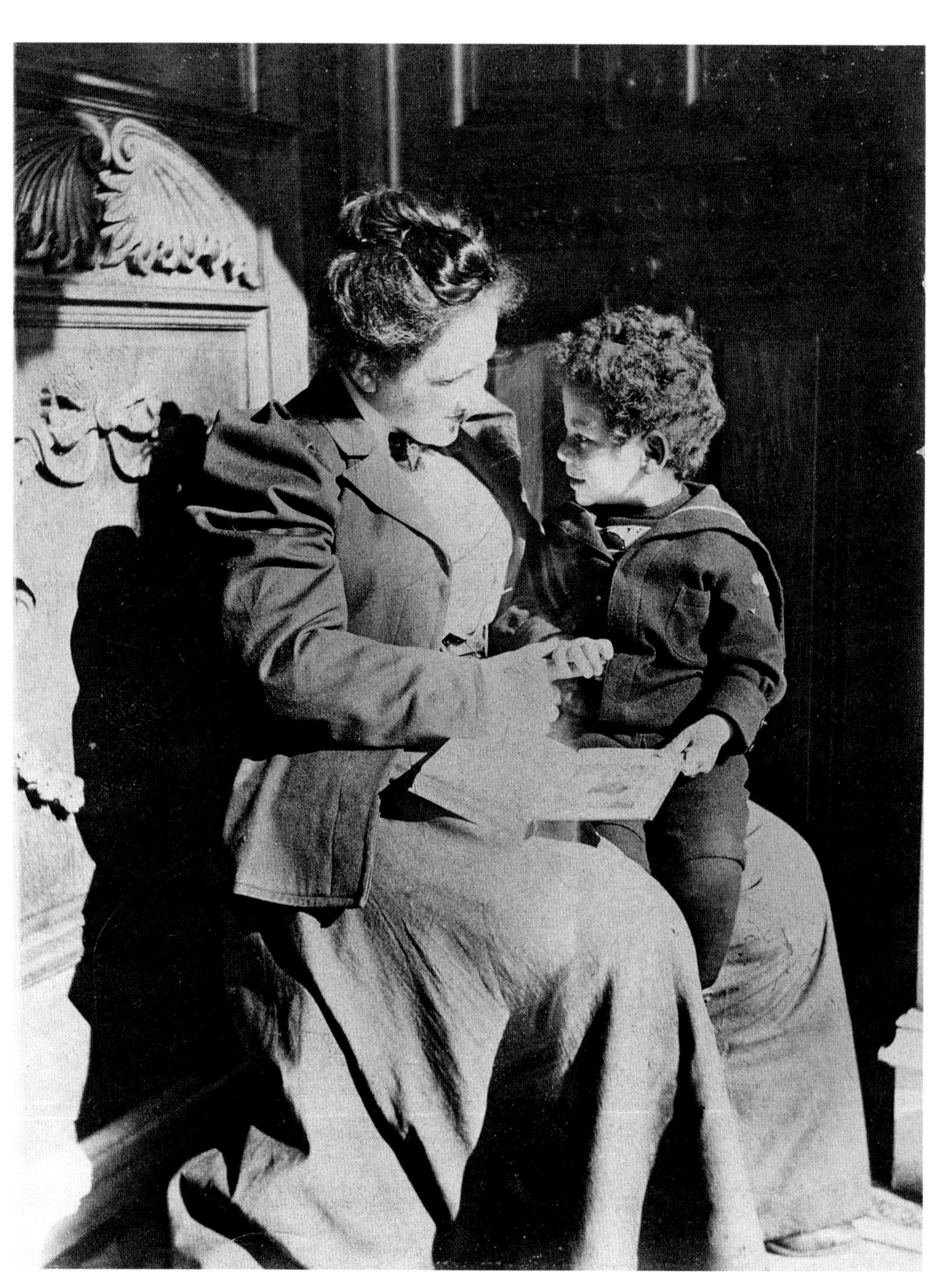

Woody Allen's 2011 fantasy comedy, *Midnight in Paris*, rests on the conceit of an American tourist who late one night decides to take a stroll through the streets of Paris, only to find himself journeying back in time. A vintage car pulls up beside him and offers him a ride – a ride that will in fact transport him back to the age of Cole Porter and Ernest Hemingway. His second nocturnal journey, undertaken the following night, takes him to an illustrious gathering hosted by a lady of considerable girth and attended by Henri Matisse, Pablo Picasso and other avant-garde artists. It turns out that the young man has time-travelled back from the early twenty-first to the early twentieth century, specifically to the famous salon of the great American art collector and writer Gertrude Stein! This anachronistic encounter is fairly bursting with comic potential. Stein, for example, scolds Matisse for selling his paintings for 'several hundred francs', which she considers grossly over-priced. On hearing this, Allen's American time-traveller promptly expresses his wish to buy a good dozen of them.

The episode demonstrates very clearly, in retrospect, how the Paris salon hosted by the sister and brother Gertrude and Leo Stein became the stuff of legend. Even today, the name Gertrude Stein is inseparable from the myth of 'the American in Paris', and some would actually place her squarely at the centre of that myth. The painters Georges Braque, Juan Gris, Pablo Picasso and Henri Matisse were all regular visitors to her apartment at 27, rue de Fleurus, as were the writers Ernest Hemingway, Sherwood Anderson and F. Scott Fitzgerald. Stein was a champion of avant-garde writers and artists, an early promoter of their art and a stern judge of quality and

**22
Gertrude Stein with her nephew Allan Stein, c. 1903–04**

Musée national Picasso, Paris (APPH 2775)

Gertrude Stein

talent. Her reputation as a patroness of the arts was rivalled only by her renown as an author in her own right, which she owed primarily to her works for a wide readership, such as *The Autobiography of Alice B. Toklas* (1933). Stein's styling of this work as the memoirs of her life partner, Alice B. Toklas, served her as a form of literary selfmystification in that it enabled her to write about herself ostensibly as seen through the eyes of another. Alone the narrative framework of the book is a rhetorical tour de force, and, writing in an informal, conversational style, Stein invites her readership to partake in all her many scrapes and adventures.

The Steins were of German-Jewish origin. The marriage of their parents, Daniel and Amelia Stein, produced five offspring, the youngest of whom was Gertrude, born in Allegheny, Pennsylvania, in 1874. The family spent a few years in Vienna, Austria, where their household included a

private tutor and a governess for the children, and when Gertrude was four years old, they moved to Paris, where they rented a house in the up-market suburb of Passy. In 1879, however, after barely a year in France, Daniel took them all back to America to take advantage of the more promising business opportunities on the other side of The Pond. Gertrude consequently spent her youth in Oakland, California, and it was there that the two themes that were to dominate her life snapped into focus: books and food, food and books. Amelia Stein died young of cancer, and after her death Daniel took care of his family single-handedly until he himself passed away, in 1891. Michael Stein, the couple's eldest son, was twenty-six by then and hence old enough to take charge of the family's financial fortunes. This he did with such skill that the Stein siblings were soon comfortably well-off. When Leo went to Cambridge, Massachusetts, to study at Harvard in 1892, his younger sisters, Bertha and Gertrude, moved in with their aunt in Baltimore. Her brother's enthusiastic accounts of college life so inspired Gertrude, however, that she soon signed on at Radcliffe College, the women's equivalent of Harvard. Among her professors there was the charismatic William James, whose book *Principles of Psychology* (1890), in which he expounded his theory of a 'stream of consciousness', was to have an enduring influence on the arts. Another of her teachers, a professor of literature, evidently found her writing style rather trying, telling her: 'I wish you might overcome your disdain for the more necessary marks of punctuation.'[1]

Following Professor James's advice, she embarked on the study of medicine, and it was while at medical school that she wrote her first short stories and that her literary interests and ambitions became apparent.

Leo Stein moved to Paris in the autumn of 1900 and there enrolled at the Académie Julian, an independent art school which taught drawing and painting from life. He also visited galleries and exhibitions and led the life of an art-loving gentleman of private means. The American Renaissance scholar Bernard Berenson introduced him to the gallerist Ambroise Vollard and it was at the latter's gallery that Leo caught his first admiring glimpse of the paintings of Paul Cézanne. Gertrude moved in with her brother at his apartment at 27, rue de Fleurus, not far from the Jardin du Luxembourg, in the autumn of 1903. Michael Stein, accompanied by his wife, Sarah, and their son, Allan, also moved to Paris in December of that year.

Unlike her brothers, however, Gertrude Stein seems not to have had any intention of settling permanently in Paris as yet. A stormy love affair with a fellow female student and her wish to pursue medicine in fact took her back to America that same winter. Before long, however, she had made up her mind to abandon medicine after all, and in June 1904 she returned to Paris, firmly resolved to make the city on the Seine her permanent place of abode.

Gertrude and Leo had a very close, almost symbiotic relationship during those early years in Paris, when the bond between them was sustained by their shared tastes and interests. It was also during those early years that Leo's preference for the fine arts

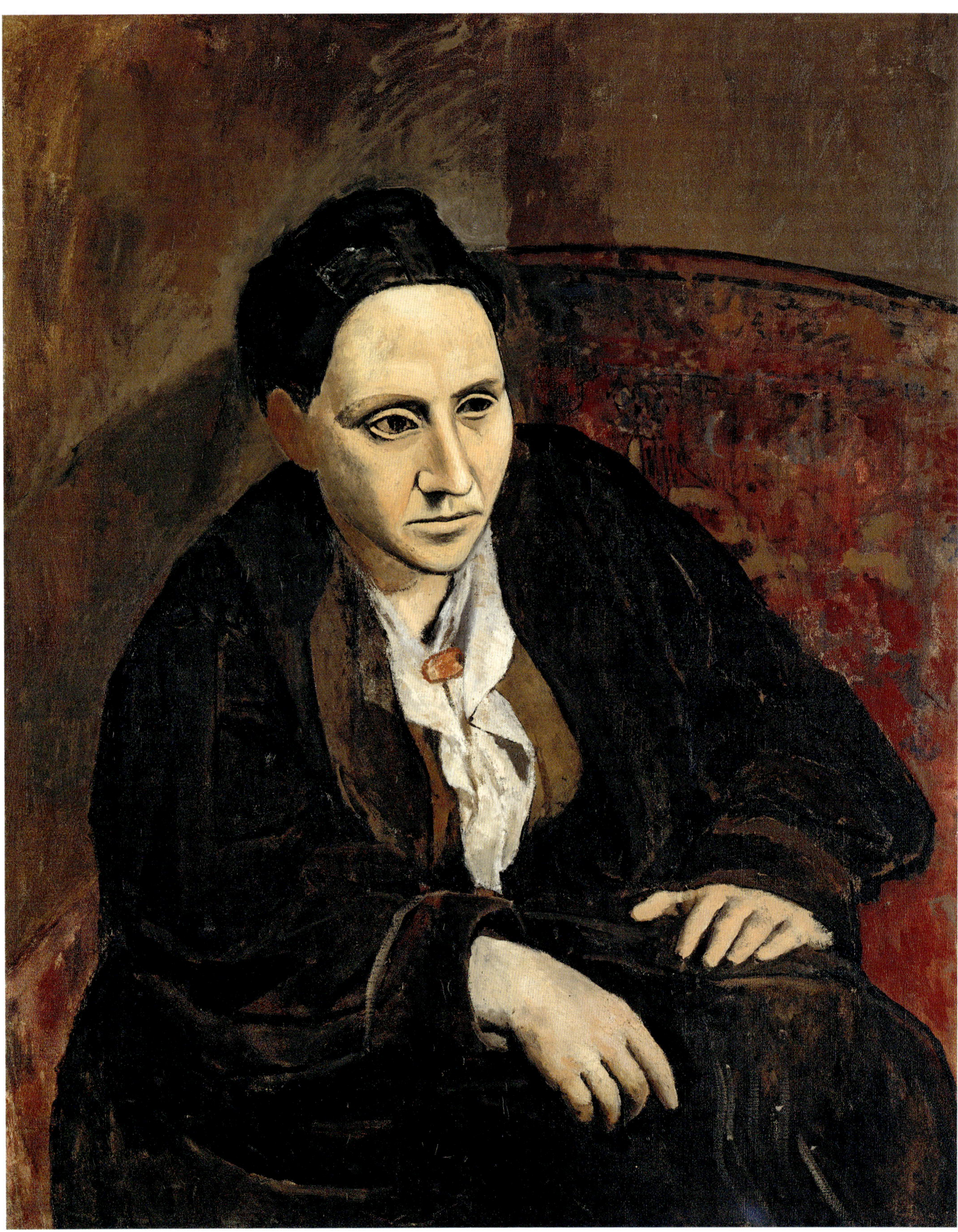

and Gertrude's for literature crystallized. That it was Leo who connected them to Paris's avant-garde artists, building up a close-knit group of friends and acquaintances, is therefore unsurprising. Following her brother's lead in matters of taste, however, Gertrude also began to take an interest in the new departures then rocking the art world. She had him introduce her to Vollard, for example, who in his memoirs painted the following picture of her:

> Gertrude Stein's is [*sic*] a very attractive personality. … To see her with her dress of coarse velveteen, her sandals with leather straps, and her general air of simplicity, one would take her at first sight for a housewife whose horizon is restricted to her dealings with the greengrocer, the dairyman and the rest. But you have only to encounter her glance to perceive in Miss Stein something far beyond the ordinary *bourgeoise*. The vivacity of her glance betrays the observer, the investigator whom nothing escapes.[2]

Stein schooled her brilliant powers of observation at all the great exhibitions held in Paris, first and foremost among them the Salon d'automne and the Salon des Indépendants, where Leo Stein bought his first works of art.

The Salon d'automne of 1905 sparked a scandal by devoting one whole gallery to the expressive, brightly coloured paintings of Henri Matisse and fellow artists such as André Derain and Maurice Vlaminck.

Undeterred by any of this, Leo Stein went ahead and bought Matisse's *Woman with a Hat* (1905) showing the painter's wife, Amélie.

The Stein siblings would henceforth count among Matisse's more important Parisian patrons and would regularly welcome the painter into their home on the rue de Fleurus. Leo Stein's forays into the Paris art world also

**23
Pablo Picasso,
Gertrude Stein,
1906**

The Metropolitan Museum
of Art, New York (47.106)

brought him into contact with Clovis Sagot, who ran a small art dealership with a bar attached to it. As Sagot the dealer was throwing his weight behind a young Spaniard by the name of Pablo Picasso, then aged just twenty-four, Leo bought a painting of his as well, and a short time later met the then virtually unknown artist in person. From that time forth, Picasso would likewise be a frequent guest at the Steins' home, becoming a special favourite of Gertrude's. Recalling her first impression of him much later, she remarked that Picasso, to her, had seemed like 'a good-looking bootblack … alive with big pools of eyes'.[3] This attractive 'bootblack' even offered to paint her portrait, which is why Stein made the long journey on foot from her home in Montparnasse to Picasso's home and studio on the rue de Ravignan in Montmartre almost daily throughout the winter of 1905–06 (fig. 23).

She must have been a highly unusual sitter, and many of those who knew her noted the conspicuous discrepancy between her bulky body and finely hewn face. As to Picasso's reasons for wanting to paint such an ambitious portrait of her, we can only speculate. Knowing that unlike her brother, Gertrude had not been all too impressed by his work at first, could it have been an attempt to win her over – an artistic seduction, as it were? Another hypothesis that warrants mention is that of Picasso and Stein as kindred spirits, which Picasso perhaps understood intuitively. Both were foreigners in Paris with no more than a rudimentary knowledge of French; both were discerning and swift to pass judgment and both shared a tendency to become dogmatic and even truculent when espousing their aesthetic convictions. Another, no less weighty motivation for the portrait might have been the fact that it was through Gertrude Stein that Picasso first made the acquaintance of Henri Matisse, several of whose works the Steins already possessed. Matisse was regarded as the 'head of the Fauves' at the time, and the

24
Gertrude Stein and Alice B. Toklas, rue de Fleurus, Paris, 1922, photographed by Man Ray

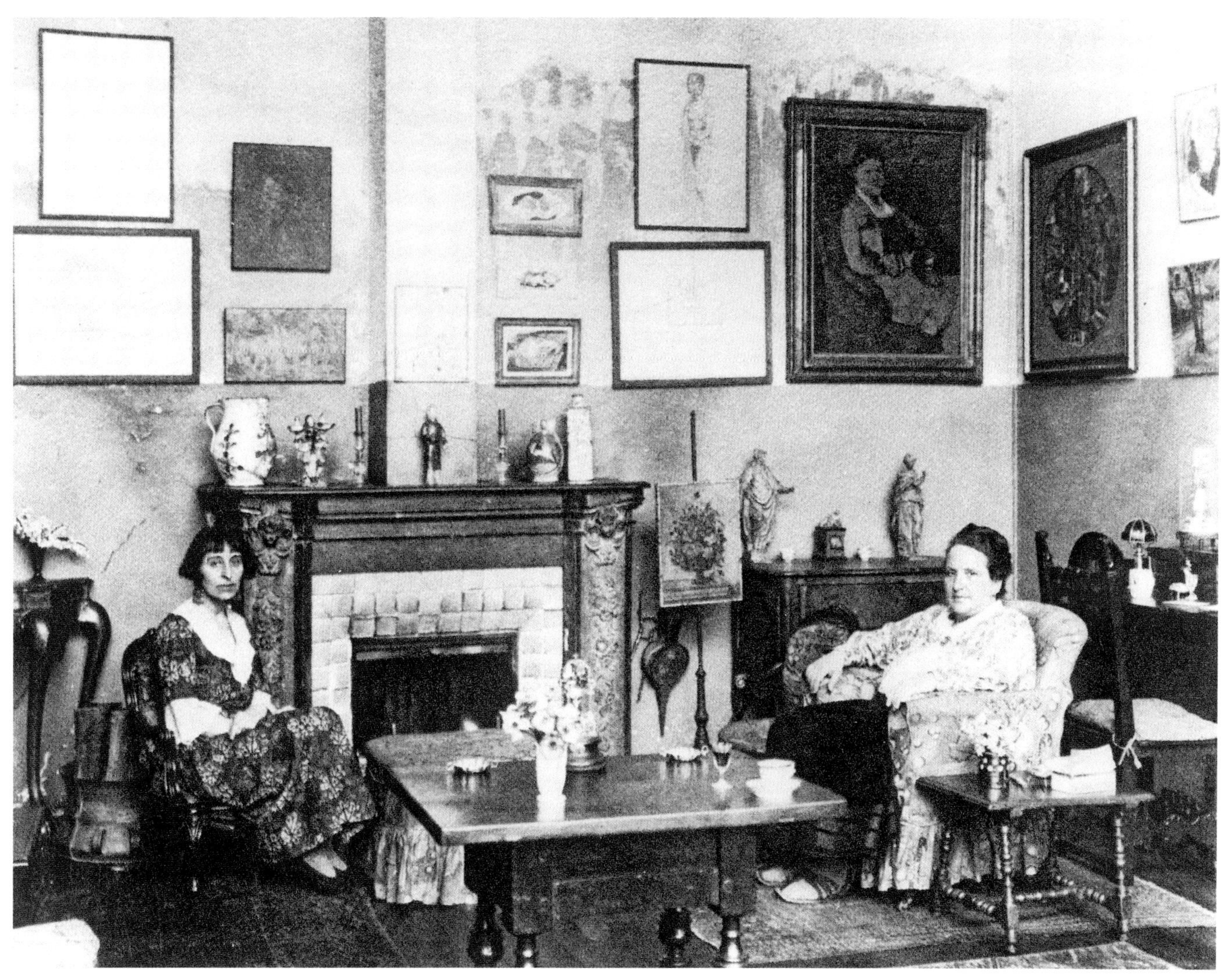

success of his works at the scandalous Salon d'automne of 1905 had given him the reputation of a great avant-garde artist who was already receiving commissions from famous foreign collectors. Picasso's portrait of Gertrude Stein might therefore have been his way of leaving his own calling card at the number one address for up-and-coming avant-garde artists in Paris. The Stein siblings made it a custom of theirs to invite artists, art lovers, writers and intellectuals to their home every Saturday evening, and their soirées took on the aura of a literary and artistic salon on a par with those famously hosted by educated noble ladies of the eighteenth and nineteenth centuries (fig. 24). *The Autobiography of Alice B. Toklas* contains Gertrude Stein's own detailed account of how Picasso's portrait of her, which now hangs in a prominent location in the Metropolitan Museum of Art in New York, came about: 'As I say', she has Alice B. Toklas say:

Gertrude Stein and Pablo Picasso immediately understood each other. Then there was the first time of posing. ... There was a large broken armchair where Gertrude Stein posed. ... Fernande was as always very large, very beautiful and very gracious. She offered to read La Fontaine's stories aloud to amuse Gertrude Stein while Gertrude Stein posed. She took her pose. Picasso sat very tight on his chair and very close to his canvas and on a very small palette which was of a uniform brown grey colour, mixed some more brown grey and the painting began. This was the first of some eighty or ninety sittings. ... Spring was coming and the sittings were coming to an end. All of a sudden one day Picasso painted out the whole head. I can't see you any longer when I look, he said irritably. And so the picture was left like that. ... As I was saying the sittings were over, the vernissage of the Independent was over, and everybody went away.[4]

Gertrude Stein goes on to relate how soon afterwards, Picasso and his companion, Fernande Olivier, went on holiday together to northern Spain, while she and Leo rented a villa in Fiesole in the hills above Florence. On their return, Picasso had a *coup de théâtre* in store for them: 'She came back to a Paris fairly full of excitement', Alice B. Toklas continues. 'In the first place she came back to her finished portrait. The day he returned from Spain, Picasso sat down and out of his head painted the head in without having seen Gertrude Stein again. And when she saw it he and she were content.'[5]

This portrait is one of the undisputed masterpieces of

Picasso's early period. And the subject herself would give it pride of place in her home throughout her life, for 'it is I and it is the only reproduction of me which is always I for me.'[6]

Yet there can be no talk of Picasso having left us an idealised picture of his American friend. The burgeoning writer's broad, bulky body is presented in canvas-filling close-up with one hand resting on her knee, the other on her thigh. In her own description of the work quoted above, Stein noted the predominantly brown-grey colour scheme, which was retained even in the final version of the work. Only the white blouse, its waterfall collar held together by a red brooch, and the subject's face and hands stand out against their largely monochrome surroundings. In the background Picasso hints at the corner of a room, which he aligns with the central axis, while the figure herself is thrown into relief by the discreetly patterned backrest of a divan. Gertrude Stein gazes out of the picture and into the distance with a rigid, seemingly unmoving, mask-like expression. Her countenance, as characterised by Picasso, is so utterly smooth-skinned that it might have been carved in wood, with the eyes sharply delineated as two slits. The impression is that of some ancient idol, whose gaze transfixes us, while remaining unapproachable and aloof. The stylistic characteristics of the work and what we know of its origins have long left Picasso scholars facing a puzzle. Given Stein's propensity to self-mystification – even self-glorification – in her own biographical writings, her account of how the painting came about should probably be taken with a hefty pinch of salt. Yet, as anyone who studies the portrait carefully will soon confirm, her literary descriptions of the work do at least match the objective reality of the painting on one key point, namely in the very obvious stylistic discrepancy between the subject's face and the remainder of the work.

Especially striking in Stein's description is her revelation of how at some point during the winter of 1905–06 Picasso must have manoeuvred himself into a dead end, as manifested in his deep dissatisfaction with his previous rendition of Stein's face. Numerous Picasso scholars believe the key to understanding this unusual creation story lies in the profound transformation that the painter must have undergone during the months he spent in his native Spain in 1906. For it was only after that extended vacation that he began synthesizing certain stylistic features of medieval Spanish art in his own works. Hence, the look on Gertrude Stein's face, which is that of a wooden mask, its parts articulated in a sharp, angular manner. This famous portrait is a work of transition that carries within it the embryonal elements of a new creative phase. It shows us Picasso assembling his stylistic palette to produce a painterly synthesis that seems to herald an imminent new departure in his work. He has

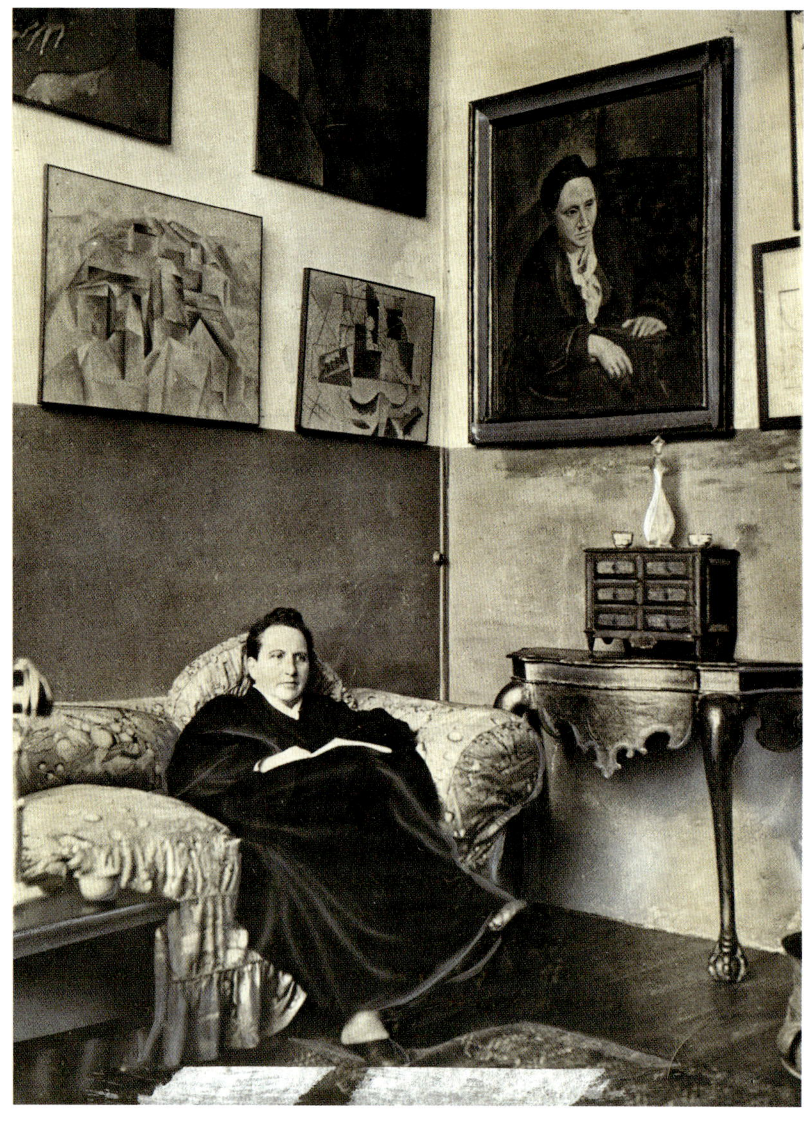

put his Rose Period with its depictions of clowns and circus artistes behind him and has appropriated the angular, stylised language of medieval – and later African – art. This fundamental reorientation will eventually lead him to cubism and with it to what was probably the greatest artistic revolution of the twentieth century (fig. 25).

Having outlined the painting's significance as a

turning point in Picasso's oeuvre, let us now turn to the history of the portrait that for years, indeed decades, has been closely bound up with the life of the subject portrayed. After all, the painting defined the image of the American patroness and promoter of the avant-garde as did no other.

Gertrude Stein had the great good fortune to meet the love of her life in 1907. The individual in question was her fellow American Alice B. Toklas, who in the company of a mutual friend had travelled to Paris in September of that year. Alice B. Toklas became Gertrude Stein's devoted life partner and moved in with her at 27, rue de Fleurus, just a few months after their first meeting. She typed up Stein's handwritten manuscripts for her and was her secretary, housekeeper, lover and life-long confidante rolled into one. For decades, the pair were inseparable. Stein was tall and of such a stocky build that the petite figure of her companion looked positively willowy alongside her. The division of roles between this unequal pair has sometimes been compared to that of a high priest and altar boy.

Yet it was not Toklas, but Stein's literary ambitions that led to the deep rift with her brother Leo, who more than once accused her of being utterly devoid of talent and advised her to abandon writing altogether. Gertrude herself naturally took a completely different view. 'It was I who was the genius', she remarked insouciantly in retrospect, 'there was no reason for it but I was, and he was not.'[7]

Leo Stein finally moved out of their shared apartment in 1913. When the siblings divided up their art collection, Leo kept the Renaissance furniture and the Renoirs and Gertrude held onto the Picassos, while each of them took a Cézanne or two. By the time of their final break, Leo was clearly exasperated, commenting: 'There is practically nothing that we agree on or that we at least regard with similar sympathies.'[8]

Gertrude Stein is often viewed as the mother of modern literature on the

**25
Gertrude Stein
in front of her
portrait,
photographed
by Man Ray**

grounds that she rose above linguistic conventions and obsolete narrative structures, blithely ignored syntax and punctuation, and made the continuous present a literary tense. Not in all quarters were these idiosyncrasies hailed as literary accomplishments, however, and more than once they were not understood at all.

Compounding violations of standard American English, moreover, was Stein's repetitiveness, which demanded both persistence and stamina on the part of her readers. A 1909 piece on Picasso, for example, reads as follows:

One whom some were certainly following was one who was completely charming. One whom some were certainly following was one who was charming. One whom some were following was one who was completely charming. One whom some were following was one who was certainly completely charming. Some were certainly following and were certain that the one they were then following was one working and was one bringing out of himself then something.[9]

Gertrude Stein herself preferred to describe her style as an authentic and free expression of her personality. On a trip to America in 1934, for example, she told the assembled journalists: 'I have not invented any device, any style, but write in the style that is me.'[10]

She would also claim that thanks to her own pared-down style, she had become a literary model for the young Ernest Hemingway. The two writers would later have a serious falling-out, not least on account of what Stein had to say about Hemingway in *The Autobiography of Alice B. Toklas*. It was a 'damned pitiful book', said Hemingway, who took exception to Stein's characterisation of him as a literary disciple of Sherwood Anderson and herself. He took revenge for what he saw as her exaggerated claims by sending her a copy of his *Death in the Afternoon* (1932) bearing the dedication 'A bitch is a bitch is a bitch', which of course is a paraphrase of Stein's famous phrase, 'Rose is a rose is a rose'.[11]

Gertrude Stein, Alice B. Toklas and the writers Hemingway, Anderson, Ezra Pound and T. S. Eliot were nevertheless in and out of each other's lives throughout the 'Roaring Twenties'. This was also the decade when Picasso would advance from poor bohemian languishing on Montmartre to celebrated artist. His marriage to the ballet dancer Olga Khokhlova had gained him entrée into bourgeois society, and he had become a sought-after guest at fancy-dress balls and soirées. Stein, too, underwent a metamorphosis around this time – one that at least superficially was to distance her from the incarnation of herself that for weeks on end had patiently sat for Picasso in the winter of 1905-06.

In 1926 she asked the ever-obliging Toklas to cut her hair, which until then she had worn pinned up in a bun. The haircut her companion gave her, at her express wish, was so short that Hemingway quipped that she looked like a Roman emperor. Following such a radical change of type, the likeness of Picasso's portrait, painted twenty years earlier, suddenly seemed in jeopardy. Picasso himself, however, was unperturbed, and is said to have reassured himself: '*mais, quand même, tout y est*, all the same it is all there' (fig. 26).[12]

When appraising Stein's literary achievements, it is important to note that she had full command of two completely different registers: first there are the avant-garde texts, written in an impenetrable, repetitive style and published in very small editions; then there are the works penned in a witty, conversational tone that were intended for a much wider readership.

Almost all the reviews of *The Autobiography of Alice B. Toklas* in the American press were positive, and in some instances even euphoric. William Troy, for example,

71

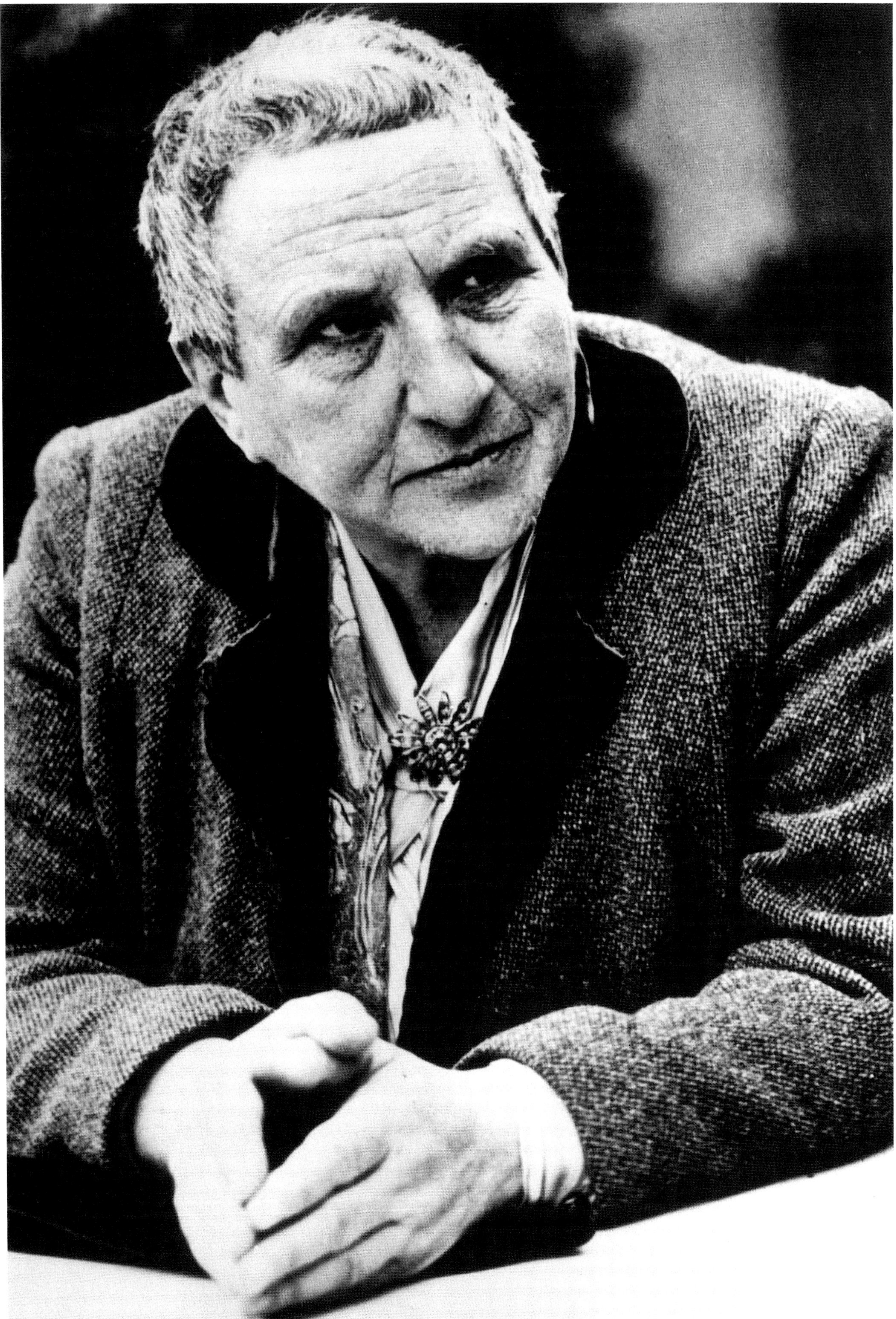

writing in *The Nation*, opined that 'among books of literary reminiscences, Miss Stein's is one of the richest, wittiest, and most irreverent ever written'.[13] Whereas Stein reached only a comparatively small audience with her other works, this was the one that assured her of enduring success with a broader audience.

The Autobiography is an account of the quarter century that that Stein and Toklas spent together in Paris. In it, their shared apartment becomes the nexus of all their many encounters with the literary and artistic geniuses of the age, who by the time the book was published had become major figures in the world of art and literature. Historical accuracy was not necessarily Stein's forte; but given the incredibly densely packed, heavily anecdotal picture that she paints of bohemian Paris, readers are inclined to forgive the author her want of accuracy.

She scored another triumph with her book about Picasso, which she wrote in French and published in 1938. The author had had the privilege of being able to follow Picasso's development close up, and when her book is read from this perspective, it does indeed have the authentic ring of an eye-witness account. The author emphasises the extent to which she and Picasso were kindred spirits, both as artists and in personality. Her early dedication to his art enabled her to style herself a prescient talent scout and patroness of the arts, who just happened to be blessed with formidable talents of her own.

The couple remained in France throughout the Second World War and the German occupation, despite the grave risks that staying there entailed. After all, both women were Jewish and could easily have returned to their native America. They had remained in Paris during the First World War, too, when both had been active and wholehearted supporters of an American aid organisation that helped

26
Gertrude Stein,
c. 1945

wounded servicemen. As Stein facetiously remarked when asked about their refusal to leave France during the Second World War: 'We always pass our wars in France.'[14]

In the summer of 1946 Gertrude Stein was diagnosed with stomach cancer that was already far advanced. After hesitating for a long time, she decided to risk surgery at the American Hospital in Neuilly-sur-Seine but died on the operating table, on 27 July. Her death robbed Alice B. Toklas of her centre of gravity. Having been Gertrude's devoted partner for so many years, unwavering in her support, and a firm believer in her friend's literary talents, she now brought that same devotion

and sheer dogged determination to bear on furthering the posthumous publication of Stein's complete works.

In her will, Gertrude Stein left all her letters and manuscripts to Yale University. Picasso's portrait of her, however, was to go to the Metropolitan Museum of Art in New York. For decades it had hung in the same place in the home the couple had shared, and Toklas tried to fill the painful gap left by its absence by hanging Picasso's *Man with a Guitar* there instead. She described the phantom pain caused by the loss of the portrait in a letter to her American friend Bobsie Goodspeed dated 10 February 1947: 'Gertrude always sat on the sofa and the picture hung over the fireplace opposite and I used to say in the old happy days that they looked at each other and that possibly when they were alone they talked to each other.'[15]

The instructions in Gertrude Stein's will are themselves a testament to the high regard in which she held Picasso's portrait of her. Her gifting of the painting to New York's most illustrious museum becomes all the more understandable bearing in mind her perception of herself as modern literature's equivalent of

Picasso: 'Twentieth-century literature is Gertrude Stein',[16] she wrote immodestly. Her gift can therefore be read as a strategic way of inscribing herself into the collective visual memory as well.

An American friend of the couple, the art collector Mabel Dodge, once wrote an essay comparing Stein's literary texts with Picasso's art. 'Gertrude Stein is doing with words what Picasso is doing with paint', she wrote. 'She is impelling language to induce new states of consciousness, and in doing so language becomes with her a creative art rather than a mirror of history.'[17]

The concept of rhythmic repetition and linguistic variation can be interpreted as a literary variant of cubism, as the translation into language of the artistic strategy of showing every facet of an object simultaneously. Stein's literary oeuvre shows her systematically deconstructing language in pursuit of a new construct that is at once artificial and wholly subjective. Hence, her view of herself as a kindred spirit of Picasso, as one who was creating a linguistic equivalent of his artistic experiments. 'I was alone at this time in understanding him', she later wrote of this period. 'Perhaps because I was expressing the same thing in literature.'[18]

When Gertrude Stein arrived in New York with Alice B. Toklas in late October 1934, the local press poked fun at her with a parody of her poetry: 'Gerty Gerty Stein Stein is back Home Home back.' Bearing in mind Picasso's magnificent portrait of her in the Metropolitan Museum of Art in that city, we might justifiably add: 'She is home forever'.

Eva Gouel

Marilyn McCully

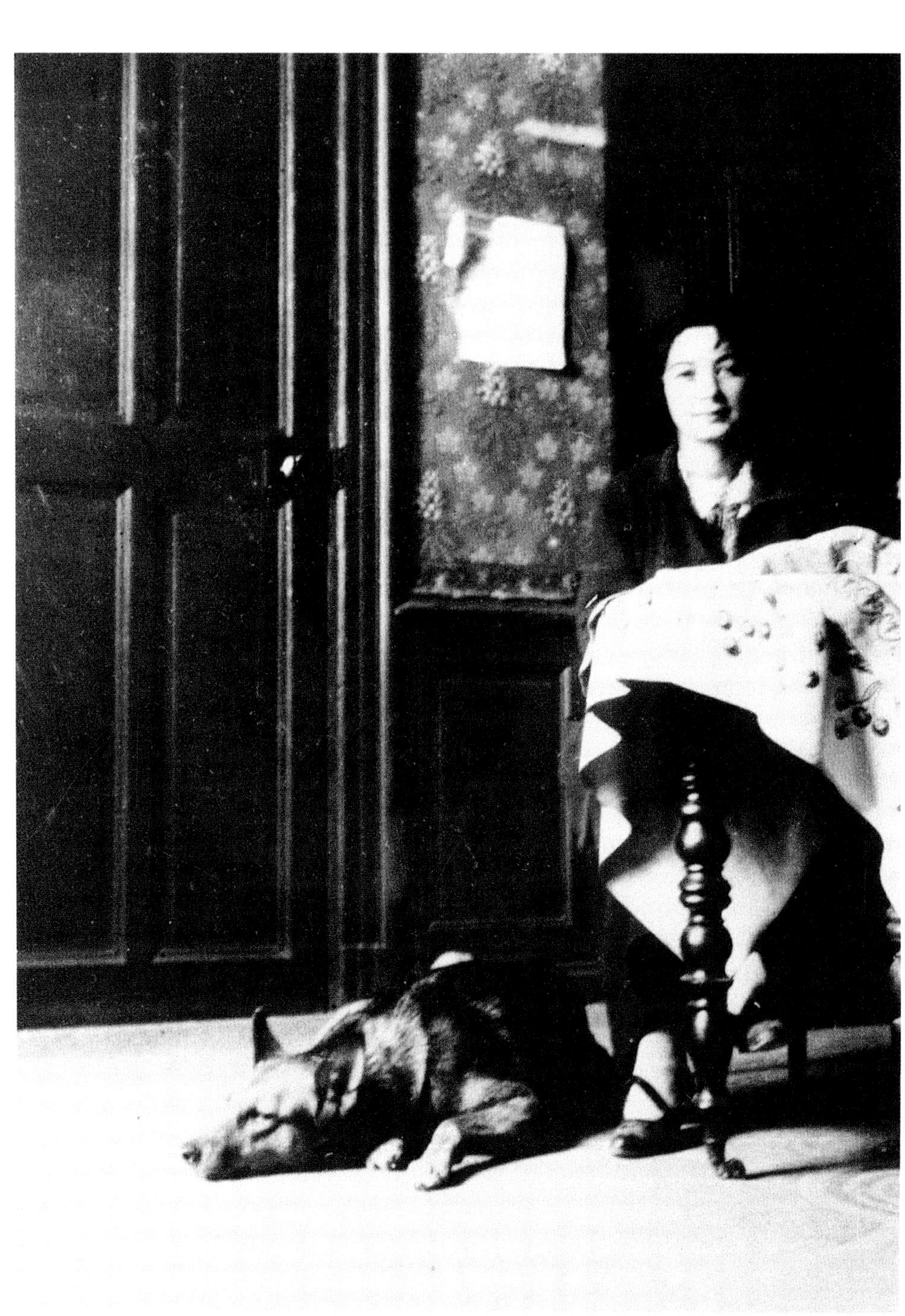

*I love her very much and I will
write this in my paintings.*
Picasso, 12 June 1912[1]

Pablo Picasso's four-year love affair with a young French-woman called Eva Gouel started off with an episode of intrigue, followed by flight from a former lover, and then the promise of a future together. Their relationship coincided with a period of extraordinary creativity for the artist, just as he was making significant advances in his revolutionary approach to cubism. Although he never painted Eva Gouel's 'portrait' in a conventional sense, he did refer to her in his cubist work. In the beginning, he wrote the title of a popular song, 'Ma Jolie', on his canvases as a code to refer to her; in other paintings, he incorporated the words 'J'aime Eva'. All of this, however, was cut short by her illness and, soon, her death.

Eva Gouel, born in 1885, was the daughter of Adrien Gouel and Marie-Louise Ghérouze, of Vincennes, who christened her Ève. When she and Picasso got together, he liked to call her Eva, the Spanish version of her name, which for him signified that she was the first woman. Before she met Picasso, she may have worked as an artist's model and gone by the name of Marcelle Humbert. It was not unusual for independent women of her generation in France to adopt more than one name, but a rumour persisted that she had once been married to a certain Monsieur Humbert. This, however, does not seem to be the case. Not much is known about her education or early associations with the art world in Paris. Did Marcelle Humbert work as a model at the Académie Humbert (and take the name from it)? The art

**27
Eva Gouel
with the dog
Sentinelle, 1914**

Musée national Picasso,
Paris (FPPH 48)

school was located at 104, boulevard de Clichy, and young artists such as Marie Laurencin and George Braque were students there. She was also the subject of a portrait painting by the artist Pierre Girieud, which was exhibited at the Salon d'Automne in 1911 and listed in the catalogue as no. 608, *Portrait*. It stated that the portrait 'appartient à Madame Markous' (belongs to Madame Markous), and at that time, the sitter was living with a Polish artist (although they were not actually married) by the name of Ludwik Kazimierz Władysław Markus. He too took on a new name: it was the poet Guillaume Apollinaire who suggested that the artist change Markus to the more French-sounding Marcoussis (the name of a market village south of Paris), and he also changed Ludwik to Louis. Marcoussis worked as an illustrator (as Markous), principally for the journal *La Vie Parisienne*, and his cartoons sometimes parodied the cubists. He and his girlfriend were mutual friends of the Italian painter Gino Severini and his wife, Jeanne, and they frequently met up at the Brasserie de l'Ermitage, where they were often joined by Picasso and Fernande Olivier. In his memoirs, Severini described 'Eva' as 'a small, spicy girl who looked like a Chinese doll. Fernande, her opposite, was a classic French beauty, with regular, well-proportioned features.'[2] The Italian recalled that he, Picasso and Marcoussis went to the Brasserie de l'Ermitage every evening, but 'involuntarily I was the cause of the drama which deeply distressed my great friend [Picasso] for quite a time. I allude to his definitive separation from Fernande in the spring of 1912'.[3]

Olivier and Picasso had already met Marcelle Humbert in the company of Marcoussis at a gathering at Gertrude Stein's (who refers to her as Eve), but Picasso's companion had no idea at the time that

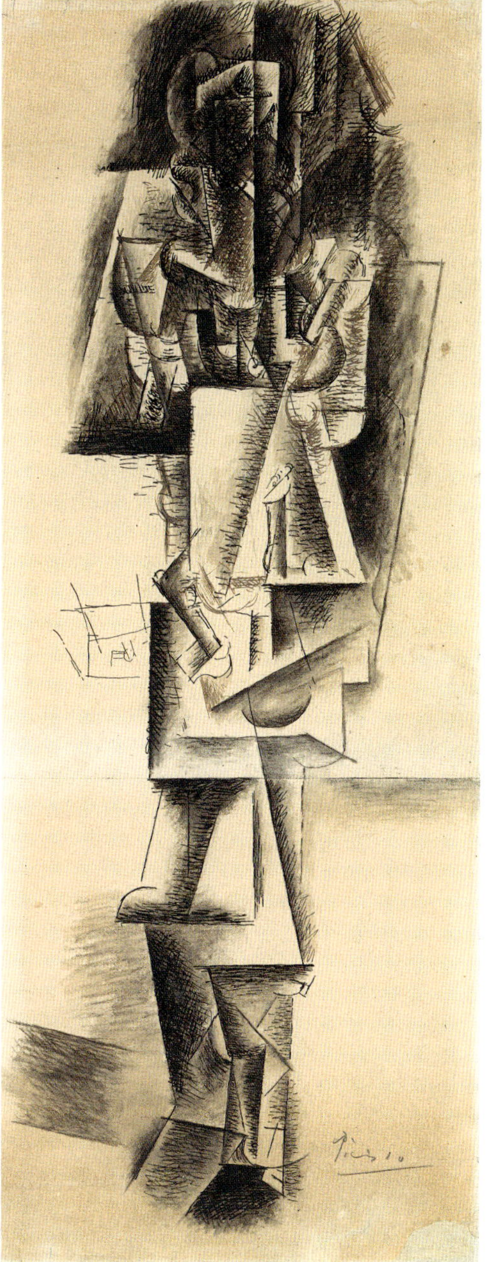

this scheming young woman would replace her in the artist's affections. According to Stein, 'I could perfectly understand Fernande's liking for Eve. … Fernande's great heroine was [the notorious American artist's model] Evelyn Thaw, small and negative. Here was a little french Evelyn Thaw, small and

perfect.'[4] Judith Cousins has dated the beginning of Picasso's undercover affair to winter 1911–12,[5] when he painted the first of a number of cubist compositions in which the song title 'Ma Jolie' (as a reference to his secret love) is added (fig. 29). Around this same time, Gertrude Stein and Alice B. Toklas visited Picasso's studio, and they noticed in another painting, *The Architect's Table* (The Museum of Modern Art, New York), the words *Ma Jolie* painted prominently at the left centre. Stein remarked: 'Fernande is certainly not Ma Jolie. I wonder who is.'[6]

The break between Picasso and Fernande Olivier, however, did not occur until the spring of 1912, after Severini

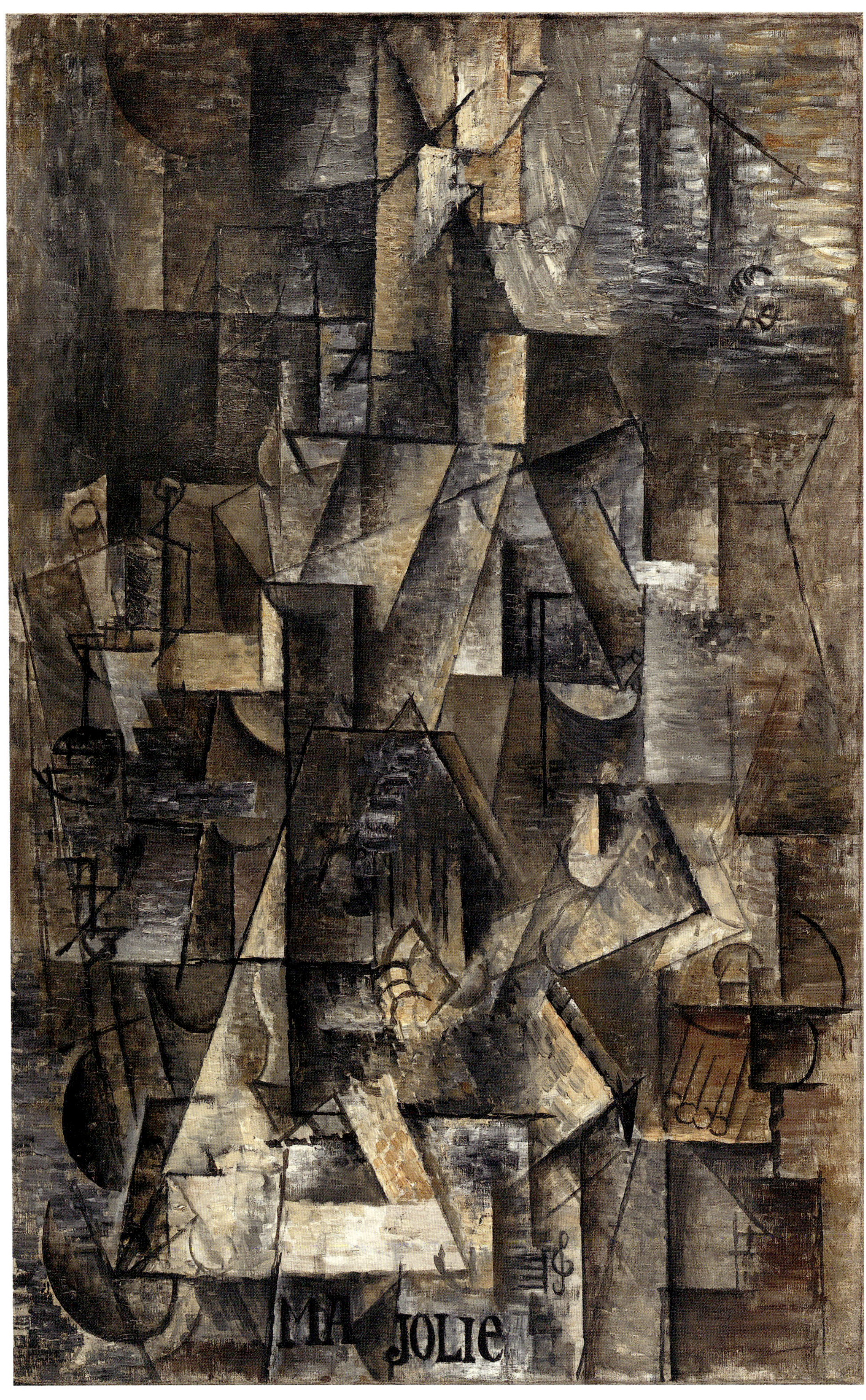
MA JOLIE

introduced the young Italian painter Ubaldo Oppi to the group at L'Ermitage. Olivier was particularly taken by Oppi's youthful good looks and embarked on an equally secret affair with him. She apparently confessed her dalliance to Marcoussis' girlfriend, who, in turn, betrayed her confidence and told Picasso. According to Severini, Picasso threw Olivier out, and 'Eva vanished at the very same time'. He goes on to say that 'the comical aspect of this drama was that Marcoussis and several others in Montmartre, aware of my friendship with Eva, thought for a time that I had kidnapped her.'[7] This of course, was not the case. Picasso wrote his great friend Georges Braque on 18 May 1912: 'Fernande has run away with a futurist. I'm going to get out of Paris for a bit. I beg you to look after Frika [the dog].'[8] What he does not say in the letter is that he was leaving with Eva Gouel. Although Picasso blamed Olivier for the break-up, in the beginning a number of his friends took her side and were reluctant to accept the artist's new partner. As for Marcoussis, he seems to have been delighted and celebrated his girlfriend's departure from his own life in a cartoon for *La Vie Parisienne* (15 June 1912), in which he depicts himself as 'the happy bachelor' and the one tied down with a ball and chain – that is, Picasso – as 'the newlywed'.

Picasso and Eva Gouel fled Paris, first to Céret in the mountains near the Spanish border, and then to Sorgues (a little town north of Avignon), where they stayed in the villa des Clochettes. The artist sent for various things, including painting supplies, from his studio (and also for his dog), and he and his new companion settled in happily for the summer (fig. 30), while Marcoussis put her things into storage. Apart from spending much of his time in the studio, Picasso sometimes took her to the theatre in Avignon, where, one night, they saw Sarah

29
Pablo Picasso,
Ma Jolie,
winter 1911–12
The Museum of Modern Art, New York (176.1945)

Bernhardt in *La Dame aux Camélias*. On another evening out, they met up at a local restaurant with a group of Montmartre friends, including Pierre Girieud (who had painted her portrait as 'Madame Markous' the previous year) and the composer Déodat de Séverac, whom Picasso had painted the previous summer in Céret. Picasso greatly anticipated the arrival in Sorgues of Braque, who, with his partner, Marcelle Lapré, was planning to join them. Once installed, the two couples sometimes shared meals, took walks together, and, on one occasion, made an excursion to Marseilles, where they hunted for African art.

Both Picasso and Braque had begun to add lettering to their canvases beginning in 1911. Braque included fragments of titles from journals and sheet music in his compositions, both to evoke café life and also music, while Picasso introduced similar elements, in addition to labels and flags with lettering, but he also continued to add references to his girlfriend. In a letter to his dealer (12 June 1912), he wrote 'Marcelle is very sweet. I love her very much and I shall write this in my paintings.'[9] In subsequent letters, he starts to refer to her as Eva rather than Marcelle, perhaps not to confuse her with Braque's Marcelle. Not only did he paint the words 'Ma Jolie' in a cubist mural on the wall of the villa des Clochettes, he also included the declaration 'J'aime Eva' in paint at the bottom of a guitar in a still life. This oil on canvas (Musée Picasso, Paris) originally had a gingerbread heart incorporated as a collage element. In its present state, both the gingerbread and the inscription are missing, and a simulated piece of paper covers the place where 'J'aime Eva' had appeared. Another example, this time done in Paris, is a very subtly coloured cubist painting of a nude (fig. 31), in which one can just make out the words 'J'aime Eva' in the

**30
Eva Gouel in a kimono, photographed at the villa des Clochettes, Sorgues, 1912**
Musée national Picasso, Paris (FPPH 152)

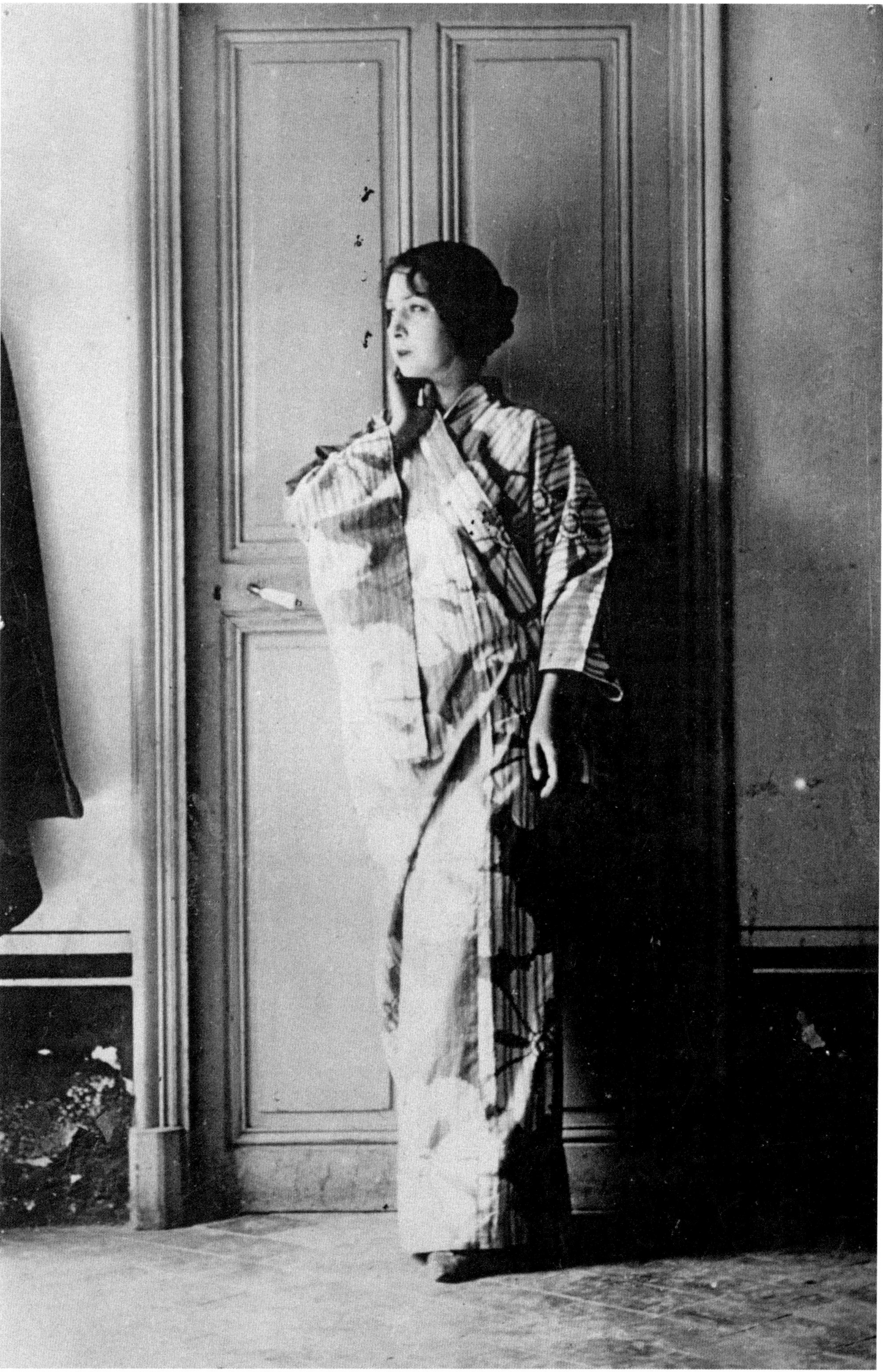

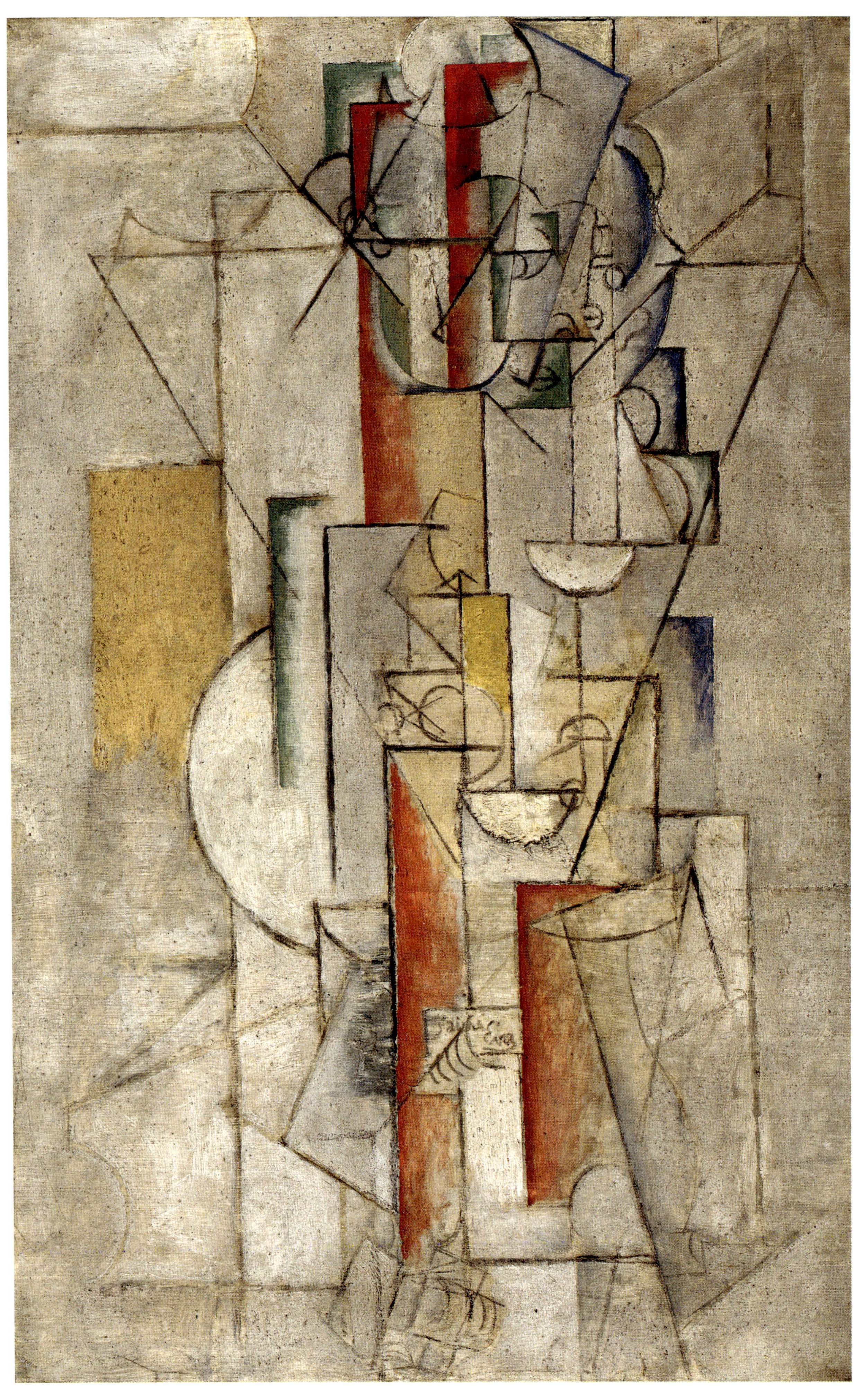

lower part of the composition between the two reddish vertical bands in the centre. On a visit some years ago to the State Hermitage Museum, Saint Petersburg, my husband and I, with the curator Alexander Babin, looked closely at the surface of Picasso's *Violin and Tenora*, 1913, in the museum's collection. We discovered, along the side of the thickly applied band of white paint at the left of the musical instruments, the name 'Eva', written vertically in minuscule letters.

When the couple returned to Paris in the autumn of 1912, they moved into a studio, which the dealer Daniel-Henry Kahnweiler had found for them, in an artists' complex, the Cité Nicolas Poussin, on the boulevard Raspail. Picasso's Barcelona friend (and future secretary) Jaime Sabartés recalled that everything changed for Picasso with Eva Gouel now in his life, and that they led a more settled existence together in Montparnasse than he had had with Fernande Olivier in Montmartre. Picasso found that the calmness of his new home situation allowed him to concentrate fully on his work. For her part, his companion was eager to establish friendships with some of Picasso's close circle of friends, including Gertrude Stein and Alice B. Toklas, who lived nearby. At the end of 1912, Stein wrote to her friend Mabel Dodge:

> I have a couple of new Picassos. We see a great deal of them. They live in this quarter and we are very chummy. The new Mme. is a very pleasant hostess and quite a cheerful person. The late lamented is gone forever. I don't know anything about her. Pablo is very happy. They are at Barcelona for Christmas, she is to be introduced to his parents as a légitime which I think she is although nothing is said.[10]

31
Pablo Picasso,
Female Nude
(*J'aime Eva*), 1912
Columbus Museum of Art,
gift of Ferdinand Howald

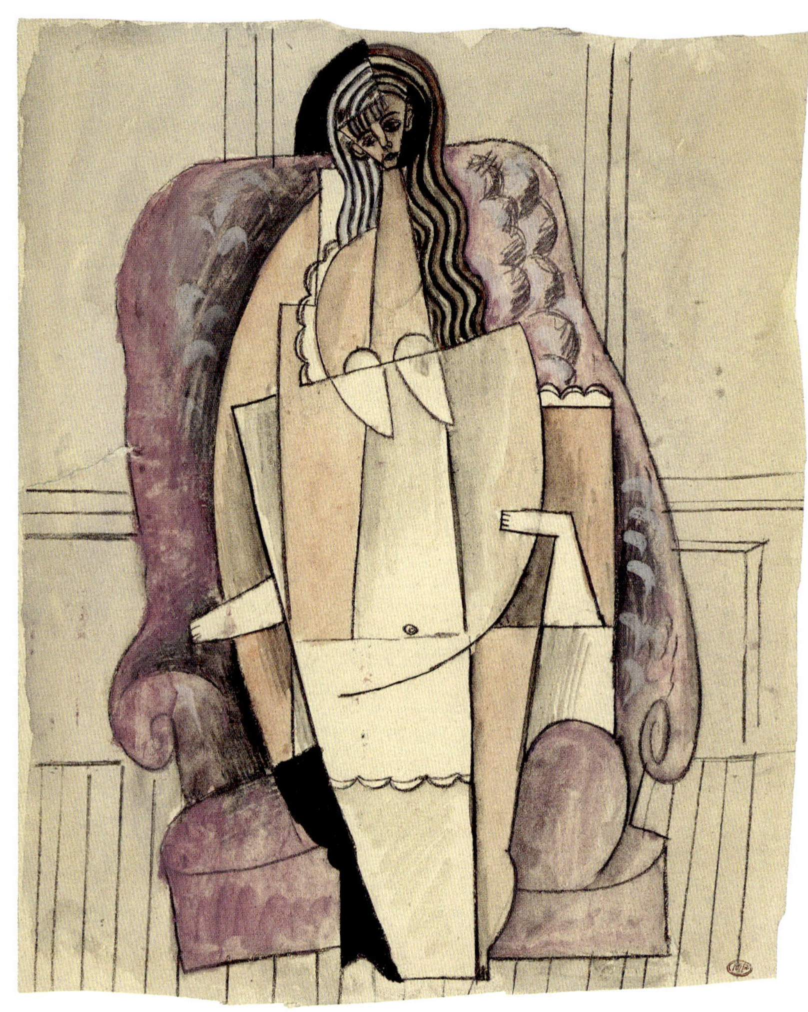

Picasso had taken Eva Gouel to Barcelona to meet his family, and Stein suggests he was going to introduce her as his fiancée. He also wanted to check on his father's health, which was in serious decline that winter. While they were there, she sent Stein and Toklas a number of postcards with views of the city. They returned to Paris around mid-January and moved once again to Céret in March. She wrote Stein from the town in the Pyrenees: 'The weather is marvelous and we've settled in.'[11] Max Jacob, who visited them in Céret that spring, commented on Eva Gouel's good-natured character and how hospitable she was to him.

Eva shows an admirable attentiveness to humble household tasks. She loves to write and laughs easily. She is even-tempered and devotes herself to looking after a guest who is naturally quite dirty and lazy when he is not being ridicu-lously crazy and idiotic ...[12]

Picasso found Céret congenial for his work, and he started a series of *papiers collés* there, which incorporated contemporary newspapers from either Paris or Céret. He was also in touch with Kahnweiler, who was having some of the artist's recent work photographed in Paris. When Picasso received the photos, he expressed his disappointment that he could not find 'the one from Paris this winter with colors, card in hand'[13] – that is, the painting in which he had inserted the phrase 'J'aime Eva'. At the beginning of May, Picasso suddenly departed alone for Barcelona, where his father died on 3 May. Gouel wrote Stein that she hoped Picasso would resume working, since that was the only way he could forget his troubles. At the same time, hints that she was not well herself were starting to emerge. In a letter to Apollinaire, for example, Max Jacob writes that they were all upset by the news of the death of Pablo's father, and he adds that Eva's health was not good.

Later in the year (1913), Picasso and Eva Gouel moved into an Art Nouveau building in Paris on the rue Schœlcher, near the boulevard Raspail and overlooking the cemetery of Montparnasse. The apartment/studio was large and full of sunlight, and Picasso became immersed in his work. There were occasional visits from friends, including Max Jacob and Apollinaire, and Picasso also reported that they had gone horseback riding with Henri Matisse through the forest of Clamart. It was in his new studio that Picasso made a few of his only 'portraits' of his companion, including several drawings (fig. 32), in which he carefully delineates her head and her long hair. These were not done just to please the sitter (if, indeed, she did model), but in preparation for a large oil on canvas, known as *Woman in a Chemise in an Armchair* (Metropolitan Museum of Art, New York). In the final version of the painting, Picasso retained some of her long hair (at the left of the head) that appears in the drawing, but he removed traces of her facial features, apart from a vertical, pin-like form, as if it were a collage element. When Pierre Daix asked the artist if the woman in the painting could be Eva Gouel, 'he shrugged and replied: "The forms just came to me like that. ... Of course, Eva was [with me] there."'[14]

The couple departed for the south of France in June 1914, and after spending some days in Tarascon, they finally settled in a house in Avignon. Their summer idyll was, however, interrupted by the news that war had been declared and that a number of their friends had been called up. Picasso saw off both Braque and André Derain (who were also in the south) at Avignon station, and Derain left his dog, Sentinelle, behind with Picasso (fig. 27). During the course of the summer, the artist painted a composition featuring a *Seated Man and an Artist's Model* (Musée Picasso, Paris), in which the model portrayed resembles Eva Gouel. This particular composition would have reverberations among Picasso's friends and critics, since it represented a departure from his recent cubist-inspired forms in favour of a more classical approach. From Avignon Eva Gouel kept in touch with a number of their friends, notably Max Jacob and Gertrude Stein, to whom she wrote frequently. She also tried, as much as possible, to keep track of the whereabouts of Apollinaire and Braque. No mention is made in her letters, however, about her own health worries.

The seriousness of her condition emerged in October 1914, when she wrote Stein with a request to find her a specialist. Picasso added to the letter that her recent operation (presumably, for cancer) had still not healed. Nonetheless, they decided to stay in Avignon until November, when they returned with Sentinelle and three cats to the apartment/studio on rue

Schœlcher. The young woman seems to have carried on fairly normally, but by the summer she confessed in a series of letters to Joséphine Haviland (the wife of Frank Burty Haviland, Picasso's good friend in Céret) that she was frail and losing weight. In June (1915) she wrote that she suspected (correctly) that Picasso was seeing someone else, but in a letter written in the following month, she says that she was happy once again. 'Pablo loves me and he has told me so.'[15] She writes that he was looking after her, and that they went out together 'like two young lovers'.[16] In order to encourage her to eat, he took her to a local restaurant on the avenue d'Orléans. She also says that they saw a few friends, including Max Jacob and the Russian artist Serge Férat, both of whom came to the apartment. However, she and Picasso were most concerned about Braque, who had been wounded in battle and trepanned in May. Once Braque was back in Paris, the couple saw him and his partner often, both in Montmartre and also when they all met up for dinner in Montparnasse. In a letter written on Picasso's birthday (25 October 1915), Gouel reports that her condition was much worse and that she could hardly write because of the trembling in her hands, and that she was just 'skin and bones'.[17] She feared that she would have to enter a *maison de santé* (nursing home).

Shortly after she wrote her last letter to Joséphine Haviland, she was indeed back in a clinic; this time, it would be final. Picasso wrote Stein in early December:

> Don't be surprised if I haven't written to you since you left [she was in Mallorca]. But my life is hell – Eva is still ill and gets worse every day and now she has been in a nursing home for a month. ... My life is pretty miserable and I hardly do any work. I run back-

wards and forwards to the nursing home, and I spend half my time in the Métro. I haven't had the heart to write you.[18]

Eva Gouel died from cancer just a few days after Picasso sent his letter to Stein, and the funeral was attended by some of their friends, including Juan Gris and Max Jacob. The poet was reported to have been drunk and misbehaved at the tomb, causing further grief to Picasso. The portrait engraving, known as *Tête de femme* (fig. 33), that the artist made shortly afterwards is a fitting evocation of the young woman whom he had intended to marry and who had shared his life for such a short, but intense, time.

33
**Pablo Picasso,
*Head of a
Woman* (*Tête de
femme*), 1915–16**
Musée national Picasso,
Paris (MP 2010); Baer 52

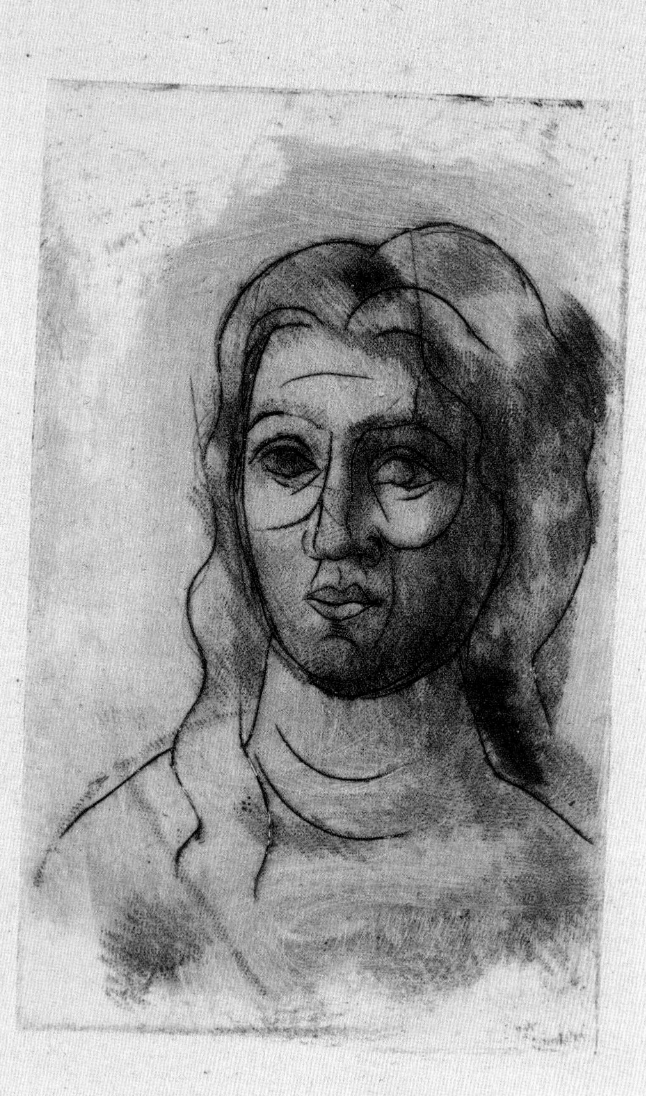

Olga Khokhlova

Markus Müller

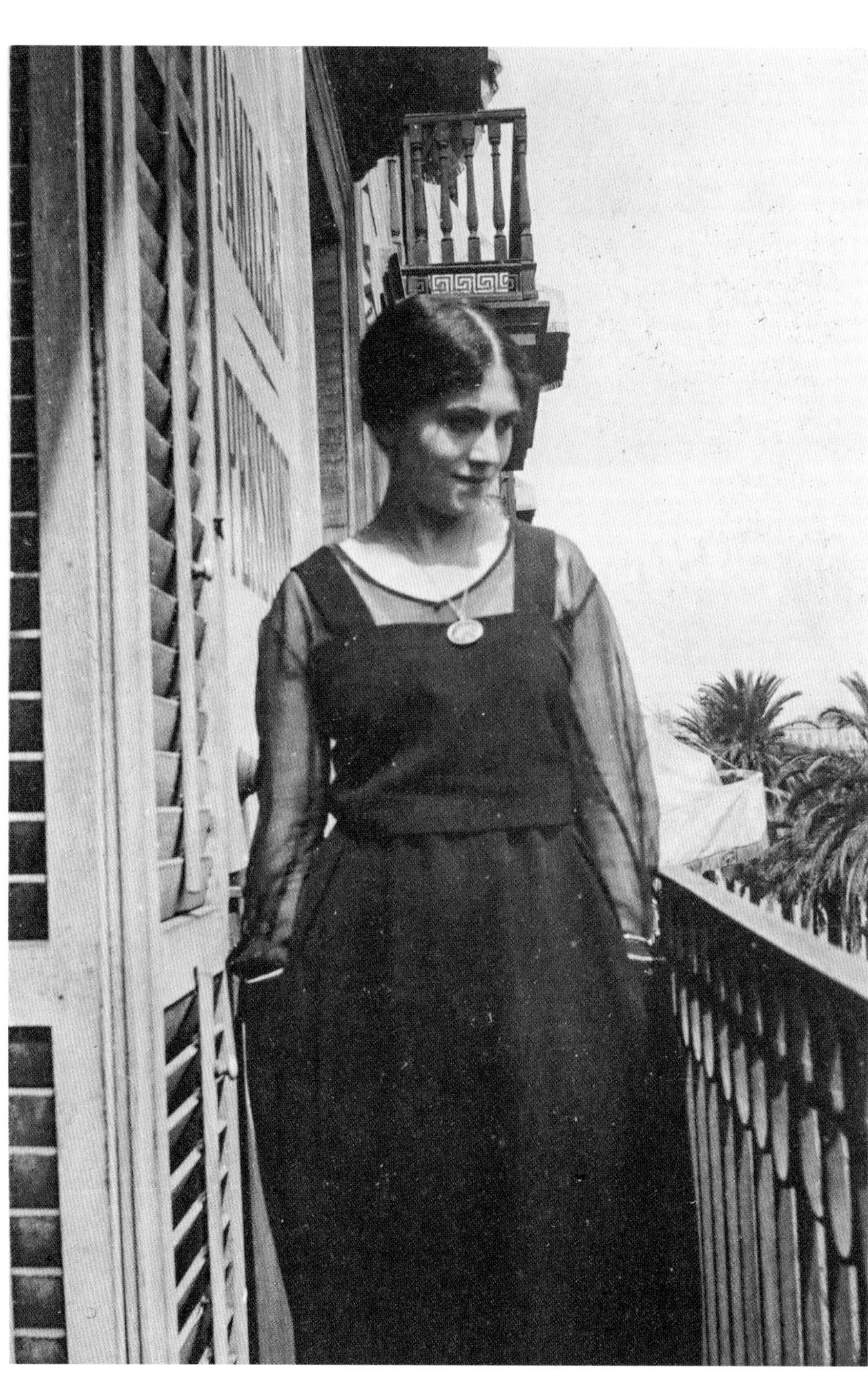

The train journey from Moscow to Paris took about fifty hours before the First World War. Eager to have his ensemble perform in Paris, however, the Russian ballet impresario Sergei Diaghilev was ready to shuttle back and forth between the two cities several times a year, if necessary. 'The Russian opera conquered Paris in one day',[1] effused one reviewer of Diaghilev's staging of *Boris Godunov* at the Opera Garnier in the magazine *Comœdia illustré* in May 1909. And Diaghilev and his Ballets Russes were to celebrate still more triumphs in the years thereafter. The then twenty-year-old Olga Khokhlova had the good fortune to be accepted as a dancer in Diaghilev's ballet company in 1911. The young lady with auburn hair had come to dance relatively late by the standards of the day. Diaghilev recruited his dancers in Moscow and St Petersburg, where he had them dance in front of an exacting jury consisting of the star dancer Vaslav Nijinsky, the famous ballet teacher Enrico Cecchetti and himself. Olga Khokhlova must therefore have been very talented indeed to win the approval of such an illustrious selection committee. Her father was a colonel in the tsarist army and her family, which was originally from Ukraine, had settled temporarily in St Petersburg. There, Khokhlova attended the ballet school of Evgenia Pavlovna Sokolova, a former prima ballerina many of whose pupils would go on to become famous ballet dancers. As a member of the corps de ballet of Diaghilev's ensemble, from early 1911 onwards Khokhlova would lead a nomadic, cosmopolitan life, performing with the Ballets Russes not only in Paris, but also in London, Rome, and several American cities.

The year 1917 brought some fundamental changes in the life of the young dancer. The Ballets Russes had taken up its winter quarters in Rome and begun rehearsing Jean Cocteau's piece, *Parade*, the music for which was composed by Erik Satie, whose score includes the clatter of a

**34
Olga Khohklova
on the balcony
of the Pension
Ranzini,
Barcelona, 1917**

Musée national Picasso,
Paris (APPH 3627)

typewriter as an integral part of his modernist soundscape. Diaghilev was astute enough to cultivate a traditional repertoire, which he then spiced up with the occasional avant-garde outlier, that being the category to which *Parade* undoubtedly belonged. The costumes and stage sets were designed by Pablo Picasso, who had travelled to Rome with Jean Cocteau to create the sets in situ. And thus, the stage was set for Picasso to meet, and become infatuated with, the then twenty-five-year-old Khokhlova, seemingly oblivious to Diaghilev's warning that as a Russian woman, she would expect him to marry her.

After premiering *Parade* in Paris in May 1917, the Ballets Russes took the production to Madrid and Barcelona, and with it Picasso, who was eager to accompany his new girlfriend. When he took Khokhlova to meet his mother in Barcelona, doña María allegedly told the young woman: 'You poor girl,

you don't know what you're letting yourself in for. If I were a friend I would tell you not to do it under any conditions. I don't believe any woman could be happy with my son. He's available for himself but for no one else.'[2]

While Khokhlova's mother-in-law has been much maligned, there can be no doubt that Señora Picasso either had an uncanny gift for prophecy or was all too familiar with how her only son ticked. Had Khokhlova heeded her counsel, however, the world would have been many a masterpiece the poorer.

One work that definitely warrants such an accolade is *Olga in a Mantilla* (fig. 35), of 1917. It was painted in Barcelona, the city of Picasso's youth, to which he returned with his new companion after a five-year-absence and was welcomed back warmly by both family and friends alike. The painting is remarkable for the artist's magisterial characterization of his partner and his superb reproduction of various fabrics and textures. Picasso portrays his future wife in three-quarter profile and has her stare back at us. Several of his biographers have interpreted the work as a psychological portrait of the young Russian, whom they describe as strict,

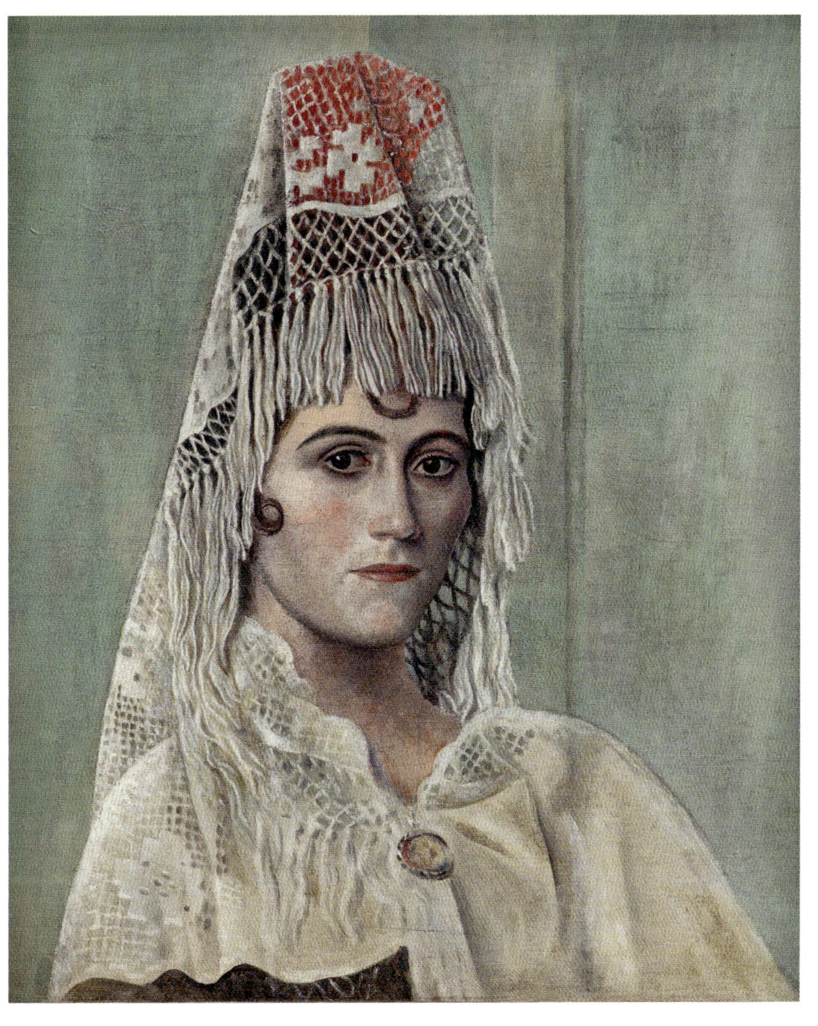

insecure, and possessive. Roland Penrose, for example, claims that 'beneath the smooth oval of the young and sensitive face we can divine a temperament already formed and unwilling to compromise. The dark discerning eyes appear to have settled on the object of their adoration with a possessive intent'[3] – comments that belong rather in the realm of psychological conjecture.

By depicting Olga as a *maja* with mantilla, Picasso was in fact upholding one of the great traditions of Spanish painting. The lace mantilla is a traditional woman's headdress, a black mantilla being an attribute of a married woman, and a white one symbolic of the wearer's virginity. As Picasso emphasised in a letter to Gertrude Stein, his latest conquest was a 'real young woman' and it seems that this was what he wanted to draw out in his portrait of her. The painting is composed as a symphony in white, the only exception being the red comb over which the mantilla is draped. That single splash of colour takes up Olga's complexion and red lips and harmonises with the hues of her auburn hair, which can be seen here and there, peeping out from under the lace. Some commentators have speculated that the mantilla was not a real mantilla at all, but rather a 'fringed lace tablecloth' that Picasso spontaneously repurposed for the portrait.[4] His subsequent partner Dora Maar

Olga Chochlowa

told John Richardson that the 'mantilla' was actually a curtain from Khokhlova's Madrid hotel room.[5]

He does seem to have taken the theme of the virginal bride very seriously, however – certainly too seriously for him to have wanted to conjure a coquettish smile playing on his future wife's lips. The importance that Picasso himself attached to this painting is borne out by the fact that he gave it to his mother, who held onto it for many years to come. The idea of giving his mother this portrait of his bride-to-be probably came to him while working on it, which could also explain why he depicted her naturalistically.

Picasso and Khokhlova parted company with the Ballets Russes and returned to Paris in late June 1917, and it was around then that Picasso painted the highly unusual *Portrait of Olga in an Armchair* (fig. 36) after a photograph

taken in his studio in the suburb of Montrouge.

Compared with the photograph, the figure of the young woman is elongated so that she looks both slimmer and more sylph-like. In the photograph, moreover, she stares straight into the camera, whereas in the painting she gazes elegiacally into the distance, as if unmindful of the viewer. And although the photo is a full-figure portrait, Picasso's

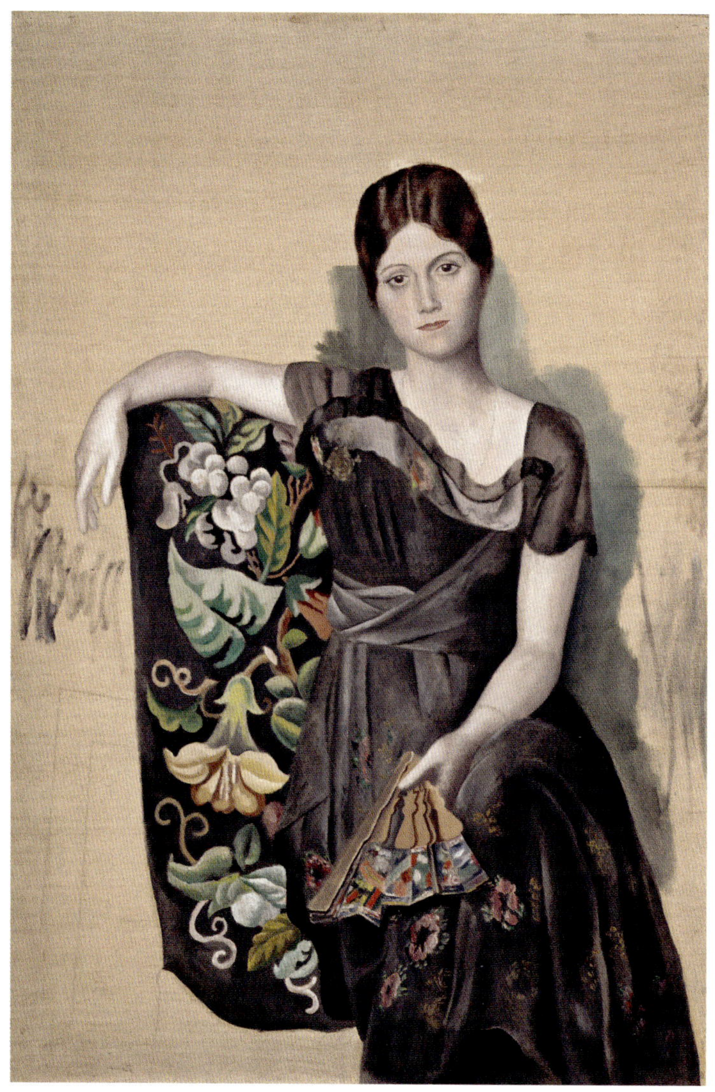

36
Pablo Picasso,
Portrait of Olga in an Armchair,
1918
Musée national Picasso, Paris (MP 55)

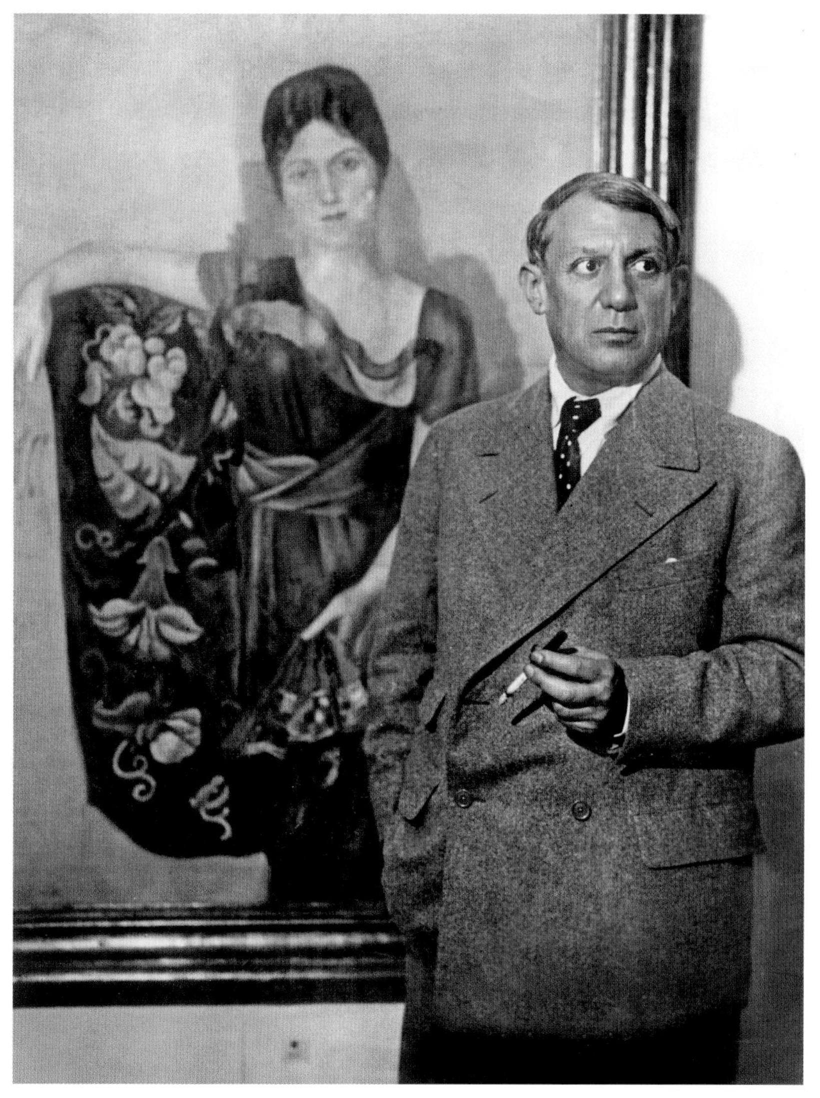

legs are no more than hinted at. The few broad brush-strokes of grey with which Picasso circumscribed the outline of the young ballerina might almost be a shadow cast by the figure on an otherwise blank rear wall. Thus the painter gave his work a look that at first glance makes it seem unfinished. Only on second glance do we detect the aesthetic cunning that brings this composition to life. For Picasso's sketchy outlining is not so much a shadow as a compositional counterweight to the all too naturalistic style of representation. Works like this prove that towards the end of the war, Picasso was not be-coming a dogmatic classicist, but was rather spicing up his neoclassical adventures with ever new changes of style and approach.

Unlike a number of Picasso's previous muses, Olga Khokhlova did not come from an artistic background. Her father was a colonel in the tsarist army, and her figure and deportment conveyed haute bourgeois propriety coupled with the elegant gestures of a ballet dancer. She was clearly talented, as can be easily in-ferred from the roles she was asked to perform. Nijinsky him-self selected her for the part

composition ends at the hem of Olga's black, floral dress. The fall of the cloth and the crossed legs were apparently important to him, since in the photograph we can see the large tome that he placed under her feet to facilitate that pose.

Both the figure of Olga and the chair on which she is sitting seem to hover over the unpainted canvas of the ground, and even the chair

of the nymph in *L'Après-midi
d'une faune* (The afternoon of
a faun) as early as 1912, and
four years later Léonide
Massine assigned her the lead
role in *Las Meninas*. Her
career came to an abrupt end
in April 1918, however, when
severe pain in her right foot
forced her to stop dancing and
to undergo surgery in Paris.
Her convalescence dragged
on for months, and she would
never again set foot on the
stage. The private photos of
the 1920s that show her in a
dancer's costume and striking
a dancer's poses thus have to
be read as mere memories
and no more than a nostalgic
reliving of the career she had
had to abandon (fig. 38).

Picasso and Khokhlova
were married in the Russian
Orthodox church on rue Daru
in Paris – then a favourite
haunt of Russian exiles – on
12 July 1918. The newly-weds
spent their long honeymoon in
Biarritz at the invitation of the
Chilean millionaire Eugenia
Errázuriz. Before being
eclipsed by the Côte d'Azur in
the early 1920s, Biarritz was
France's most urbane seaside
resort – 'urbane' being the
adjective that best describes
the young Picassos in the early
years of their marriage.

Picasso's ascendancy as
an internationally acclaimed
artist became visibly meteoric
after the First World War.
Since Daniel-Henry Kahnweiler,
as a German national, now
counted as an enemy alien,
Picasso signed on with the
Paris-based dealer Paul
Rosenberg and agreed to have
Georges Wildenstein represent him in the United States.
Rosenberg found an elegant
abode for the young couple at
no. 23, rue La Boétie, next
door to his own business
premises at no. 21. For the
newly married Picasso, the
change of address reflected a
radical change of lifestyle.
Having formerly lived a bohemian life among the artists of
Montmartre and Montparnasse, he now became a respect-
able bourgeois citizen. While
he used the *côté rue* (street
side) as a makeshift studio
pending the availability of one

38
Pablo and Olga
Picasso on the
beach near
Antibes (Alpes-
Maritimes),
c. 1924

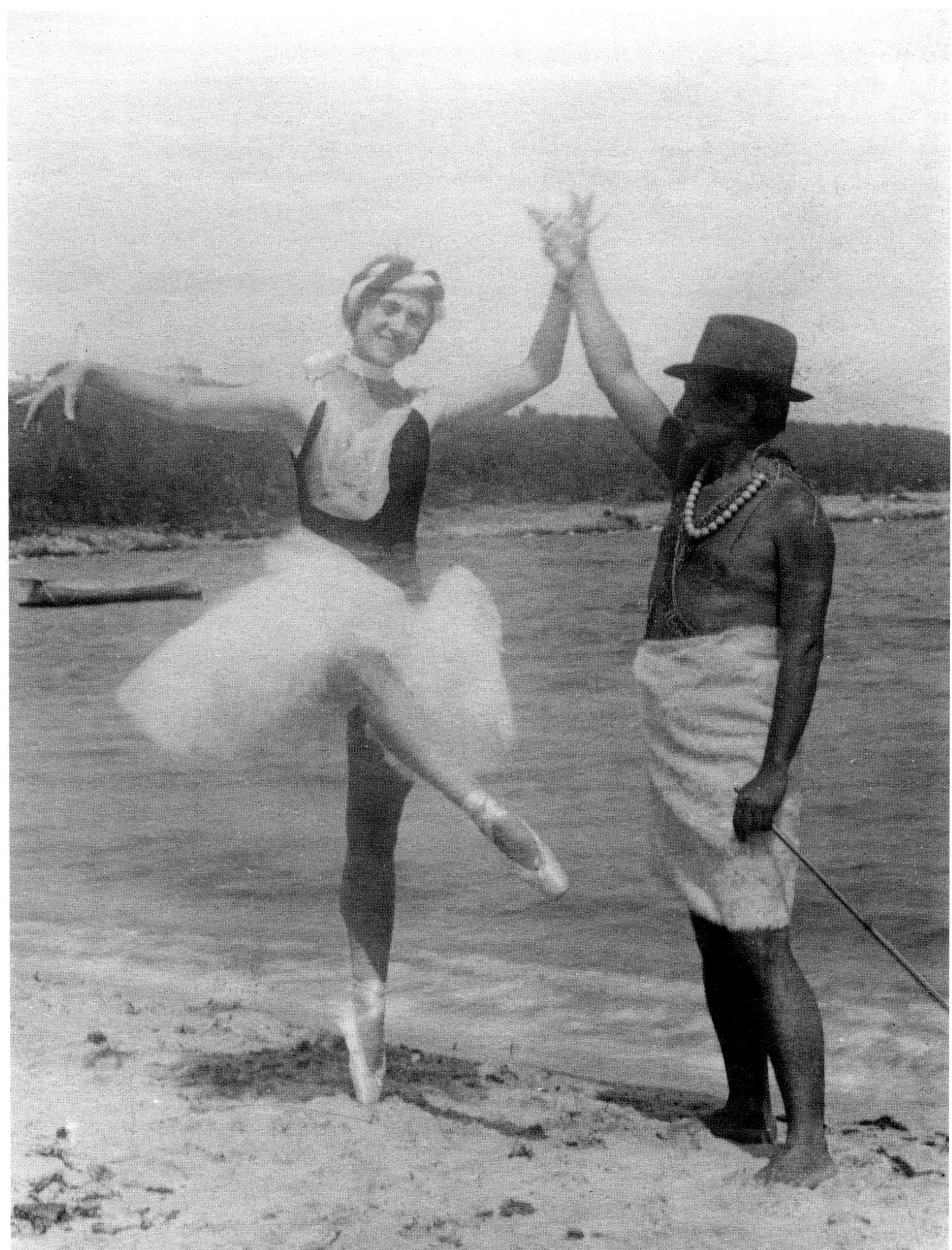

of the upper floors of the building, his wife busied herself with
turning the *côté cour* (court-
yard side) into an elegant,
bourgeois home.

The photographer
Brassaï, who by then had
known the artist for many
years, described the new living
situation in his *Conversations
with Picasso*:

> This middle-class apart-
> ment was completely un-
> like his usual surround-
> ings. There were none
> of the extraordinary
> furnishings he was so
> crazy about, none of the
> strange objects he liked
> to have around him,
> there were no piles,
> nothing scattered about,
> as was his wont. Olga
> jealously made sure that
> Picasso did not impose
> the powerful imprint of
> his personality on a
> realm she considered
> hers alone.[6]

A drawing dated 21 November
1919 (fig. 39) presents Olga's
universe as viewed by her
husband. It is a delicate outline
drawing of a herring-bone
parquet floor and on it four
figures, casually grouped in
two pairs rather like a conversation piece. Olga herself is
sitting crossed-legged in an
armchair next to Jean Cocteau,
while Erik Satie and the British
writer and art critic Clive Bell
are seated in front of the fireplace, which has a mirror
hanging over it. The latter described sitting for this group
portrait in one of his letters:
'We were set in a row, for all
the world as though we were
posing for the village photographer, and then Picasso took
our like-nesses.'[7] The stiffness

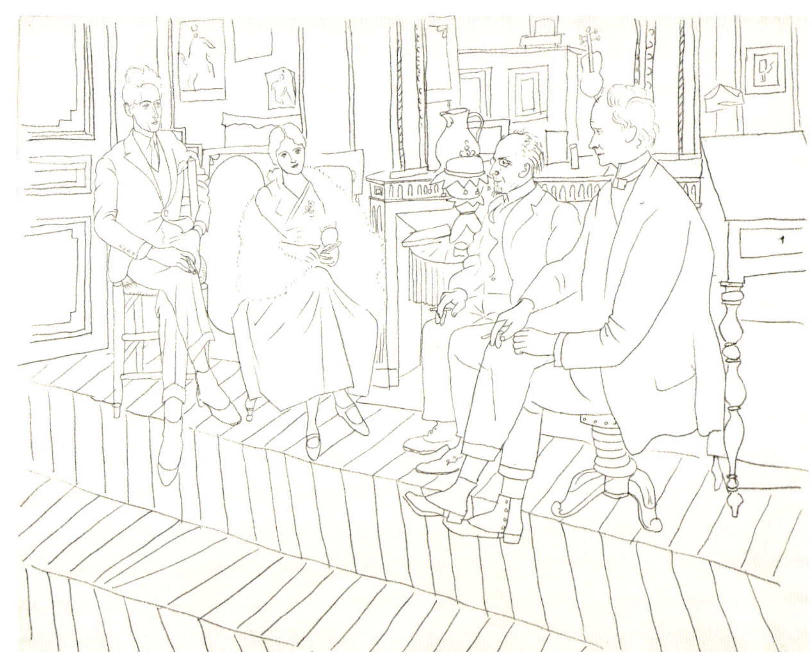

**39
Pablo Picasso,
*The Salon of the
Artist, Rue de
la Boétie,*
21 November 1919**

Musée national Picasso,
Paris (MP 869)

and artfulness of the drawing are not without an element of subliminal comedy. Such is the graphic verve and precision that Picasso accords every dado, every moulding, every item of furniture, that the four protagonists come across as four bright islands in a sea of haute bourgeois decorative art. The work is thus a graphic staging of an art lover's salon in which the young Madame Picasso takes centre stage, Cocteau and Satie represent poetry and music respectively, and Clive Bell is cast in the role of cosmopolitan art connoisseur. The drawing thus fulfils two functions at once: it celebrates friendship while at the same time asserting the artist's status.

Cocteau and Satie, both of whom had known Picasso for many years, posed for him in his new home at a time when other old friends of his were turning away from him. Without so much as a hint of irony, the poet Max Jacob spoke of his former friend's *époque duchesse* – 'duchess

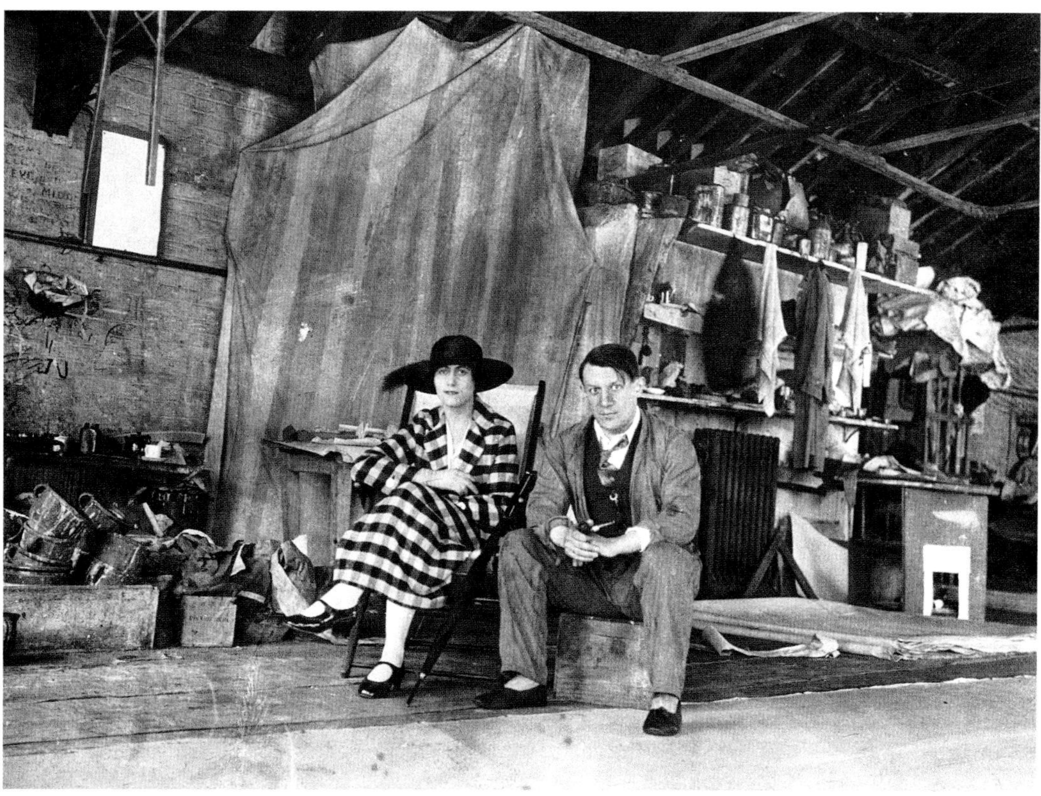

40
Olga and Pablo Picasso in the studio in London where he made the curtain to *Le Tricorne* **(***The Tricorne***), 1919**

Musée national Picasso, Paris (APPH 4776)

period'; and in a letter to their former dealer Kahnweiler of 3 September 1918, Picasso's compatriot Juan Gris poured scorn on his former friend: 'Picasso still produces fine things, if he can find the time for them between all that Russian ballet and fashionable portraiture' (<u>fig. 42</u>). [8]

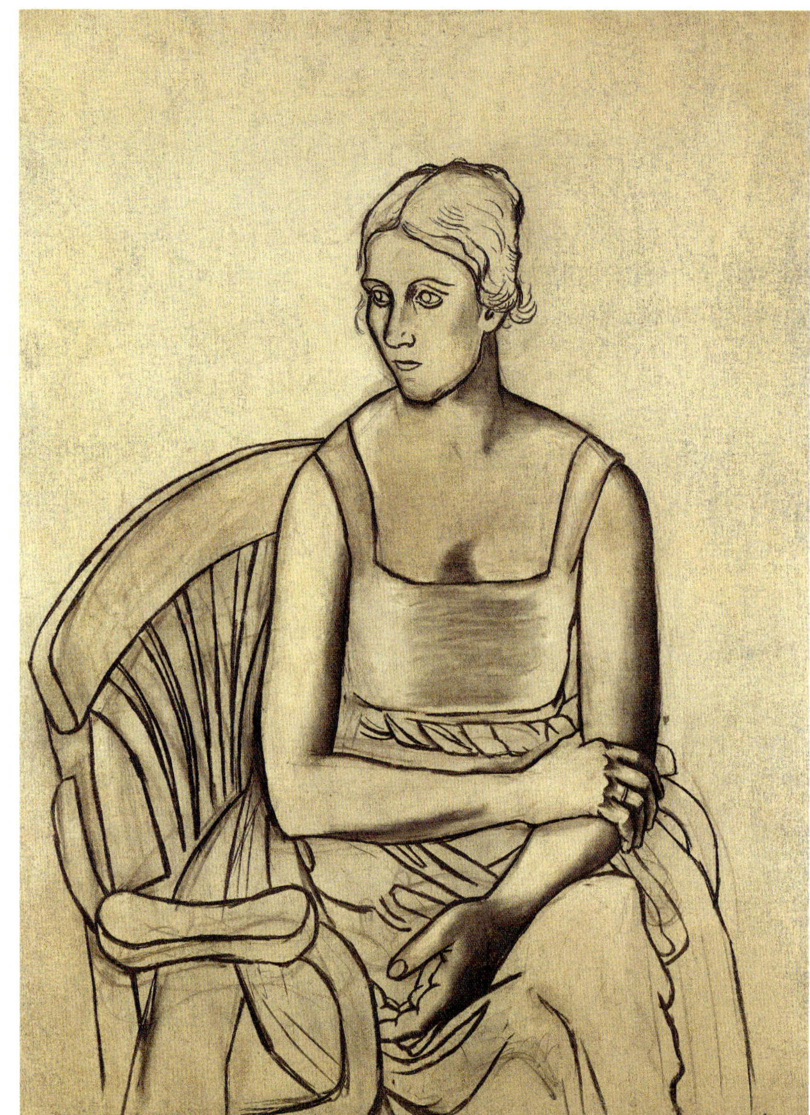

Picasso's capacity for self-reinvention troubled more than just one of his former artist friends. Once the First World War was over, the great revolutionary and destroyer of painterly certainties trained his sights on the museum and on history. Some critics derided these works harking back to the French classicists as op-portunistic, even sycophantic. Picasso was evidently trying to paint his way to French citizen-ship, sneered the critic André Fermigier. Some biographers preferred to follow the dictum *'cherchez la femme'*, however, and identified the artist's new wife as the true motivation for his sudden change of taste. During his years with her, they argued, Picasso became a reactionary and turned his back on the avant-garde. To them, the neoclassical inter-lude between his cubist and Surrealist periods was a time of stagnation – a negative verdict that coloured their judgment of Olga Picasso, too.

Some well-known biographers, such as Roland Penrose, Pierre Cabanne and John Berger, even accused her of having tamed Picasso and corrupted his very essence by forcing him to live according to her own bourgeois norms.[9] Under her influence, they argue, the bohemian artist had become a mere crowd-pleaser, a gentleman painter who adapted his art to the prevailing taste. Yet the very idea that Picasso would have allowed himself to be moulded by his wife is hardly plausible and difficult to reconcile with what we know of his character. Accounts of Khokhlova's biography, like those of Picasso's other muses, have tended to focus on her inspirational value to the artist, rather than on her as an individual and artist in her own right. Yet such a one-dimensional view can scarcely do justice to the complexity of her life story.

It was a proverbial 'attic find' that at last shed light on the tragic dimension of Olga Picasso's life at the side of her world-famous husband. Her grandson Bernard Ruiz-Picasso chanced upon a large trunk bearing his grandmother's initials in an uninhabited room of Château de Boisgeloup, which Picasso had made over to her and where she lived occasionally after they separated. The trunk contained those personal effects and mementos that Olga Picasso had had with her at the time of her death, at the Beau Soleil clinic in Cannes. It follows that these were items that were of immense sentimental value to her. Among them were the letters that she had exchanged with the family she left behind in Russia. She lost contact with them altogether after the October Revolution of 1917 and heard nothing more until 1919, when a French intermediary tracked them down for her. The account of what had happened to them was deeply distressing.

Her father had gone missing while fighting the Red Army

41
Pablo Picasso,
***Portrait of Olga Khokhlova*, 1920**
Private collection

25 August 1925. 'His pictures fill three whole rooms. … People come in hordes to see Picasso's paintings.'[10]

Throughout the 1920s, Olga Picasso must have been tormented by the fact that while she herself, as the wife of an artist of international renown, had been climbing the social ladder, her family in post-revolutionary Russia had been moving in the opposite direction. Her mother, who suffered from a heart condition, never lost hope of seeing her daughter once again, but died in the summer of 1927 without that wish being fulfilled.

The conflicting claims on the former ballet dancer left her emotionally torn for years to come, for she knew that while she and Picasso were living in comfort in France and had even started a family together, her mother and her siblings were barely scraping by. Her husband was also emotionally torn, though for a completely different reason. In 1927 he met the young Marie-Thérèse Walter, who was to become his new girlfriend and muse. While unfaithful husbands in bourgeois circles were typically found out by tell-tale signs such as lipstick on a shirt collar, Picasso gave himself away by the content of

during the civil war, although it later transpired that he died in mid-December 1919, probably of typhus, and her brothers, who likewise fought on the side of the Whites, also disappeared from the radar during those years of turmoil. Starting in 1919, however, Olga Picasso was at least able to write regularly to her mother, Lydia, and her sister, Nina, who by then were living in Tbilisi, and she also began sending them money, earning her the sobriquet of the family's 'good fairy'. The letters from Russia also tell of the spread of her husband's fame far beyond France. 'I went to the Shchukin Museum today and was at last able to see your husband's paintings', wrote her brother Vladimir in a letter dated

42
**Pablo Picasso,
*Portrait of Olga
Picasso*, 1923**
Private collection

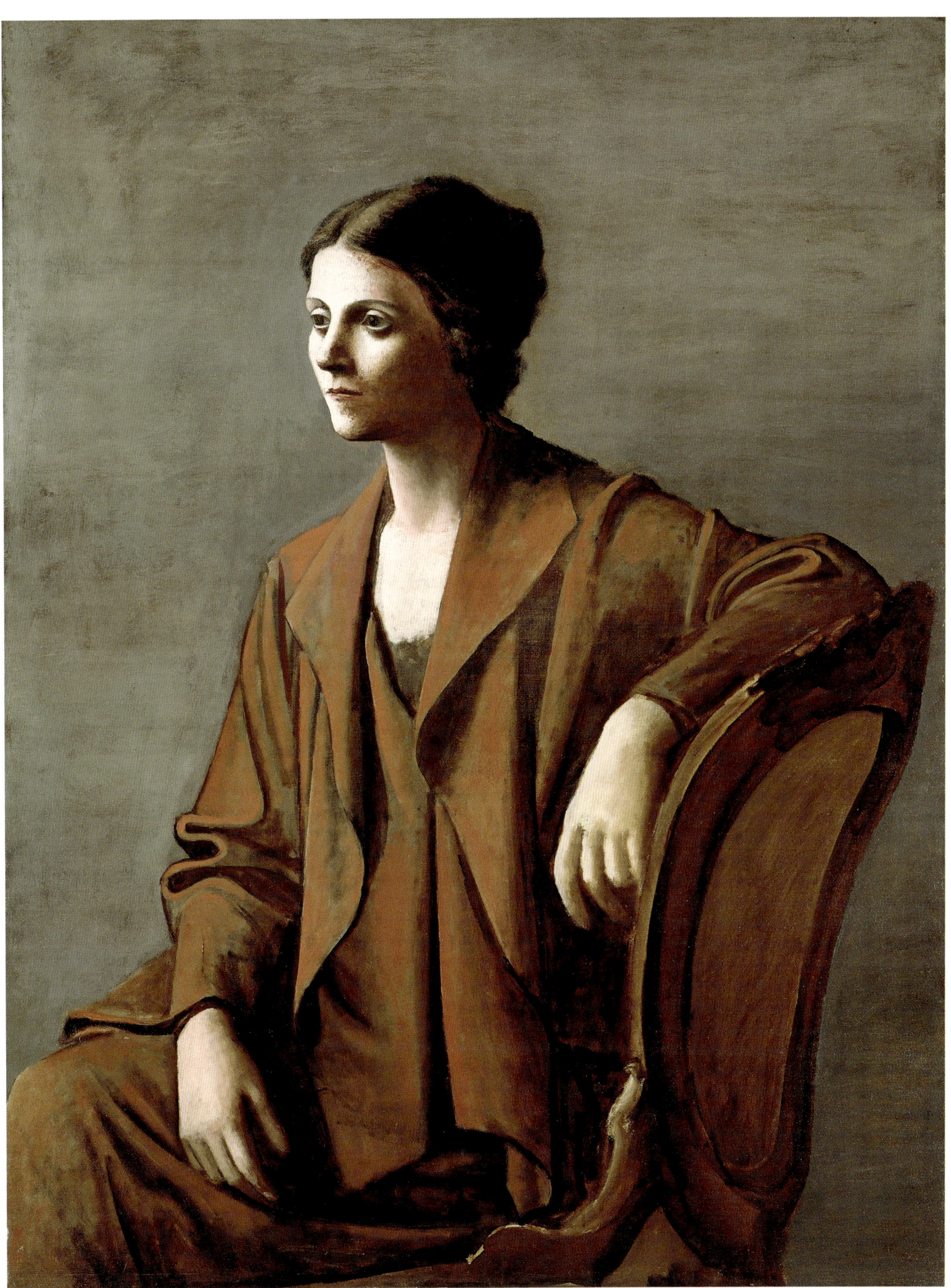

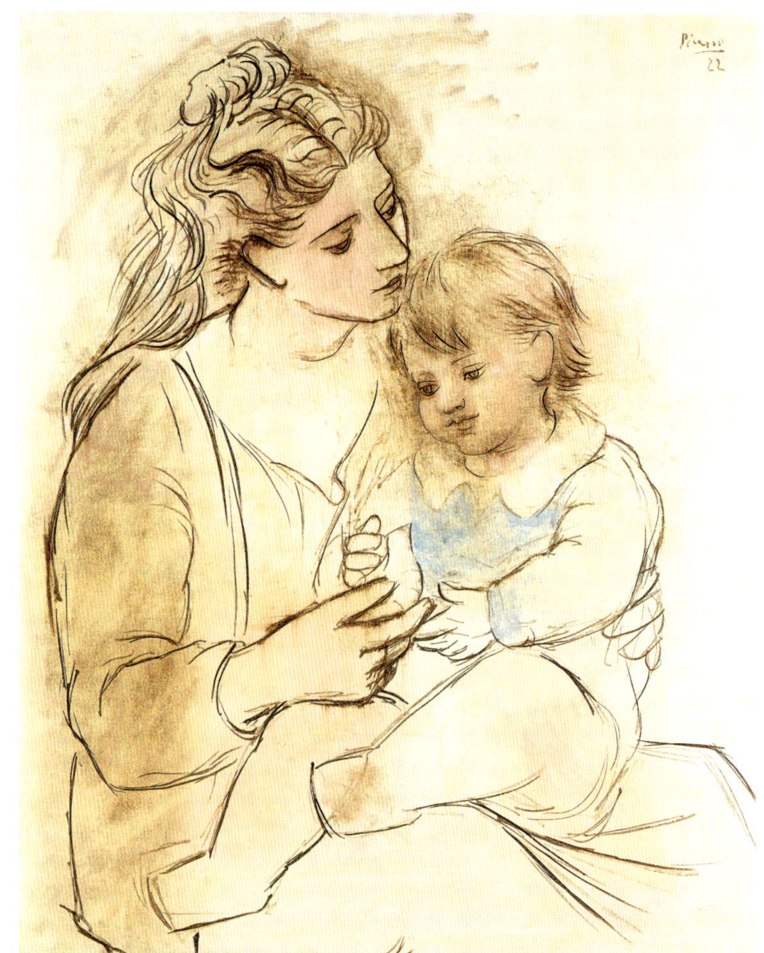

his own oeuvre. By 1931 at the very latest, the painterly evidence of the new woman in her husband's life, on public display at exhibitions, must have been impossible for Olga to deny.

When Marie-Thérèse Walter gave birth to a daughter, Maya, in September 1935, the rift between Picasso and his wife became unbridgeable. Olga Picasso moved into a Paris hotel, taking with her their son, Paulo, born in February 1921 (fig. 43). In later years, Picasso would look back on this period as the 'worst time' of his life. Yet the couple would never formally divorce, and for legal purposes the marriage ended only with Olga Picasso's death, in 1955. Presumably it was the vagaries of this situation that prompted the behaviour that Françoise Gilot

describes in her memoirs. Olga Picasso, she says, followed both the artist and his new companions around and made embarrassing scenes in public.

Through their son, Paulo, Olga generally knew where Picasso was currently living, which is why she was able to spy on Françoise Gilot and Pablo in the south of France. She even sunned herself on the same beach as them and accused Gilot of having stolen her husband. Françoise Gilot undoubtedly had no great interest in presenting Picasso's previous partners in a favour-able light; yet we know of Olga's obsessiveness from Cocteau, too.

Olga Picasso spent her final years at the Beau Soleil clinic in Cannes, to which she was admitted in 1952. It seems to have been a fashionable establishment, as many other famous women chose to end their days there, among them the American author and publisher, Margaret C. Anderson, who can be credited with having brought authors such as Ezra Pound and T.S. Eliot to the attention of a much wider reading public.

The private clinic was housed in a very grand, three-storey, late-nineteenth-century building which originally served as the Hôtel de Voyageurs. Yet the only travels that Olga Picasso would henceforth take were those in her imagination. The physician treating her was one Doctor Kruger, whose calling card described him as a specialist in *maladies nerveuses*. Olga Picasso's sufferings were indeed both mental and physical, and her physician updated her husband on her state of health – discreetly enclosing his bills in the same envelope as his reports. Olga Picasso's diary for those final years provides

moving testimony to the love and care of her son, Paulo, and grandson Pablito, who visited her regularly.[11]

Olga Picasso died of cancer in Cannes on 11 February 1955. Once her romantic vision of a bourgeois life at Picasso's side proved illusory, she continued dreaming her dream without him, so that the hoped-for *pas de deux* with her husband turned into a long and lonely trudge towards death.

**43
Pablo Picasso,
*Mother and
Child*, 1922**
Private collection

Marie-Thérèse Walter

Markus Müller

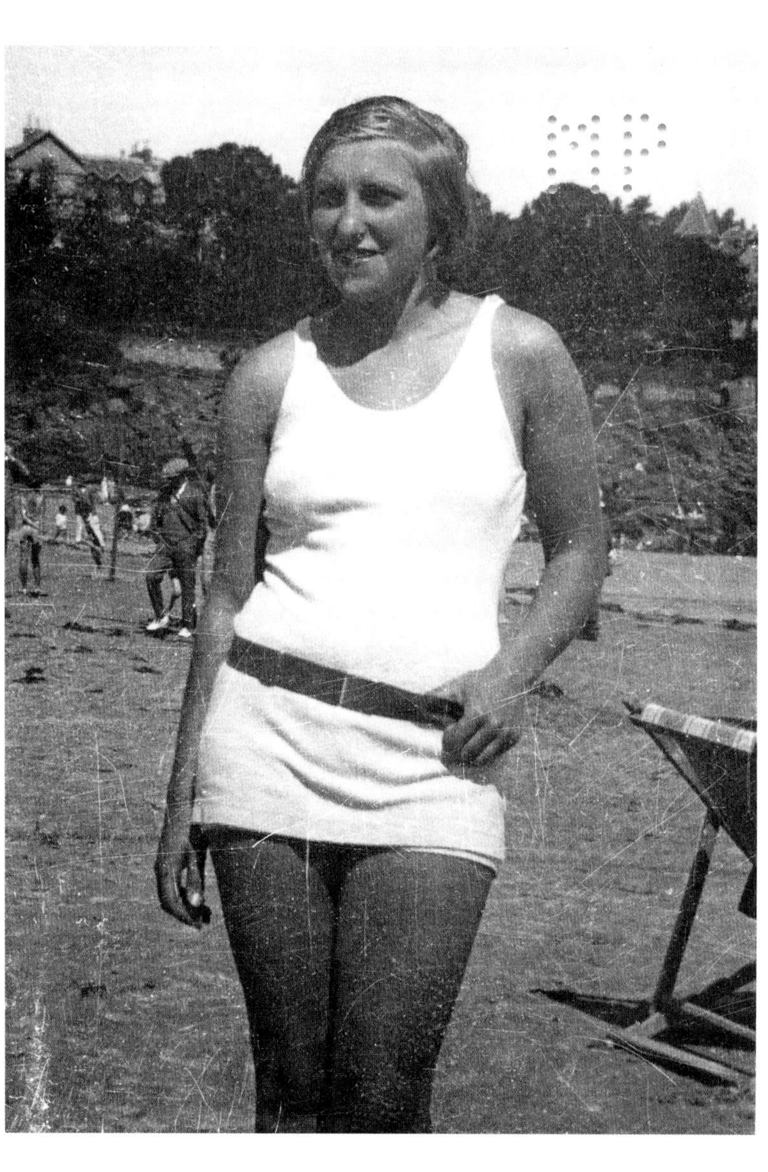

Beauty
and
the
Beast

Standing at an entrance to the Galeries Lafayette department store in the heart of Paris at 6 o'clock in the evening on Saturday, 8 January 1927, was a young woman who had gone there to buy a collar for her blouse. She was approached by a complete stranger, a man who looked to be in his mid-forties and addressed her directly with a winning smile: 'Mademoiselle, you have an interesting face. I would like to paint your portrait. I'm sure we shall do great things together.' He then introduced himself: 'I'm Picasso.'[1] Since the person thus addressed showed no glimmer of recognition at the utterance of this name, Pablo Picasso showed her a monograph about him in an Asian language that he happened to have with him. Given that nowhere in this work was his name spelled out in roman letters, the young woman might well have dismissed this ostensible proof of a reputation spanning the globe as a simple con trick; but as it happens, she was charmed by it and readily assented to Picasso's wish to see her again. The young woman in the crowd was Marie-Thérèse Walter, who lived with her mother and sisters in Maisons-Alfort on the outskirts of Paris. She was one of the many thousands of faces thronging the Galeries Lafayette that Saturday evening.

'I would like to see you again', Picasso said. 'I'll meet you at 11 o'clock on Monday at Saint-Lazare Métro station.' On the said Monday, Picasso took Marie-Thérèse Walter to a café, then to lunch, and then to his studio, where he carefully scrutinised her profile and her face. He then bid her farewell and asked her to come again at 11 o'clock the following day. When the meetings became a daily ritual, she pretended to her mother that she was commuting to Paris because of a new job.

Her young age – she was seventeen at the time – has led to all manner of speculation, recriminations, and far-fetched justifications on the part of Picasso's biographers. For the fact is, the forty-five-year-old Picasso was entering into a love affair with a minor. His own version of the beginning of their relationship is related by Françoise Gilot in her book *Life with Picasso*. Marie-Thérèse Walter for her part chose to confide first in the American art historian Lydia Gasman and two years later, in April 1974, in the French art critic and journalist Pierre Cabanne, to whom she gave her only radio interview.

Marie-Thérèse Walter was a young woman of athletic build who was an excellent swimmer and loved rowing, cycling, and doing gymnastic exercises with a medicine ball (fig. 45). She was also passionate about riding and hiking. She owed her German-sounding surname to her grandfather from Heidelberg, who had settled in France in the mid-nineteenth century.

There was no moral opprobrium attached to an extramarital affair in her eyes; after all, she herself and her three sisters were the product of their divorced mother's affair with the married industrialist Léon Volroff.[2] Reflecting on the discretion of her relationship with Picasso many years later, she bathed it in an aura of intimacy and mutual contentment: 'My life with him was always secret. Calm and peaceful. We said nothing to anyone. We were happy like that, and we did not ask anything more.'[3]

Even old friends like Gertrude Stein and Picasso's dealer Daniel-Henry Kahnweiler were left in the dark, so that the first pointer to the existence of a new girlfriend were the initials 'MT' worked into a depiction of stylised guitars later in 1927. 'MT' was how Picasso addressed his muse and mistress in their voluminous correspondence, while

45
Marie-Thérèse Walter in Juan-les-Pins, July 1932

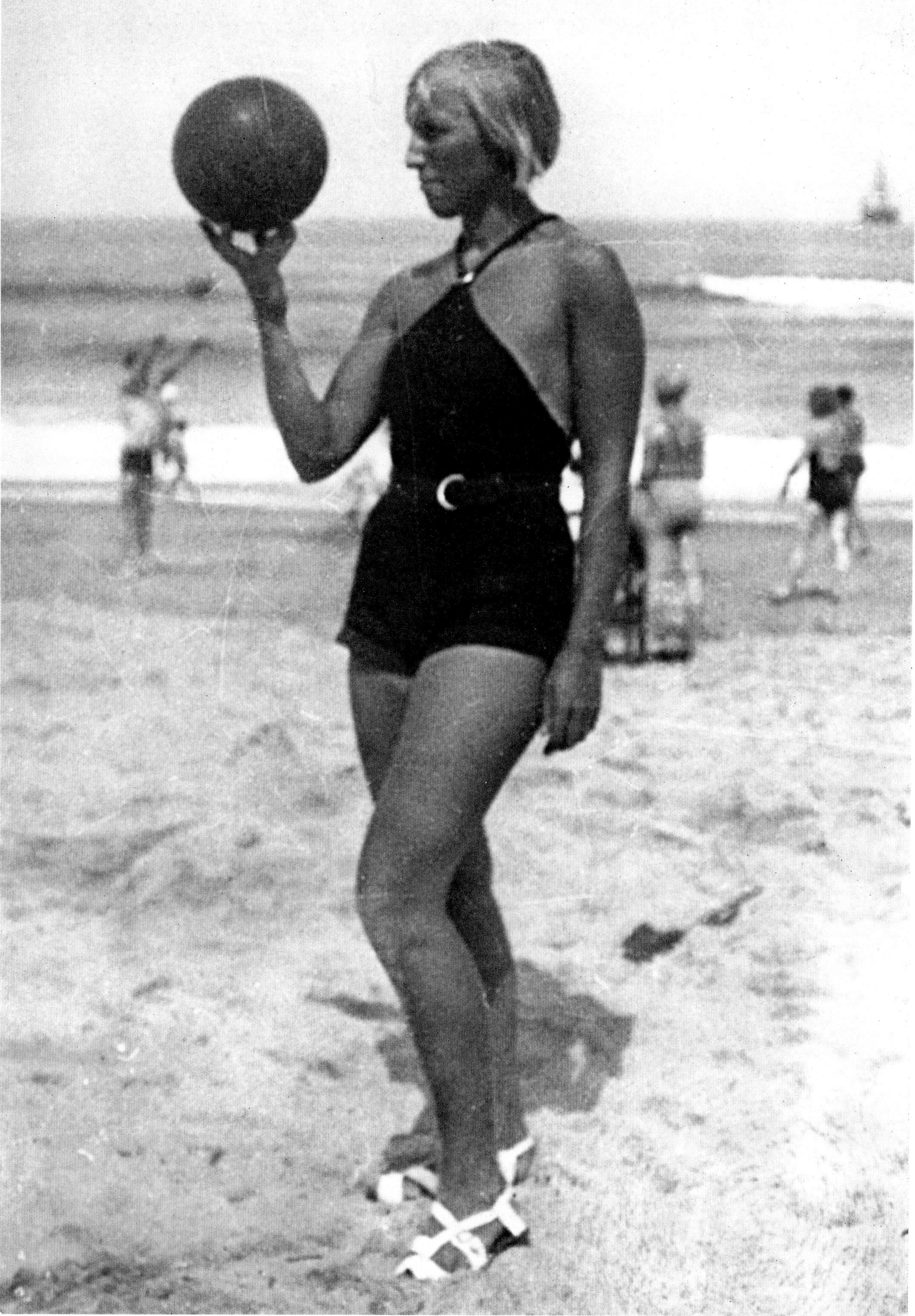

Marie-Thérèse's term of endearment for him was simply 'PIC'.

Picasso spent the summer of 1927 in Cannes together with his wife, Olga, and son, Paulo, but returned regularly to Paris to see his new mistress. Henceforth, he would install her in nearby lodgings wherever the Picassos were vacationing, as well as arranging a comparable set-up closer to home by renting an apartment for her in the centre of Paris so as to have her within easy reach at all times.

Marie-Thérèse Walter entered Picasso's art in the passive, dreamy pose of the 'sleeping woman' (fig. 46). John Berger noted that 'among the five hundred or more of his own past paintings which Picasso owns, over fifty are of

Marie-Thérèse. No other person dominates his collection a quarter as much', concluding from this that she was the most important sex partner Picasso ever had.[4] It is in these works, more than those inspired by any other muse, that the quasi-symbiotic relationship between Picasso's sexuality and his creativity as an artist is most clearly in evidence. Sexual potency for him was creativity, just as creativity fuelled his libido. His works of

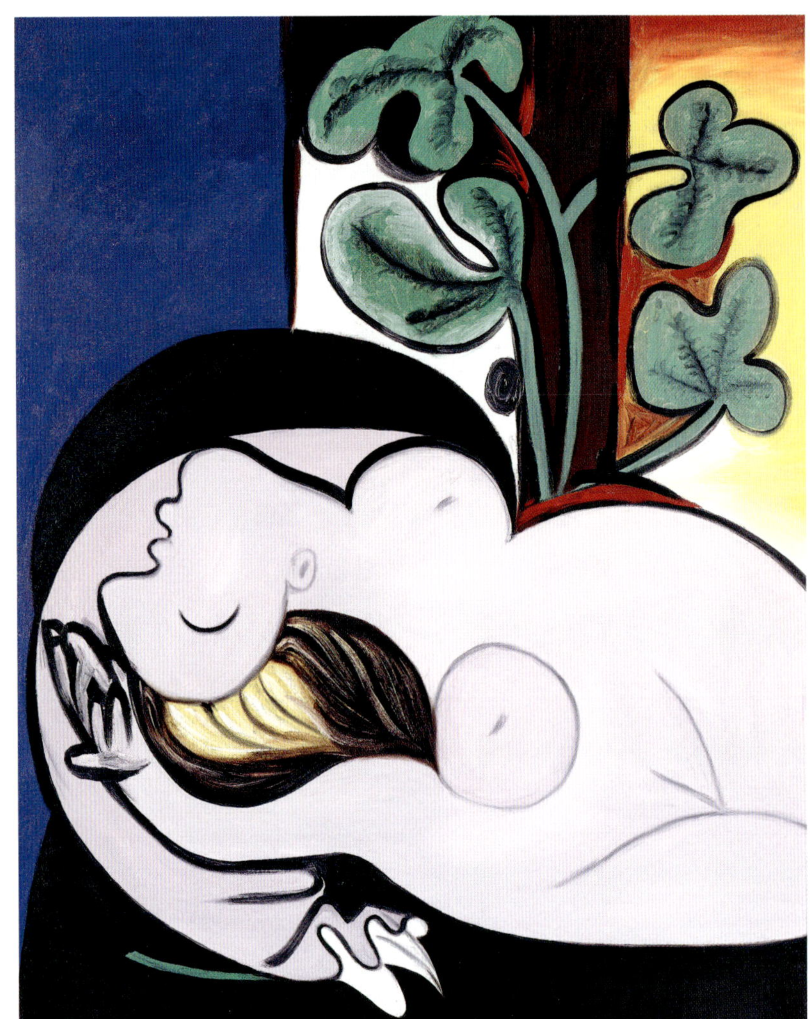

46
Pablo Picasso,
Nude in a Black
Armchair (*Nu au*
fauteuil noir),
9 March 1932
Private collection

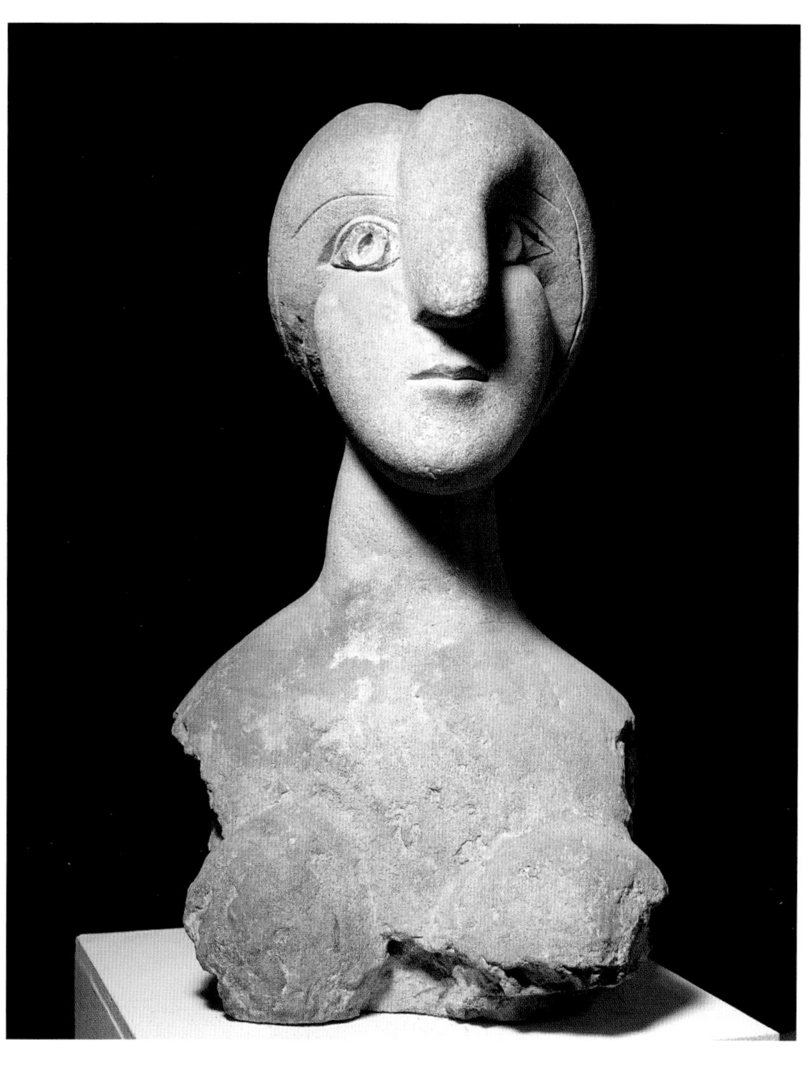

**47
Pablo Picasso,
*Bust of a
Woman*, 1931**
Musée national Picasso,
Paris (MP299)

the early 1930s are painted and sculpted paeans to his young lover. They show him finding ever new metaphors for desire and worshipping her body in lines and brushstrokes. 'Never had Picasso celebrated a woman in this way', wrote one eye-witness, Picasso's biographer Pierre Daix.[5]

In June 1930 Picasso became seigneur of the Château de Boisgeloup in Normandy, which he acquired with the intention of converting its extensive stables into a sculpting studio. Daix suspects that the true motive behind this purchase of a second home was to have a refuge for himself and his muse located at a safe distance from the French capital. The château would indeed serve him as a love nest for himself and his young partner on numerous occasions, and the sculptures that he produced there in the early 1930s all bear the imprint of Marie-Thérèse Walter's physiognomy and above all her classical profile. Among them are both sculptures in the round and classically inspired reliefs, as well as works in which Picasso depicts his muse as an aloof, idol-like figure with elongated neck and a face articulated as an agglomeration of swollen forms. What makes these works so troubling is the way the artist invests the feminine facial forms with a potential for sexual association – as when Walter's striking nose is given a phallic shape (fig. 47).

Picasso's sculptural orbiting of his young muse shows him feeling his way forwards in more than one stylistic direction at once: she inspired him to both neo-classical forms and to bold experiments in surrealistic transfiguration. If Picasso's art of the late 1920s and early 1930s has one defining characteristic, then surely it is the polarity between the serene grandeur of neoclassicism and his resolutely anti-classical creations.

Pablo Picasso turned fifty in October 1931, and two major exhibitions were held in honour of that milestone the following year: a large retrospective at the Galerie Georges Petit in Paris in the early summer of 1932 and Picasso's first-ever museum exhibition at Kunsthaus Zürich in September of the same year. The Zurich show featured 181 of the 225 Paris exhibits supplemented by a further forty-three works from other sources. To ensure the success of the presentation, Picasso had painted some thirty new paintings between December 1931 and April 1932, twenty-two of which were exhibited that summer in Paris. The majority of them are depictions of Marie-Thérèse and in the words of Jack Flam are 'an ecstatic outpouring of painted love poetry' to her.[6]

As Picasso himself acknowledged in an interview of 1932, producing works of art was a way of keeping a visual diary.[7] The vast panoply of works on show in Zurich had the effect of baring his soul for all to see. Here, indeed, his intertwining of life and work is self-evident. The Paris exhibition, meanwhile, was an opulent arrangement of over two hundred paintings, seven sculptures, and six artist books. The clandestine affair with Marie-Thérèse Walter had

**48
Pablo Picasso,
Face (*Marie-
Thérèse*), 1928**
Kunstmuseum
Pablo Picasso Münster

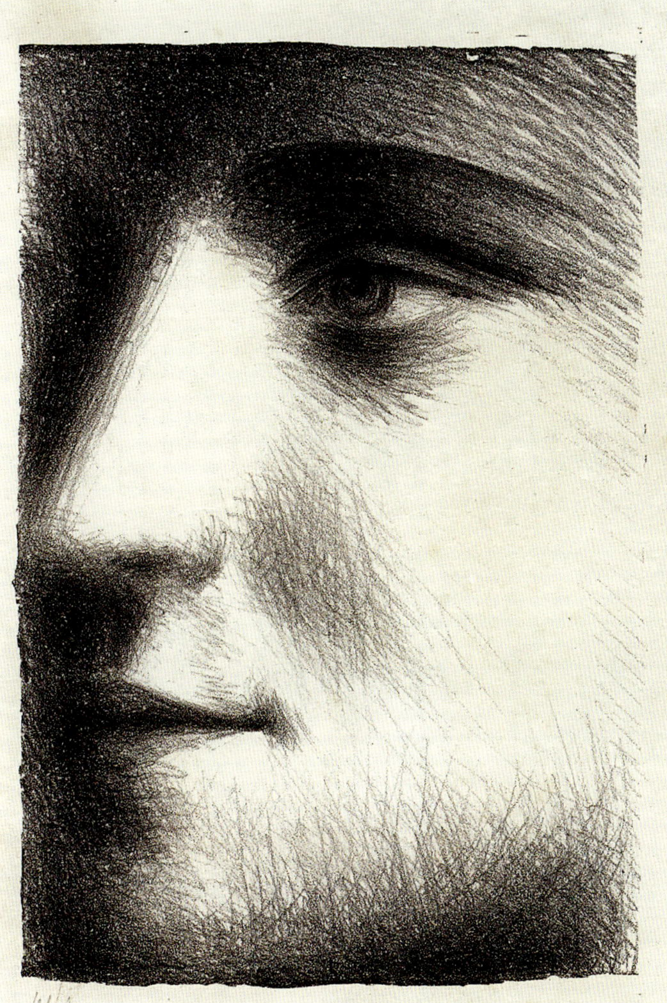

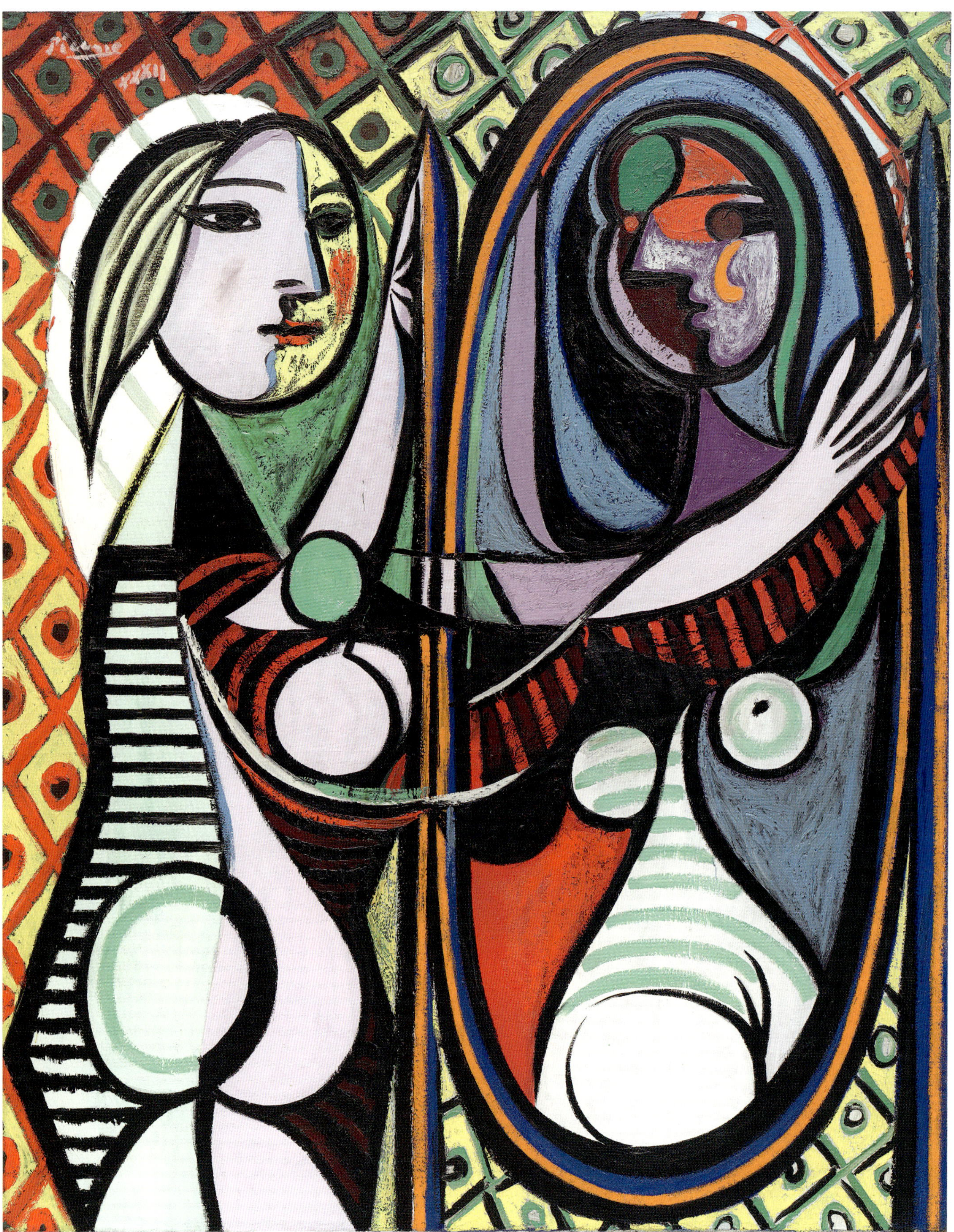

greatly enriched Picasso's art, firing his imagination to great cascades of creativity. But if the retrospective was a revelation, then inevitably it would also be a revelation for his wife, Olga Picasso. 'How horrible for a woman to look at a work of mine and to realize that she has been supplanted' Picasso once said.[8] Presumably it was for strategic reasons, therefore, that he decided not to show his most recent sculptural renditions of his young partner's large, idol-like head. The retrospective of 1932 was nevertheless the pivotal event that led to Olga Picasso's discovery of her husband's extramarital affair. Bernard Picasso, grandson of Olga and Pablo, naturally doubts whether his grandmother could really have been fooled for all those years prior to that and argues that her jealous temperament and distrust of her husband would surely have led her to have suspicions much earlier than this.[9]

In the early summer of 1933 Picasso agreed to design the front cover of the new Surrealist magazine *Minotaure*. True to the title, he chose as his motif a crouching, muscular Minotaur, holding a phallic-looking dagger in his raised right hand. Picasso's appropriation of the Minotaur as his personal emblem had begun in the late 1920s, and the mythological creature that is half-man, half-bull would henceforth serve him as a figure of projection for biographical disclosures. The Minotaur is also the protagonist of the *Vollard Suite*, the series of etchings that Picasso created for the art dealer Ambroise Vollard between 1930 and 1939, in which he is shown as both a lecherous participant in euphoric, Dionysian festivities and as a pathetic creature warranting nothing but pity. The aquatint *Blind Minotaur Led by Girl through the Night* (fig. 50), for example, shows the creature fumbling along with the aid of a stick and leaning heavily on a girl whose distinctive profile is recognizably a play on Marie-Thérèse Walter's

49
Pablo Picasso,
Girl before a Mirror,
14 March 1932
The Museum of Modern Art, New York, gift of Mrs Simon Guggenheim (2.1938)

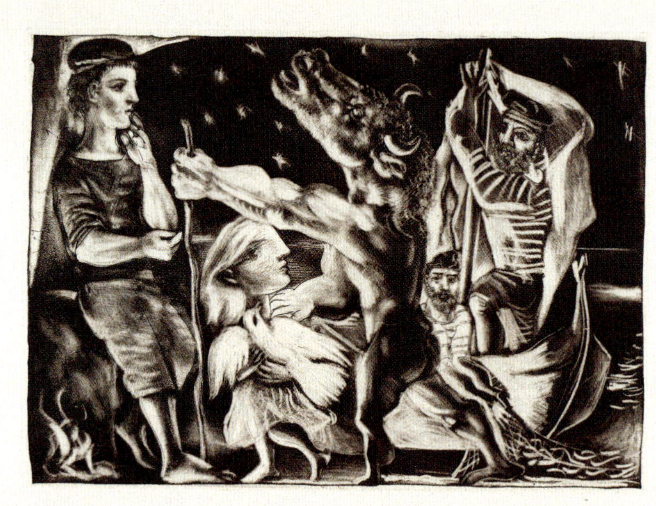

physiognomy. The Minotaur's stocky, sinewy build – fairly bursting with virility – makes for a striking contrast with his attitude of needy fragility. Picasso integrates this central group in the larger pictorial context of a nocturnal fishing expedition. The scene is brought to life by the virtuoso choreography of light, while the drama of the composition itself reflects the scandalous circumstances under which it was created – just a few days after Walter told him that she was pregnant.

Picasso's cloaking of something deeply personal in ancient myth allows the Minotaur's blindness to be read metaphorically, as an expression of the artist's having lost his way. The dreaded monster notorious for devouring women has mutated into a helpless, groping creature. Picasso's British biographer, John Richardson, coined a most apposite term for this meshing of biography and art: he called it 'secret exhibitionism'

and adduced the *Vollard Suite* as an exceptionally haunting example of it. In retrospect, Picasso would refer to the time of the series' creation as the 'worst time' of his life. It was in the autumn of 1933, incidentally, that he first consulted a lawyer on the question of whether and how his marriage to Olga might be dissolved.[10] As the Picassos had not entered into any kind of prenuptial agreement, for legal purposes their marriage was a community of acquests and gains, which naturally included Picasso's works. In the event of divorce, therefore, all their property would have to be divided equally between them. Marie-Thérèse Walter's pregnancy in 1935 dramatically accelerated the Picassos' estrangement from each other, and in June 1935 Picasso obtained a court order establishing their irreconcilability in the belief that this would enable him to pursue a divorce. He filed the official divorce petition in July 1935 but had his hopes of a swift resolution dashed almost immediately. A letter of 13 July 1935 addressed to Jaime Sabartès, an old Catalan friend, contains a despairing cry for help: 'I am at home alone. You can imagine what has happened and what still is ahead of me.'[11] On 5 September 1935 Marie-Thérèse Walter gave birth to a girl, who was named after Picasso's prematurely deceased sister, María de la Concepción – soon shortened to 'Maya'. As Picasso, being a married man, had no means of acknowledging his paternity of an illegitimate child, he and one of Marie-Thérèse's sisters went to Paris city hall and there registered the birth of a daughter, 'father unknown'.[12]

On coming to power in Spain, General Francisco Franco revised the country's divorce law with the result that Picasso, as a Spanish citizen, no longer had the right to get divorced at all. In early 1940, the artist therefore changed his petition for divorce into a petition for judicial separation instead.[13] He would not be able to honour the prospect of marriage that he had dangled before Marie-Thérèse Walter when she first told him of her pregnancy. What Picasso did do, in November 1935, was take his new family to live at a house owned by Vollard in Tremblay-sur-Mauldre, not far from Paris. And at almost exactly the same time he began an affair with the young photographer and artist Dora Maar. Throughout those first few months of Maya's life, Picasso demonstrated a sincerely paternal care and affection for his daughter. As Marie-Thérèse Walter herself said, recalling those early days of their short-lived 'family life' in the aforementioned radio interview with Pierre Cabanne: 'He was with me all day. He was the one that did the washing, cooked the meals; he looked after Maya; he did everything, except perhaps make the beds.'[14]

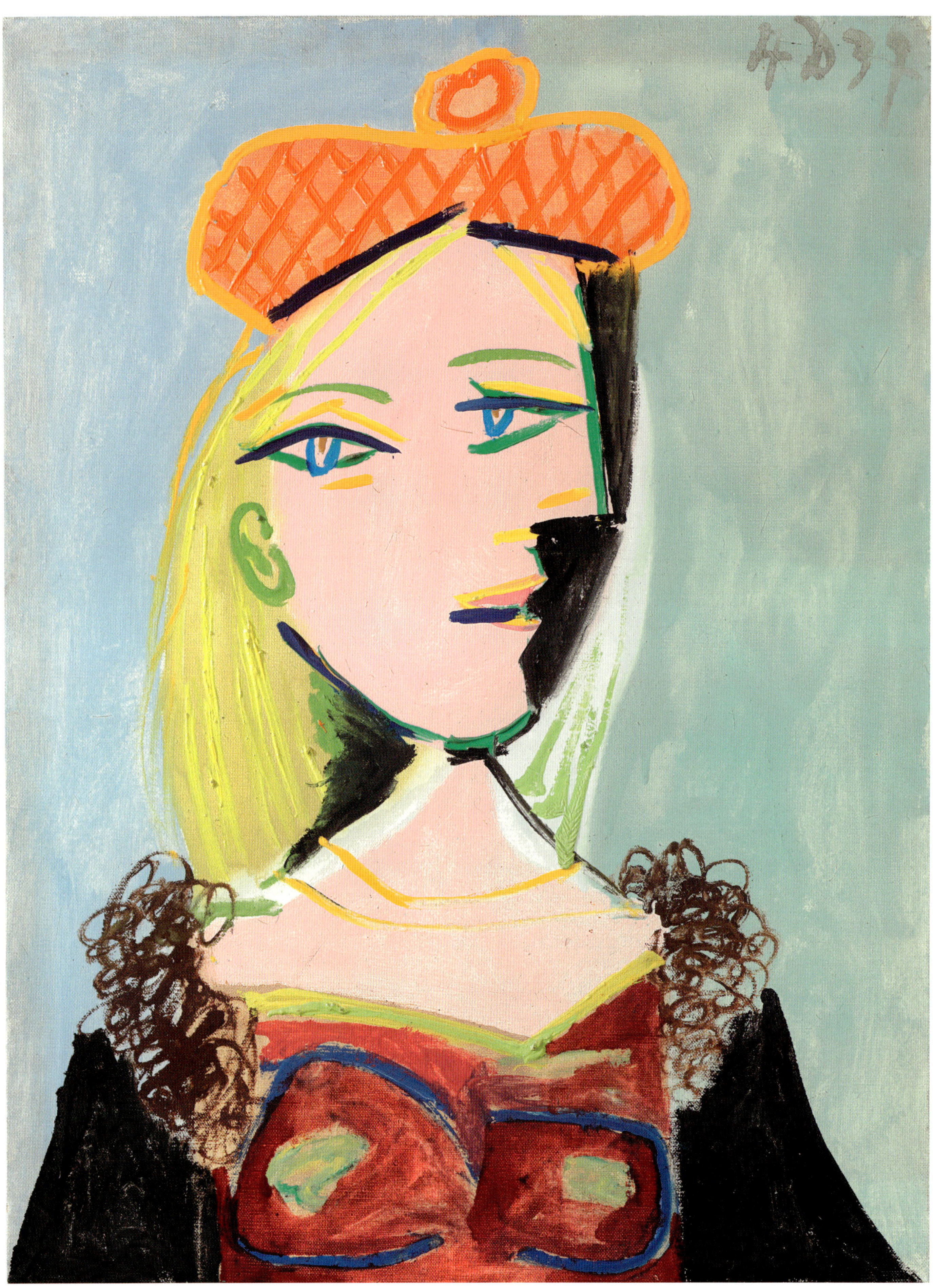

Dora Maar would soon be taking her place at Picasso's side. And Picasso himself, having rented an apartment for Marie-Thérèse and Maya on the boulevard Henr IV on the Ile Saint-Louis in Paris, would have to spend a good deal of time crossing from one side of the Seine to the other. His relationship with Marie-Thérèse Walter did not, however, descend into a sordid *scène de ménage* – to use the French term for a domestic dispute – and Picasso was clearly very caring and solicitous towards both his former partner and their daughter. Much later he would accede to a meeting of at least two parts of his patchwork family when Marie-Thérèse Walter and Maya came to Vallauris on a visit shortly after Françoise Gilot had given birth to Paloma in 1949. Maya frequently visited her father during the school holidays, and Picasso made sure that both she and her mother had enough to live on. When Maya married Pierre Widmaier, in 1960, and the young couple settled in Marseille, Marie-Thérèse Walter likewise decided to turn her back on Paris and move south. After living in Castellane and then Menton for a while, she finally chose Juan-les-Pins as

a permanent abode. Was it her wish to be close to her daughter and grandchildren that drove her there, or was she rather motivated by the fact that Picasso, too, now lived exclusively in the south of France – in fact, just twenty kilometres away to the west, in Mougins? Picasso had given her around a hundred works over the years, and by selling one or the other of these from time to time she was at least able to spare herself any material worries. The death of Picasso, on 7 April 1973, destroyed once and for all what his grandson Olivier Widmaier-Picasso describes as the 'emotional fiction'[15] that his former muse and partner had managed to keep alive – at least in her imagination – for

On 20 October 1977, nearly fifty years after she first met Picasso, Marie-Thérèse Walter took her own life by hanging herself at her home in the south of France. The inner turmoil that prompted this drastic act we will never know, as it was prosecuted in absolute privacy. What remains are the painted and drawn pages of Picasso's visual diary in which he sings the praises of his most sensual of muses. Pierre Cabanne surely comes close to the mark when he concludes that of Picasso's 'five "official" wives ... none was to be as discreet as Marie-Thérèse Walter, nor any benefit less from his fame'.[16] In that one radio interview that Marie-Thérèse Walter gave, she captured the essence of Picasso's personality by describing him as 'wonderfully terrible'.[17]

years, if not decades. After all, since Picasso had never 'officially' left her, it was not beyond the bounds of possibility that he might one day return to her. The song 'J'attendrai' by Rina Ketty was a big hit in France in 1938, and during the war years its lyrics, 'J'attendrai, le jour et la nuit, j'attendrai toujours ton retour' ('I will wait, day and night, I will always wait for your return'), became the mantra of those French women whose men had gone to war and who were hoping for their safe return from the front. Marie-Thérèse Walter, too, seems to have lighted upon 'J'attendrai' as the elegiac leitmotif of her adult life.

52
Pablo Picasso,
Reclining Woman Reading (*Femme couchée lisant*),
21 January 1939

Musée national Picasso, Paris (MP 177)

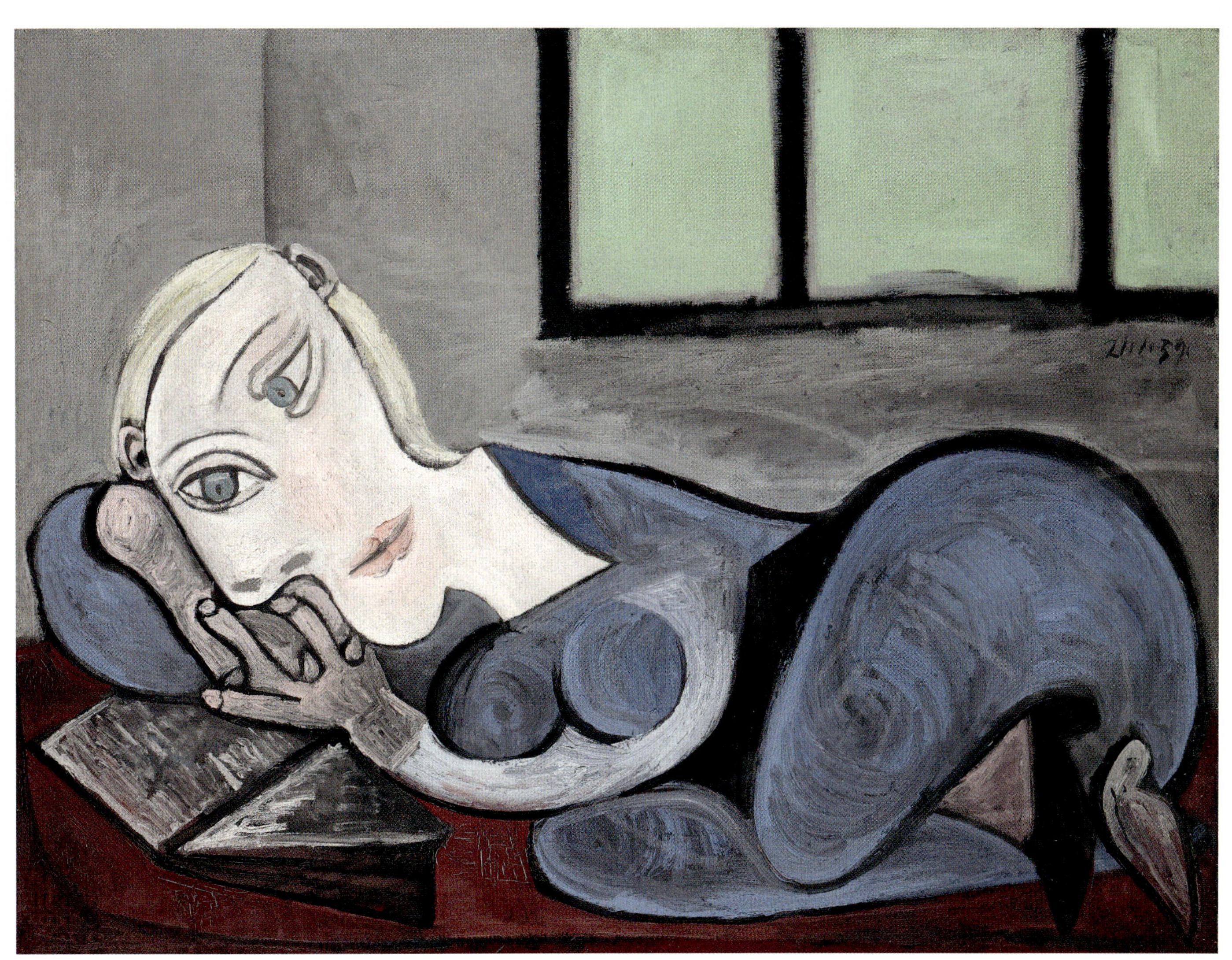

Dora Maar

Markus Müller

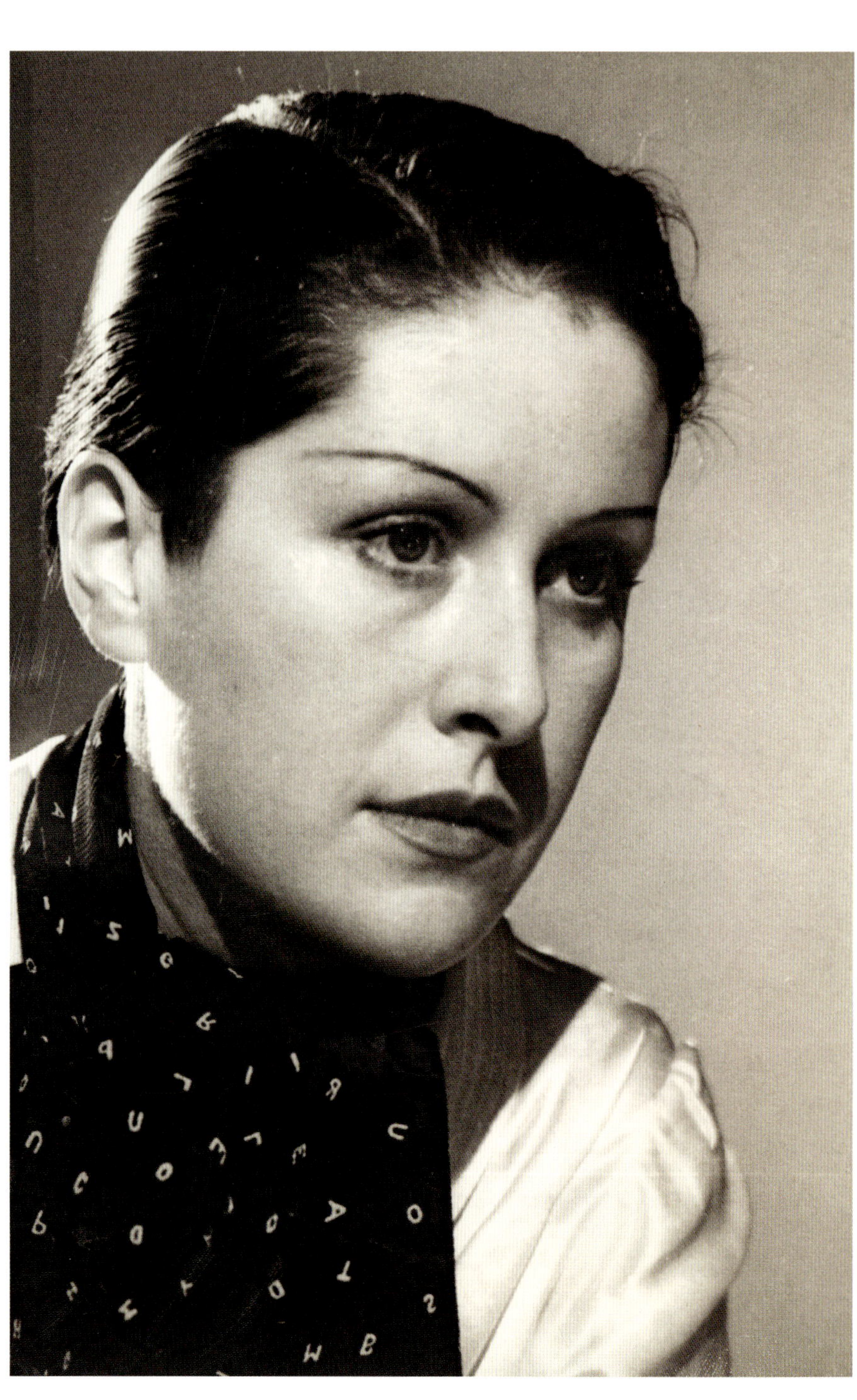

Dora Maar and Françoise Gilot are biographically united by the fact that even as Picasso's muse and partner, both women were active as artists in their own right. Yet their connection to one of the greatest artistic geniuses of the twentieth century inevitably had the effect of eclipsing the recognition of their own art – so much so that if it is mentioned at all, then only by the by, most biographers being too preoccupied with the two muses' inspirational value to Picasso's own output to pay their work any serious attention.

Not until 1995 was Maar's photographic work accorded an exhibition of its own. That first show, *Dora Maar: Fotógrafia*, in Valencia, was followed by a second exhibition of her work in Munich, Marseille and Barcelona in 2001-02, and, more recently, by the first presentation of the full breadth of her life's work in a wide-ranging show at the J. Paul Getty Museum in Los Angeles in collaboration with the Tate Modern in London and the Centre Pompidou in Paris in 2019.

Born in Paris as Henriette Theodora Markovitch on 22 November 1907, Maar was the daughter of a French mother from Tours and a Croatian architect and hence grew up in a multilingual, cosmopolitan home. When she was three years old, the family moved to Buenos Aires, where her father had been commissioned with several major building projects. During her school days in Argentina, Theodora learned to speak both Spanish and English. She began her study of art at the Union Centrale des Arts Décoratifs and the Ecole de Photographie after the family's return to Paris in 1926. She also enrolled at the Académie Julian, a private art school for life drawing and painting founded in the nineteenth century, and there took painting lessons with the French cubist André Lhote, as well as making the acquaintance of

53
Dora Maar in three-quarter profile, 1935
Musée national Picasso, Paris (MP 1998-147)

Light in the Darkroom

the not yet famous photographer Henri Cartier-Bresson.

On graduating, Maar opted for photography as the more profitable art medium. In 1931, at the age of twenty-five, she and the photographer Pierre Kéfer opened a studio together near Paris, where her focus at first was on fashion photography, portraits and nudes. That in those early years she also did work for forty magazines and periodicals proves that she was adept at harnessing her creative impulses to commercial projects. She also made frequent use of the technique of photomontage, which would play an even greater role in her Surrealist works. In a 1934–35 study for an advertisement for the French manufacturer of haircare products Pétrole Hahn, for example, she has a miniature ship navigate the 'ocean' of a woman's wavy coiffure (fig. 55). This, and her other early commercial photographs are virtuoso prefigurations of a stupendous blending

of several different registers of reality that Dora Maar instrumentalized in her dream-inspired Surrealist works. Her first photo to be signed with the name 'Dora Maar' dates from 1932, when she relinquished her birth name altogether.[1]

Another facet of her work were her photographs of people living on the fringes of urban society in Barcelona, London and Paris. Those early works, taken with a Rolleiflex,

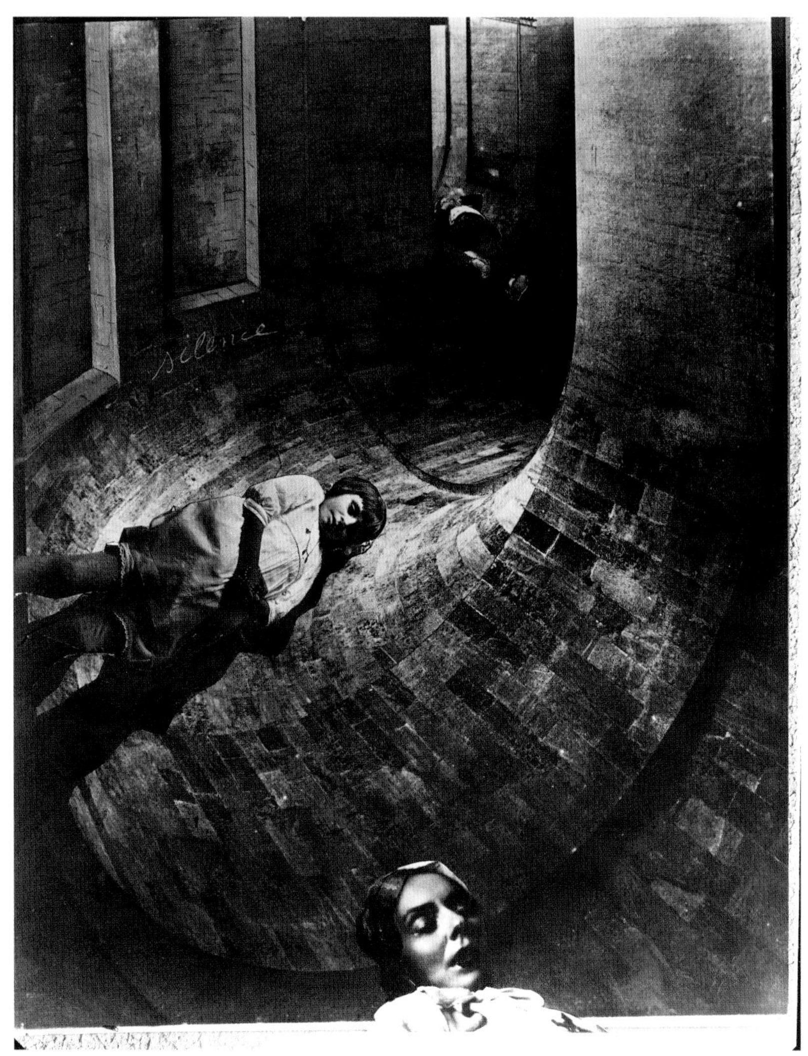

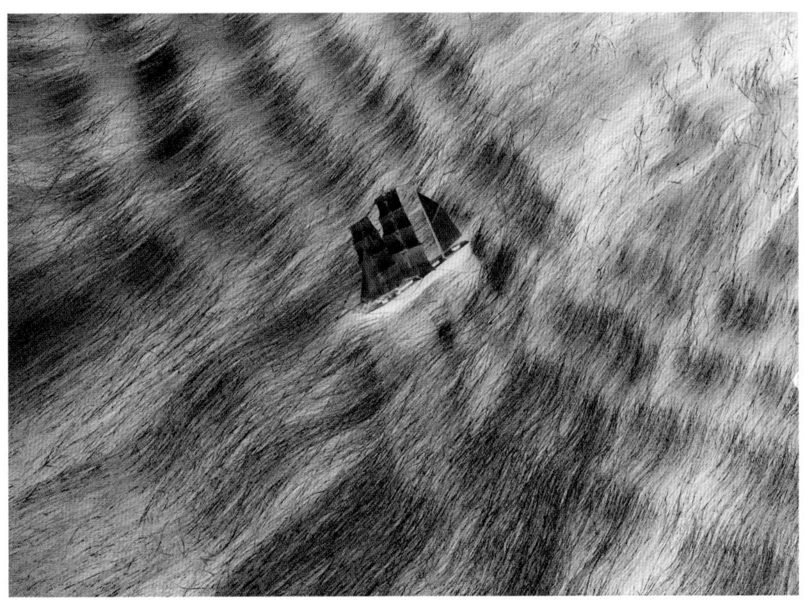

55
Dora Maar,
photomontage
(study for an
advertisement
for Pétrole
Hahn),
1934–35

Brassaï spoke admiringly of how Maar inched towards her photographic subjects like a hunter stalking its prey. Another of her contemporaries, Jacques Guenne, praised her work in a similar vein, in 1934 describing her as 'a brunette hunter of images ... with the openness of a man and the curiosity of a woman'.[3]

The Kéfer–Maar studio did not last long and must have disbanded in 1934 or 1935, when Maar moved into a studio of her own at 29, rue d'Astorg, in Paris. The address is significant to the extent that it was next door to the Galerie Simon, run by Daniel-Henry Kahnweiler, Picasso's erstwhile art dealer. In spite of this physical proximity, however, Maar and Picasso would not actually cross paths until they met at a restaurant in the Quartier Latin in the autumn of 1935.

Surrealism looms large in Maar's artistic work of the ensuing period, as is apparent from the way she superimposed different layers of reality to

**55
Dora Maar,
photomontage
(study for an
advertisement
for Pétrole
Hahn),
1934–35**

reveal an artistic hand in which the influence of role models such as Eugène Atget and Brassaï is undeniably apparent. But they are also articulations of social critique, attesting to a political stance that was finding an outlet in photography. Maar was indeed politically active during the 1930s and belonged to Georges Bataille's anti-fascist, far-left group Contre-Attaque. 'Death to the slaves of capitalism', was one of the key slogans of its founding manifesto. It was also during this time of her intense political commitment that Maar and Bataille became lovers. 'Unlike today, at the age of twenty-five I was pretty far left', reflected Maar in 1994, towards the end of her life, 'though I never belonged to the Communist Party.'[2]

create works that are perplex-ing and sometimes even dis-turbing. The dreamlike atmos-phere that she was so expert at staging more than once took on the unpleasant after-taste of a nightmare.

She had mastered the relevant techniques during her training, even if she had been working according to rather different aesthetic norms at the time. For her Surrealist works, she assembled collag-es of single elements on photographic paper and after retouching them, where necessary, photographed the whole work with a large-format camera.[4]

She was able to publish her first works of this kind in 1933, when they appeared in the Surrealist poetry review *Le Phare de Neuilly*. Her works of this period belong unmistak-ably to the tradition of the Surrealist collage novel, which Max Ernst had helped estab-lish with books such as *La*

femme 100 têtes (1929), known in English as *The Hundred Headless Woman*. André Breton, the leader of the Surrealist movement, described them as *trompe l'œil* representations of dreams. Maar had been a close friend of Breton's wife, the artist Jacqueline Lamba, ever since their student days, and by the time Picasso met her, the art photographer was already a fixture of the Paris circle of Surrealists. At the time, Picasso was in the midst of what he would later describe as the 'worst time of his life'. He had been having an affair with the young Marie-Thérèse Walter since 1927, and the birth of their daughter, Maya, on 5 Sep-tember 1935, had precipitated the final rupture with his first wife, Olga Picasso. The year 1935 was thus a turning point in Picasso's life – and that in more respects than one.

According to Brassaï:

It was not at Le Flore, however, but at Les Deux-Magots that, one day in autumn 1935, he met Dora Maar, just as Marie-Thérèse Walter was bearing him a daughter, Maya. On an earlier day, he had al-ready noticed the grave, drawn face of the young

56
Dora Maar,
Untitled, 1934

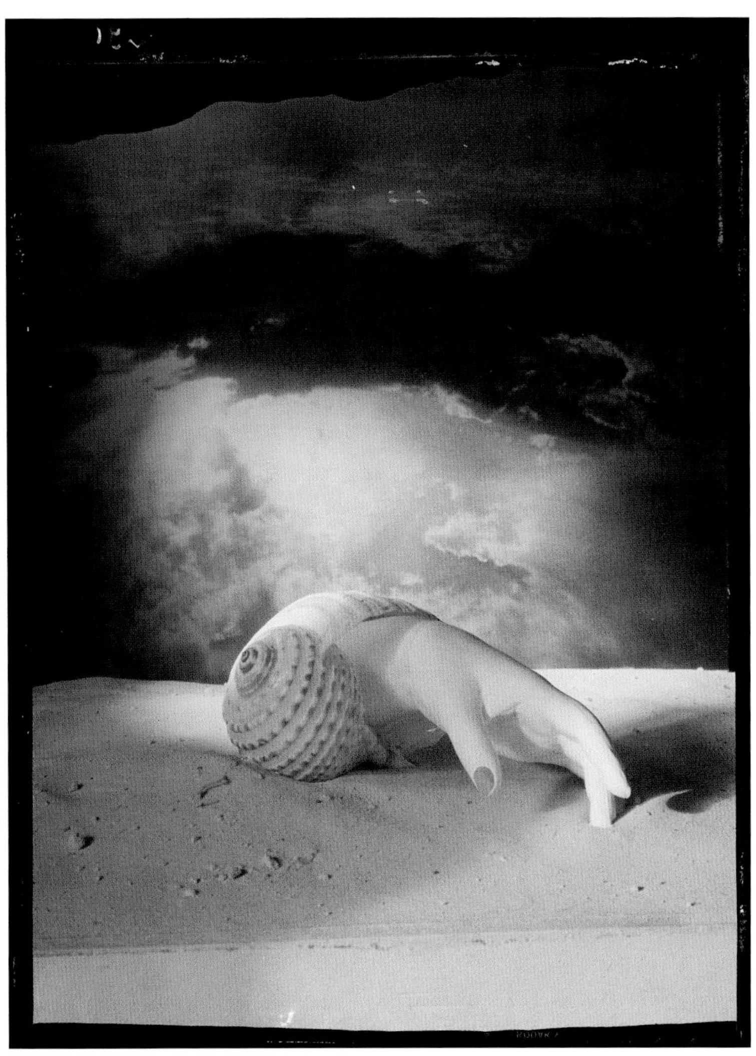

woman at a nearby table, the attentive look in her light-colored eyes, sometimes disturbing in its fixity. She had been moving in surrealist circles since 1934. When Picasso saw her again in the same café in the company of Paul Éluard, who knew her, the poet introduced her to Picasso.[5]

Françoise Gilot, who was to succeed Maar as Picasso's

partner, would later flesh out Brassaï's account with recollections of her own, including the following highly revealing detail:

Pablo told me that one of the first times he saw Dora she was sitting at the *Deux Magots*. She was wearing black gloves with little pink flowers appliquéd on them. She took off the gloves and picked up a long, pointed knife, which she began to drive into the table between her outstretched fingers to see how close she could come to each finger without actually cutting herself. ... before she stopped playing with the knife, her hand was covered with blood. Pablo told me that was what made up his mind to interest himself in her. He was fascinated. He asked her to give him the gloves and he used to keep them in a vitrine at the Rue des Grands-Augustins, along with other mementos.[6]

The key element in this description is not Maar's appearance, but rather the bizarre, masochistic game of manual dexterity that attracted Picasso's attention. Entirely missing from this account, however, is the Surrealist poet Paul Éluard, who is said to have introduced them to each other. Picasso, of course, had an interest in characterising Maar as mentally unstable, which presumably explains the emphasis he gave to this disturbing detail when describing his first encounter with her to Gilot.

Picasso's new companion was enthroned in his work in the summer of 1936, even if Marie-Thérèse Walter would still inspire many a painterly tour de force articulating the soft and sensuous forms of her voluptuous body in the years to come. These works of the late 1930s combining cubism's multi-perspective views with the visual strategies of Surrealistic transfiguration have frequently been described as Picasso's hallmark style. And just as the two muses would continue to co-exist in Picasso's works, so the artist would never truly sever his ties to Walter. On the contrary, every Wednesday and Sunday he made a point of visiting his former partner and their daughter, Maya, at the house

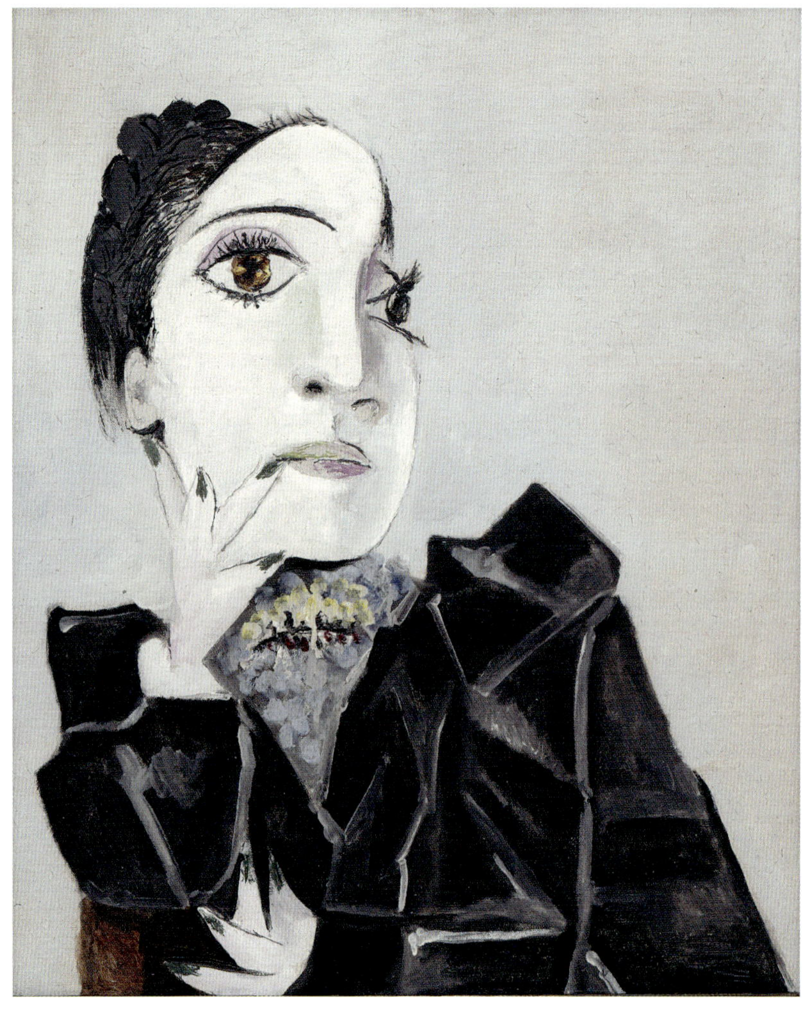

57
**Pablo Picasso,
*Dora Maar with
Green Finger-
nails*, 1936**
Museum Berggruen, Berlin

in Tremblay-sur-Mauldre, in the west of Paris, that had been placed at their disposal by Picasso's dealer Ambroise Vollard.

How ironic that it should have been Françoise Gilot, of all people, who in her memoirs *Life with Picasso* hailed his portraits of Maar as the finest works he had ever painted, and who described Maar herself as a 'majestic Amazon' – at least in matters of fashion![7] Nor could anyone who has contemplated the *Portrait of Dora Maar* of 1937 that now hangs in the Musée Picasso in Paris (fig. 59) disagree with that verdict. Picasso's paean to his partner is a dazzling firework display of a painting, in every inch of which a rarefied variant

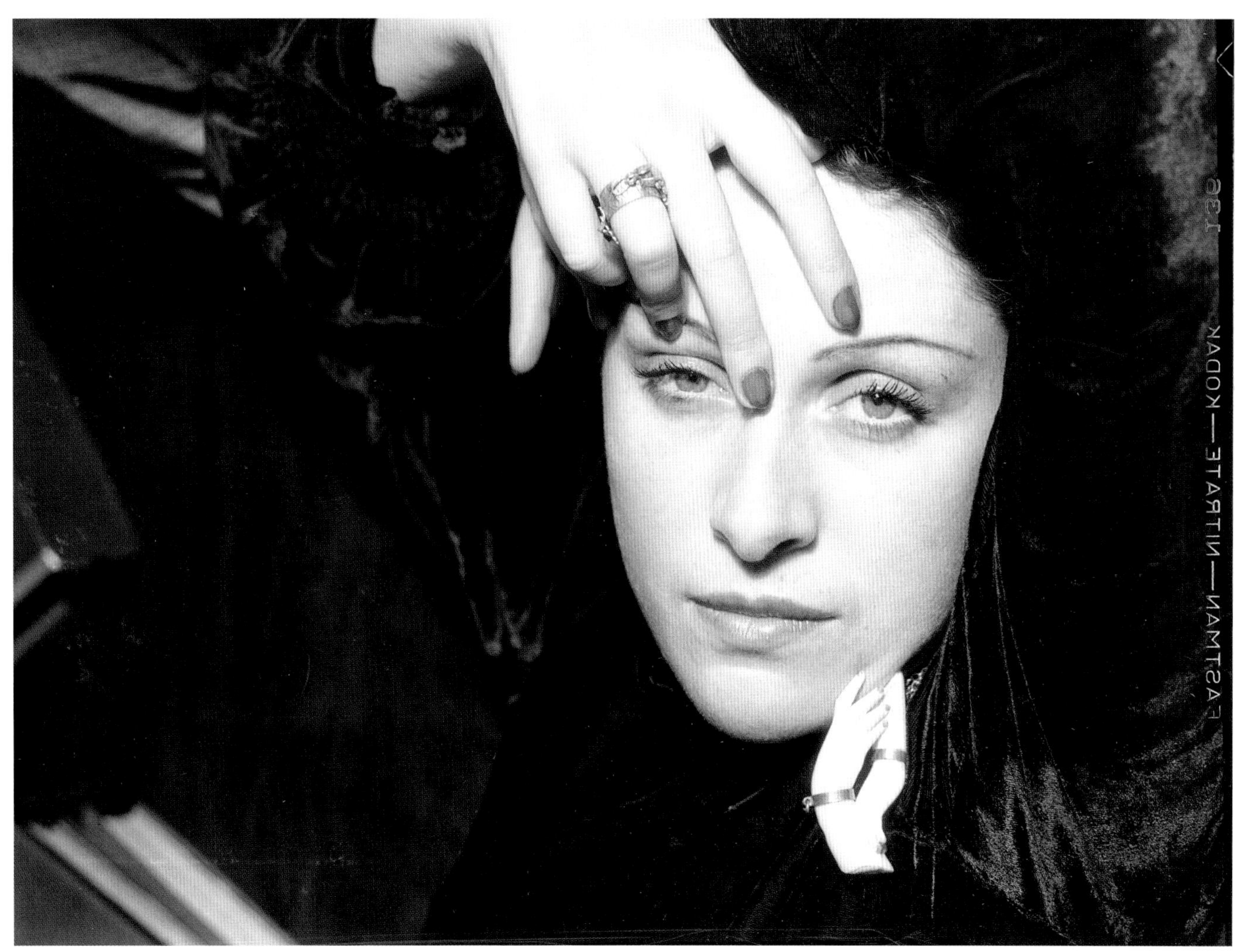

131

of cubism holds sway. While
the face is a composite of a
frontal and profile view, the
chair on which the subject is
sitting and the rather artificial-
looking, box-like interior in
which Picasso positions her
are also shown from multiple
perspectives. The pointed
fingers with their long red nails
lend the figure an aspect at
once both unapproachable
and feminine that is characteristic of Maar during this period.
She was certainly fond of
wearing expensive nail polish
and almost everyone who met
her in person remarked on her
very slender, exceptionally elegant hands.

But it was in the painting
Weeping Woman (fig. 60) that
Picasso truly immortalised
Maar. 'The first image I ever
saw of Picasso's work was the
Weeping Woman. I can never
forget it', wrote the British artist David Hockney, recalling his
first momentous glimpse of it
at the Tate Gallery in London.[8]

The idiom of that work painted
on 26 October 1937 is indeed
both expressive and harrowing.
Picasso zooms in on the countenance of a woman wracked
by pain. Never before had a
painter been able to depict a
fractured human face much as
he might an aggressively
smashed window. The patch of
white representing the hand-
kerchief that the subject is
holding up to her face stands
out in stark contrast to an
otherwise multi-coloured
composition.

Picasso painted *Weeping
Woman* by way of an epilogue
to *Guernica*, which had been
presented to the public in the
pavilion of the Spanish Republic
at the 1937 world's fair in Paris.
Picasso's monumental painting
is a searing indictment of
Franco's Nationalists and the
Nazis who supported them
and who on 26 April 1937
bombed the Basque town of
Guernica, killing countless
civilians.

Maar photographed the
various phases of the genesis
of *Guernica*, thus bequeathing
to posterity a priceless visual
record of how the twentieth
century's most famous anti-
war painting came about.
Picasso repeatedly opined that
to fully understand an artist's
creative process it was neces-

59
**Pablo Picasso,
*Portrait of
Dora Maar*, 1937**
Musée national Picasso,
Paris (MP 158)

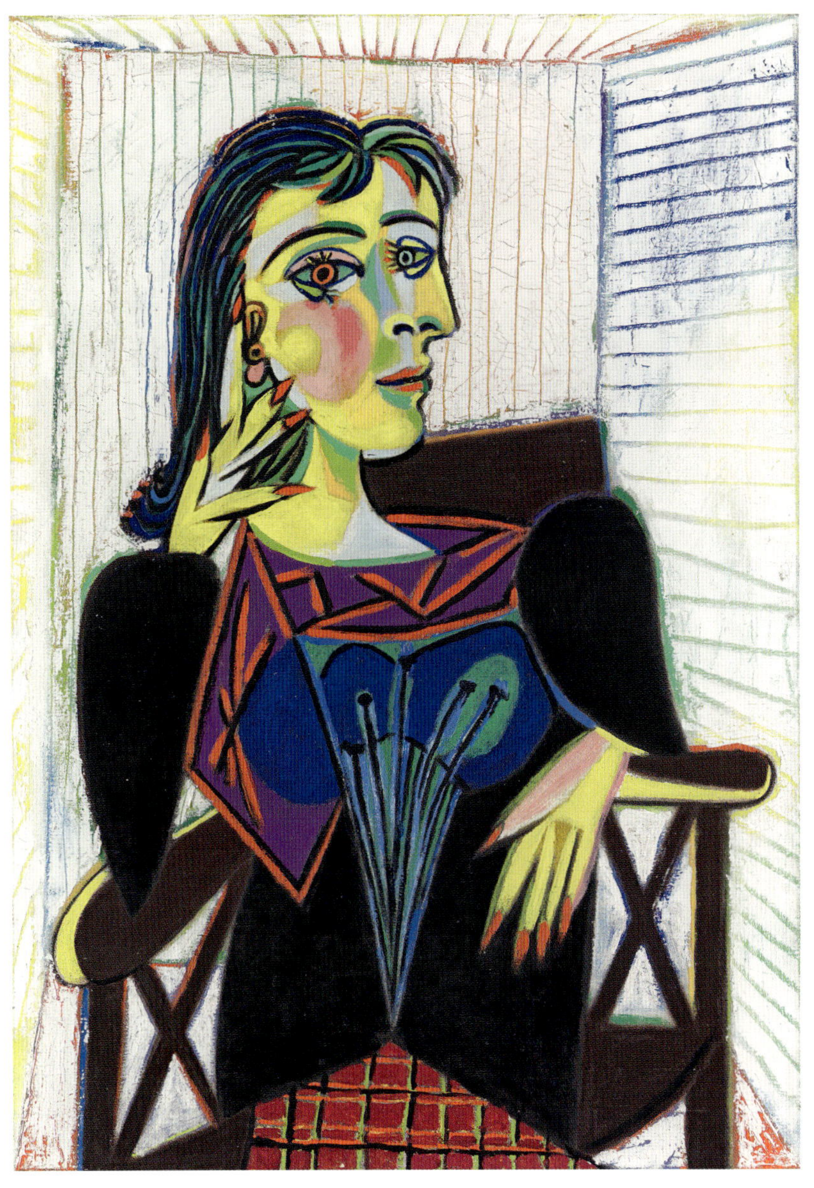

influence on him as a photographer.[9]

The motif of the *Weeping Woman* had previously featured in another of Picasso's overtly anti-Franco works: the print cycle *The Dream and Lie of Franco*, which he began work on in January 1937. Yet he also pursued the theme independent of that particular context, which explains how *Weeping Woman* came about. That Maar's own facial features were of great inspirational value to the various versions of *Weeping Woman* is beyond dispute, even if the paintings and prints were conceived not as portraits as such but as visual metaphors of physical and mental anguish.

Through Picasso's art, in other words, Maar became a timeless archetype of suffering humanity. She herself claimed not to recognize herself in any of these works and told her friend James Lord that: 'All his portraits of me are lies. They're

sary to see the 'picture behind the picture'. Maar's images of every critical stage in *Guernica*'s genesis apparently accorded with Picasso's own wish to leave behind some record of his own invention. She later contended that Picasso's decision to banish colour from the work had been prompted by black-and-white photography – and hence not least her own

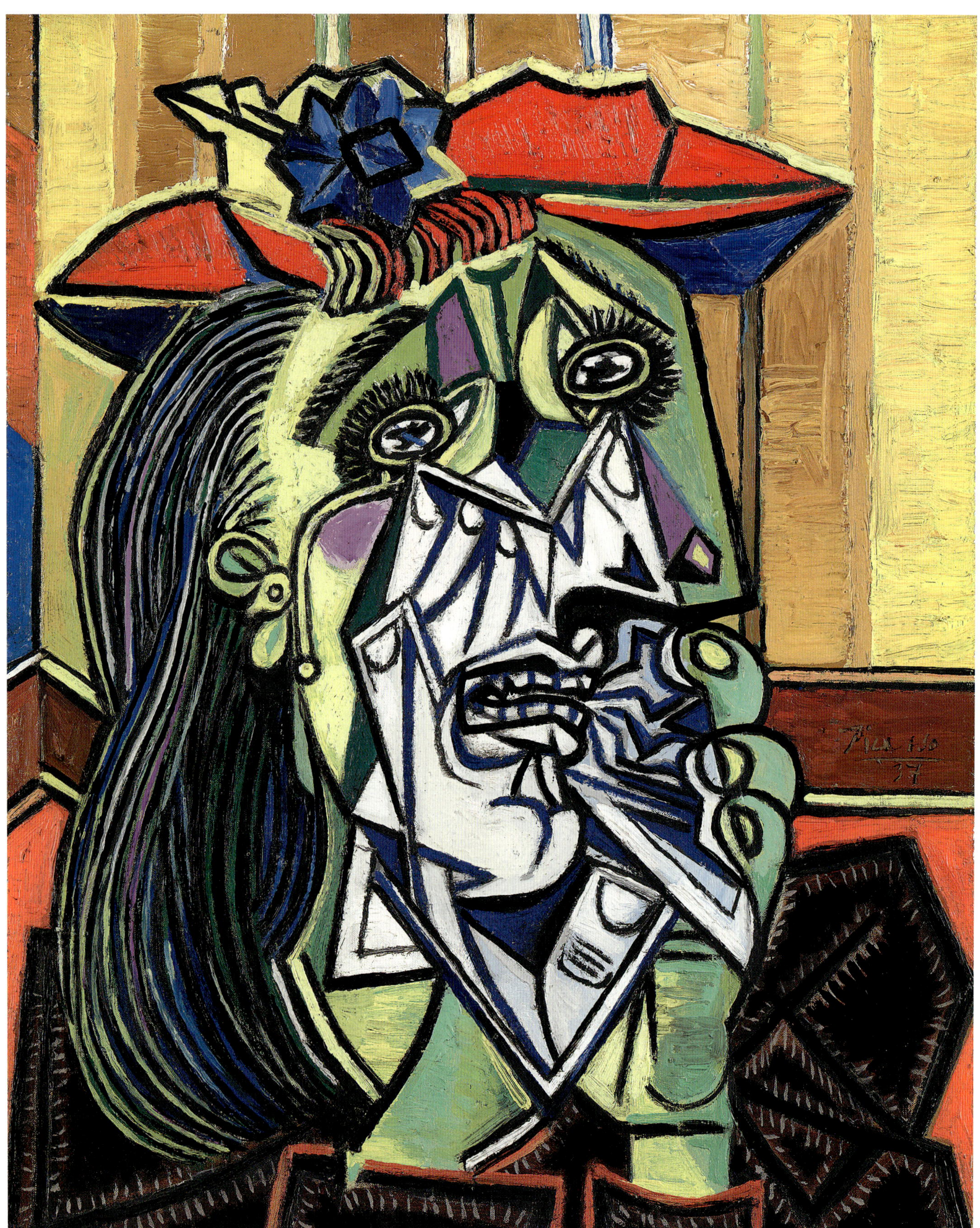

all Picassos, not one is Dora
Maar.'[10] This damning verdict
should certainly not be dismissed as mere wounded
vanity; after all, modernist
portraiture is often atavistic
given that the avant-gardes
of the twentieth century were
no longer concerned with likeness or with the principle of
mimesis.

Viewed in this light,
Picasso's *Weeping Woman* is
rather a modern-day, wholly
secular Mater Dolorosa.
Picasso's biographer John
Richardson saw the inspiration
both for it and for other works
like it less in then contemporary events than in the artist's
own private life. The real reason
for Maar's tears, he argued, was
not General Franco, but rather
the trauma of the artist's abusive treatment of her. Jean-
Paul Crespelle takes a similar
view, arguing that 'never was a
woman treated worse by her
lover than was Dora Maar!'[11] –
by which he meant above all
the way Picasso immortalised
his muse in his art. Unlike
Richardson, however, Crespelle
quotes Picasso himself on the
subject: 'For me she is the
weeping woman. For years
I painted her with tortured
shapes. This was not because
of sadism, but not because of
any particular pleasure either.

I was simply obeying a profound vision that had imposed
itself on me.'[12]

The early 1940s saw the
relationship between Picasso
and Maar deteriorate. They
lived apart, Maar having in
1936 found a studio apartment
for Picasso on the rue des
Grands Augustins and then in
1942 rented a place of her own
just a stone's throw away on
the rue de Savoie. That is where
she spent the years – and then
the decades – following their
final separation, after Picasso
met an aspiring young artist by
the name of Françoise Gilot in
May 1943. As he became ever
more infatuated with the then
twenty-two-year-old Gilot,
so his relationship with Maar
became ever more fraught
with tension.

Maar's behaviour
frequently seemed strange,
and in May 1945 she suffered
a nervous breakdown that re-
sulted in her being admitted to

60
**Pablo Picasso,
*Weeping
Woman*, 1937**
Tate Gallery, London
(T05010)

a psychiatric hospital in Paris. The psychiatrist Jacques Lacan, who was also Picasso's physician, later had her transferred to a private clinic on the outskirts of Paris, where he treated her himself with psychotherapy. Picasso denied any causal link between their fraught relationship and his partner's mental instability and breakdown and instead pinned the blame firmly on the Surrealists, alerting his new companion Gilot to the many other cases of mental illness to be found in that circle. 'And, added Picasso, she had always been crazy.'[13] John Richardson quotes him as saying: 'She always had a sense of the occult, and look what happened.'[14] Picasso even claimed to have been frightened of her, confiding in Richardson: 'I left her out of fear. Fear of her madness.'[15]

His separation from his former companion and the inspirational force of the new one could scarcely be more tellingly articulated than in an engraving at the Musée Picasso in Paris (fig. p. 182). The work in question, dated 1946, is a wonderful portrait of Gilot executed as a drypoint etching on top of the *Weeping Woman* composition of 1 July 1937. The slim, elongated neck, the slightly asymmetrical eyes, and the voluminous, generously outlined hair all breathe the stimulating freshness, energy and verve of the early Gilot portraits. Picasso, moreover, deliberately 'airbrushes out' the pain-contorted face of his former muse, superimposing the new love of his life on the ignominiously upended *Weeping Woman*. Turning an existing image or visual element on its head prior to reusing it is an ancient practice and equivalent to a symbolic devaluation. That this archaic conjuring trick tickled Picasso's fancy seems a much more plausible explanation for his palimpsest than any shortage of printing plates.

The shadowy existence to which Picasso condemned his erstwhile companion in this work parallels the life that she led after Picasso abandoned her for good, in 1946. This, at least, is the view of many of his older biographers, for whom the fifty years of her life that

61
**Pablo Picasso,
Dora Maar in an Armchair, 1939**
The Metropolitan Museum of Art, New York, The Mr and Mrs Klaus G. Perls Collection, 1998 (1998.23)

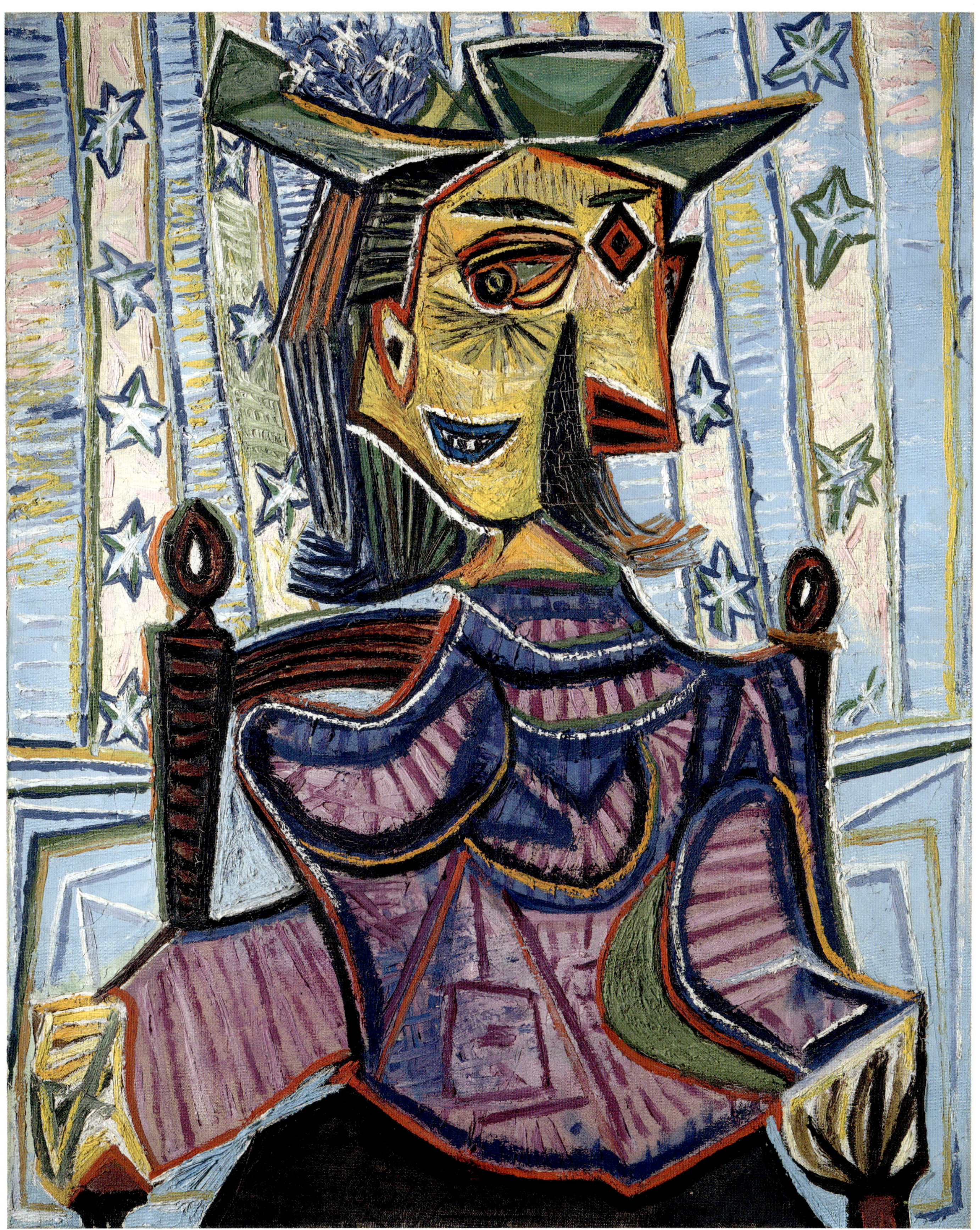

came after that calamitous event were just one, long, painful epilogue. The Paris art dealer Heinz Berggruen, for instance, once remarked that for all the vicissitudes of her life, Maar – whom he knew personally – had remained a creature of what he called 'Planet Picasso'.

Whether assertions such as these are fair to Maar or serve primarily to promote the mystification of Picasso must remain a moot point. Friends of Maar and others who had contact with her after the late forties and fifties refuted the widely circulated rumour that she had become a mere shadow of her former self and was now just sleepwalking through life. Not only did Maar visit old friends such as the artist Balthus and the Surrealist Léonor Fini, they argued, but she also dined at Le Catalan or invited friends over to her place. The American writer James Lord, who was among the servicemen to liberate Paris, visited Picasso at his studio and also became a close personal friend of Maar's. In his *Picasso and Dora: A Memoir* he describes her as a woman of great sensitivity and intellectual sparkle, even if her irritability and unpredictability do not go unmentioned.

For decades after their split, the erstwhile lovers still sent each other birthday presents and such like, even if their choice of gift seems to have been motivated more by thoughts of revenge or outright malice than by any residual fellow-feeling or kind-heartedness. Maar, for example, acknowledged Picasso's seventy-fifth birthday by sending him a devotional tract by a Dominican pater. While that particular work was undoubtedly missing from the library of such an avowed atheist, it does reflect the spiritual transformation that Maar herself underwent from far-left activist to fervent Catholic in the years after her relationship with Picasso ended.

Indeed, many older Picasso scholars paint Maar as an ultra-pious religious recluse – a picture that seems far too extreme for what we actually know of her life. She was certainly an active and astute businesswoman – at least when it came to capitalizing on her own art collection. Not only did she regularly sell drawings and paintings by Picasso to tide herself over or to supplement her income, but even at an advanced age she is said to have scrutinised auction catalogues to have a better idea of the current value of her art assets. Thus, she was neither a hapless negotiator, nor easy prey for art dealers like Kahnweiler or Berggruen, anxious to relieve her of some of the treasures in her possession. On the contrary, such was her business acumen that the haggling sometimes dragged on for months before a price acceptable to both parties was found. That an exceptional provenance can push up the price of a work was something that Maar herself was acutely aware of; hence her readiness to make strategic use of her own name and relationship to Picasso in sales negotiations. 'On the walls of a gallery, maybe they're worth only half a million', James Lord quotes her as saying. Maar adds:

> On the walls of Picasso's mistress they're worth a premium, the premium of history. A Fragonard, for example, that belonged to Madame de Pompadour is worth much more than one that belonged to Madame Dupont. I've sold quite a few things through the years, and I always get the premium.[16]

While the fact of being the muse whom Picasso deserted placed a great burden on Maar psychologically, at least materially she could regard her association with him as a 'premium of history' that upgraded her collection – as proven by the record prices fetched by the works of hers auctioned off after her death.

Picasso had once swapped a painting for a dilapidated old farmhouse in Ménerbes that Maar took over from him, and it was there, tucked away in the Vaucluse, that she generally spent the summer months. Among her neighbours were the art collector Douglas Cooper and his partner, John Richardson, who lived at the nearby Château de

Castille and frequently got together with Maar and her companion, James Lord. It was at one such dinner party in November 1954 that there was a memorable encounter between Maar and her former partner. Picasso, who was well aware of Lord's homosexuality, wanted to know if they were now married, to which Maar, 'with equanimity', according to Lord's account, retorted that no, they were as yet 'only engaged.'[17]

Maar's own art was greatly influenced by her ties to the Surrealists. She had trained as both a photographer and a painter, and Picasso is said to have encouraged her to do more painting. After all, other artists such as Wols and Raoul Ubac had started off as photographers and then, once in Surrealism's orbit, moved steadily in the direction of painting. Maar's paintings of the 1940s are original crea-

tions in a refined, late-cubist style. While many biographers are inclined to see the influence of Picasso in these works, it should not be forgotten that Maar's very first painting teacher was the dogmatic cubist André Lohte.

In the late 1950s and 1960s she made a name for herself in the art world with semi-abstract landscapes inspired by the countryside around Ménerbes (fig. 62). The Berggruen gallery in Paris frequently exhibited such works by Maar, while the Leicester Galleries in London staged a show of thirty-three of these paintings in the spring of 1958.

As an artist Maar, went on breaking new ground right up to the 1980s, as evidenced by her experimental photograms and artistic reworkings of old negatives. These works can be viewed as lending material form, as it were, to the symbiosis of photography and painting that had been a lifelong preoccupation of hers. The reworked negatives, moreover, show her creating graphic, abstract structures, whose highly charged bundles of lines seem to be a nod in the direction of gestural abstraction. Her association with the painter Nicolas de Staël, whom she

62
Dora Maar,
monotype
(untitled),
c. 1960

140

first met in 1954 and who also lived in Ménerbes, doubtless warrants mention in this regard. Maar's artistic forays into a non-figurative cosmos can certainly be judged a hallmark of her mature work. What they also represent, however, is her definitive detachment and emancipation from Picasso, who not only loathed abstraction but never tired of trying to discredit that particular permutation of modernism.

In his foreword to the catalogue of the exhibition of Maar's work at the Leicester Galleries in London, the British art historian John Russell argued that her paintings quite clearly represented the worldview of a loner.[18] His judgment was to prove prophetic, especially for Maar's final years, when she increasingly cut herself off from the outside world. So deep was her need for privacy that she communicated with others primarily by telephone, even if several of her interlocutors have since stressed how chatty she was and how long and wide-ranging their telephone conversations with her were. She also had an elaborate system of strings and pulleys installed to enable her to operate various devices from her bed.

As much as Maar's final years might seem like a scene out of Samuel Beckett's tragicomic one-act play *Endgame*, they also attest to her indomitable strength of character and independence of mind. On 16 July 1997, a neighbour called an ambulance after discovering that the artist's health had deteriorated dramatically. Maar was taken to a hospital in Paris, where she died later that same day, aged eighty-nine.

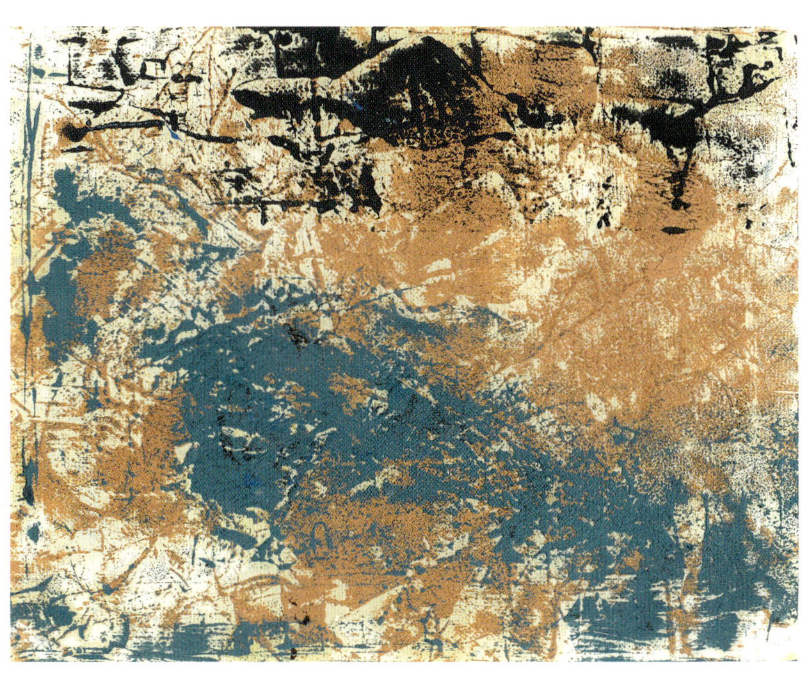

Françoise Gilot

Markus Müller

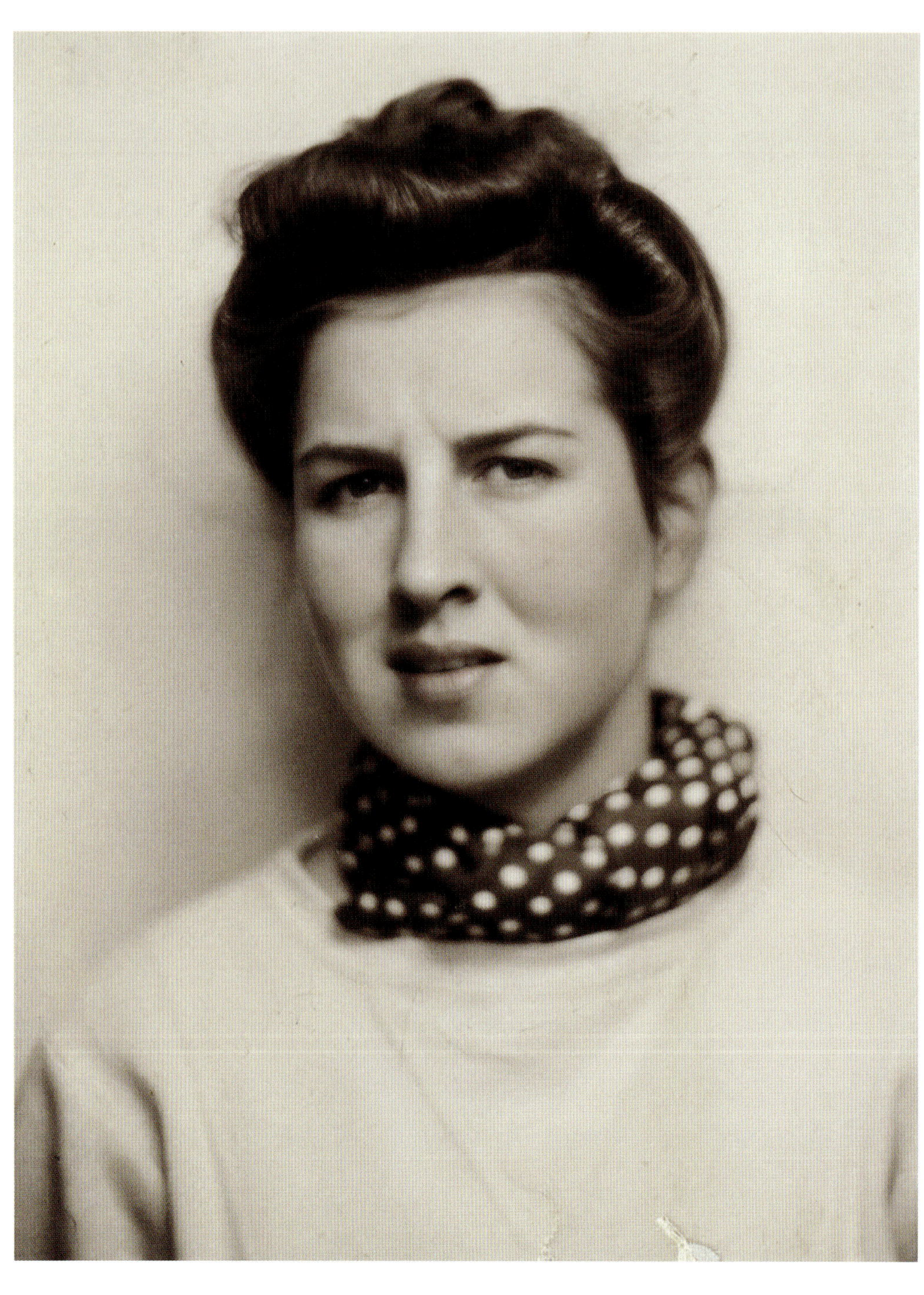

Picasso was the one who called the shots in his relationships with women; very few of his companions took matters into her own hands and walked out on him. One of them was the young Marie Françoise Gilot, who was twenty-one when she first met the sixty-one-year-old Picasso in German-occupied Paris in May 1943. The liaison that ensued lasted ten years and ended with her leaving him in the autumn of 1953.

Françoise Gilot, the only child of Madeleine Renoult-Gilot and Emile Gilot, was born in Neuilly-sur-Seine, a middle-class suburb of Paris, on 26 November 1921. Her father ran a perfume factory acquired by his widowed mother. He was also a great lover of literature with an impressive library, while his wife was passionate about the fine arts. It was therefore Madeleine Renoult-Gilot who taught the young Françoise how to draw and paint with watercolours and by doing so kindled her life-long passion for art. Françoise installed her first studio in her grandmother's attic in the winter of 1937–38, though her authoritarian father was insistent that she study law. While she reluctantly complied with his wishes at first, she did not abandon her artistic aspirations.

Some of the young woman's English friends introduced her to the Jewish-Hungarian painter Endre Rozsda, who took on the role of artistic mentor – at least until March 1943, when the Nazis' ever-tighter grip on the French capital forced him to flee. Two months later, the actor Alain Cuny invited Gilot and her bosom friend, and fellow artist, Geneviève Aliquot, to join him for dinner at Le Catalan, a restaurant in the Latin quarter that was a popular haunt of writers and artists. Sitting at the neighbouring table was Pablo Picasso in the company of his then partner, Dora Maar. Picasso, who already knew Cuny, asked to be introduced to his two guests. The two young women were

63
Passport photo of Françoise Gilot, 1940s

Musée national Picasso, Paris (APPH 4353)

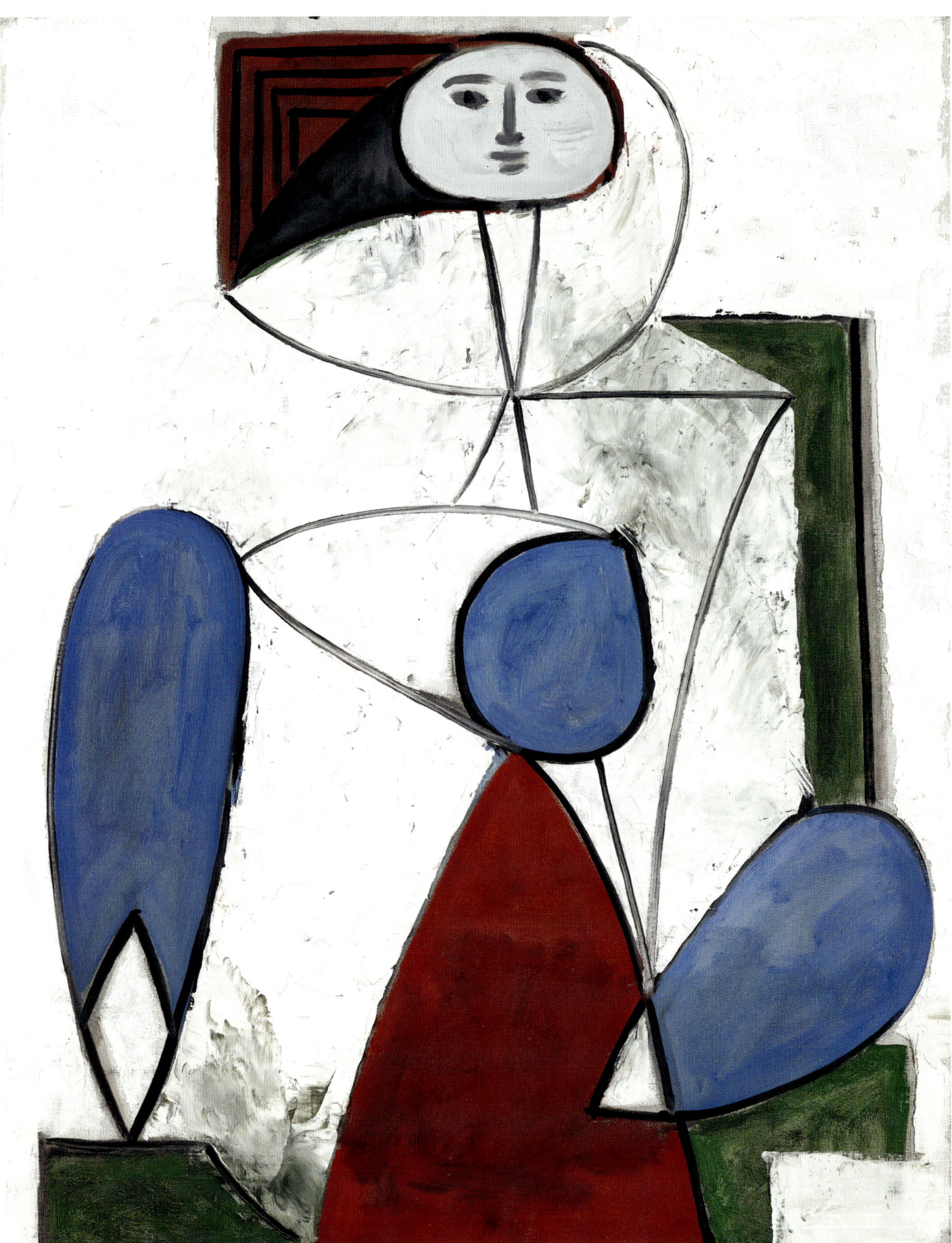

exhibiting some of their works at a Paris art gallery at the time and boldly suggested that Picasso stop by and take a look at their pictures. He, for his part, invited them to visit him at his studio.

As a teenager Françoise Gilot had collected photos of Picasso, something she herself later admitted. Hence, for her, encountering this near-legendary figure in the flesh must have been a long-cherished dream come true.[1] In retrospect, she claimed that she was very well aware of what she was getting herself into when she began the affair with Picasso and was definitely not naïve. 'I knew it was going to be a catastrophe', she told the German journalist Malte Herwig, 'but a catastrophe that would be worth living.'[2] When reflecting on that time, she often speaks of Picasso's 'Bluebeard complex', a reference to the French folktale *Barbe bleu*, known mainly through Charles Perrault's seventeenth-century retelling of it. The tale's eponymous protagonist, Count Bluebeard, is a rich and powerful nobleman whose wives mysteriously disappear. Entrusting his seventh wife with the keys to his castle before setting off on a journey, Bluebeard explains to her that there is only one room that she is strictly forbidden from entering. The new wife disregards his injunction and on entering the locked chamber discovers to her horror the lifeless bodies of her six predecessors. 'Don't forget that I was Bluebeard's seventh wife', Gilot later remarked in an interview.[3]

'I instantly thought that what I would have to avoid above all else was the ego-trip of being painted by Picasso.'[4] Hence her claim that she forbade Picasso from attaching her name to any of his depictions of her, no matter what form they took. 'They were Picassos, that's all!'[5] she said, as if to drive the point home. Knowing the fate that had befallen her predecessors, Gilot seems to have developed self-protection strategies very

**64
Pablo Picasso,
*Woman in
an Armchair*,
2 April 1947**

Musée national Picasso,
Paris (MP 1990-23)

early on. She also took her time before accepting Picasso's offer to come and live with him. Eventually she relented, and while he took on the role of her artistic mentor, the torrent of creativity that her arrival unleashed in him is evident from the flurry of new works orbiting and exalting his new companion that he produced during this period.

Gilot's artistic sympathies in fact lay less with Picasso than with Henri Matisse, whom she met in person when she accompanied Picasso on a visit to the painter's home in Vence in the summer of 1946. This is how she came to be sucked into the vortex of Picasso's possessiveness; because Matisse seems to have found Gilot inspiring, too, and began to chat about how he would depict her if she were to sit for him. It was presumably in response to the colour scheme floated by Matisse that Picasso created his work *Woman with Green Hair.* Looking at the works that he produced immediately after this visit to Matisse, it is hard not to believe that he was trying to beat his rival with Matisse's own weapons. Seized by a frenzy of creativity, he spent June 1946 exploring his young partner's face in ever new variations, though always articulating her right eyebrow as a circumflex –an idea that likewise seems to have been supplied by Matisse (figs. 65, 67).[6]

If fellow artists like Wassily Kandinsky saw Picasso as belonging to the realm of drawing and Matisse to the realm of colour, Gilot's inclinations and talents quite clearly belong in the latter domain. Not only does she frequently evoke Matisse when writing about her art; her painterly sensors are also unmistakably those of a born colorist. To interpret her oeuvre primarily as an engagement with the art of Picasso would therefore be wrong at the most fundamental level. On the contrary, Gilot was far more drawn to the work of Matisse and Georges

65
Pablo Picasso,
Portrait of Françoise,
20 May 1946

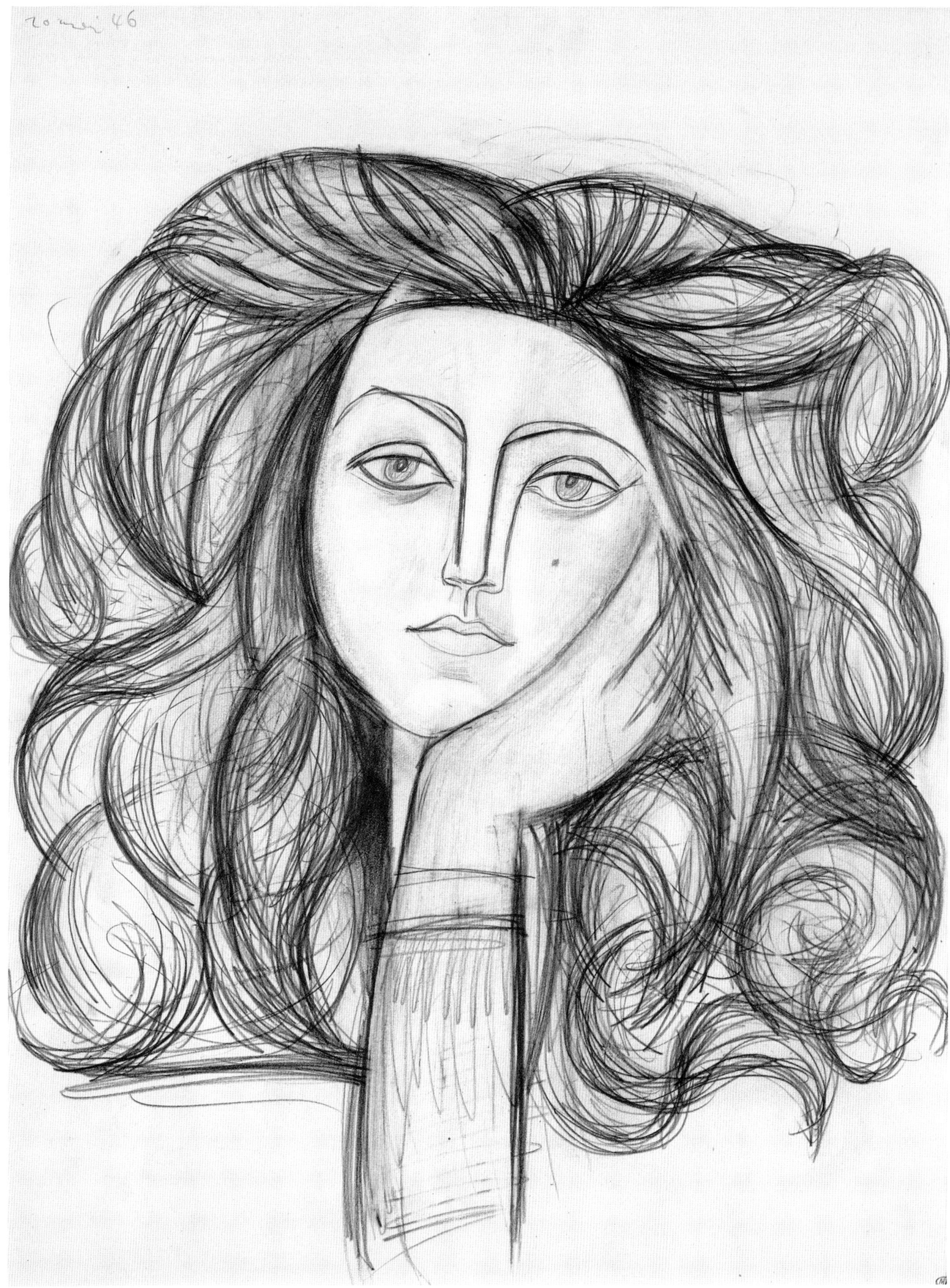

20 maggio 46

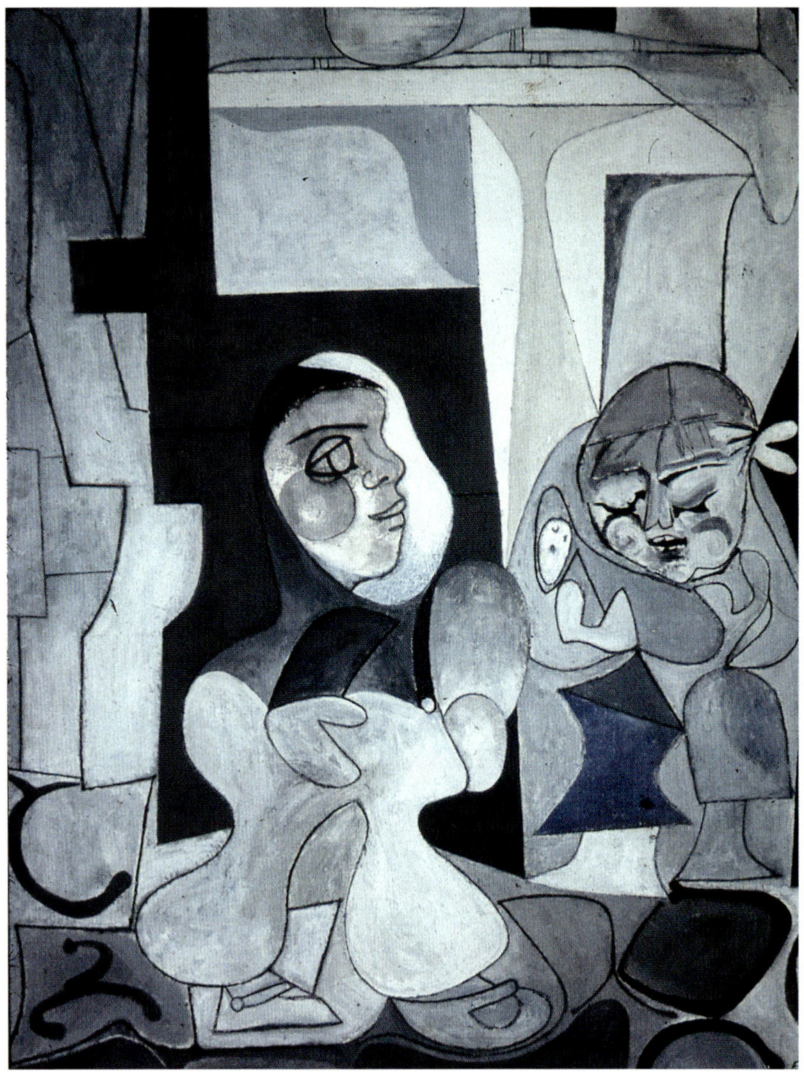

Braque than to that of Picasso, and being eager to assimilate the visual strategies of post-war French abstraction could not possibly content herself with swimming along in Picasso's stylistic wake.

In her visual world, figurative modes of representation alternate with abstract tendencies. She had become caught up in the abstract currents even while in Paris, where she made the acquaintance of Nicolas de Staël and developed a fondness for his inspiring visual idiom. Not that she ever placed her art in the service of an aesthetic dogma. On the contrary, she has consistently adapted her painterly language to the subject being painted.

'I do not paint what I look at, but what looks at me',[1] was her artistic motto. True to this maxim, her children take pride of place in her early works, in which it is the large and watchful eyes of little Paloma and Claude that transfix us. Also striking is the way Gilot captures their soft, plump features in convoluted, intersecting lines.

Claude was born in the spring of 1947 and named after Claude Gillot, the teacher of the French Rococo painter Antoine Watteau. Paloma, born two years later, owes her name

**66
Françoise Gilot,
*My Children in
the Kitchen*,
1950**
Private collection

**67
Pablo Picasso,
*The Woman
with a Hair Net
(La femme
à la résille)*,
30 May 1949**
Kunstmuseum
Pablo Picasso Münster

148

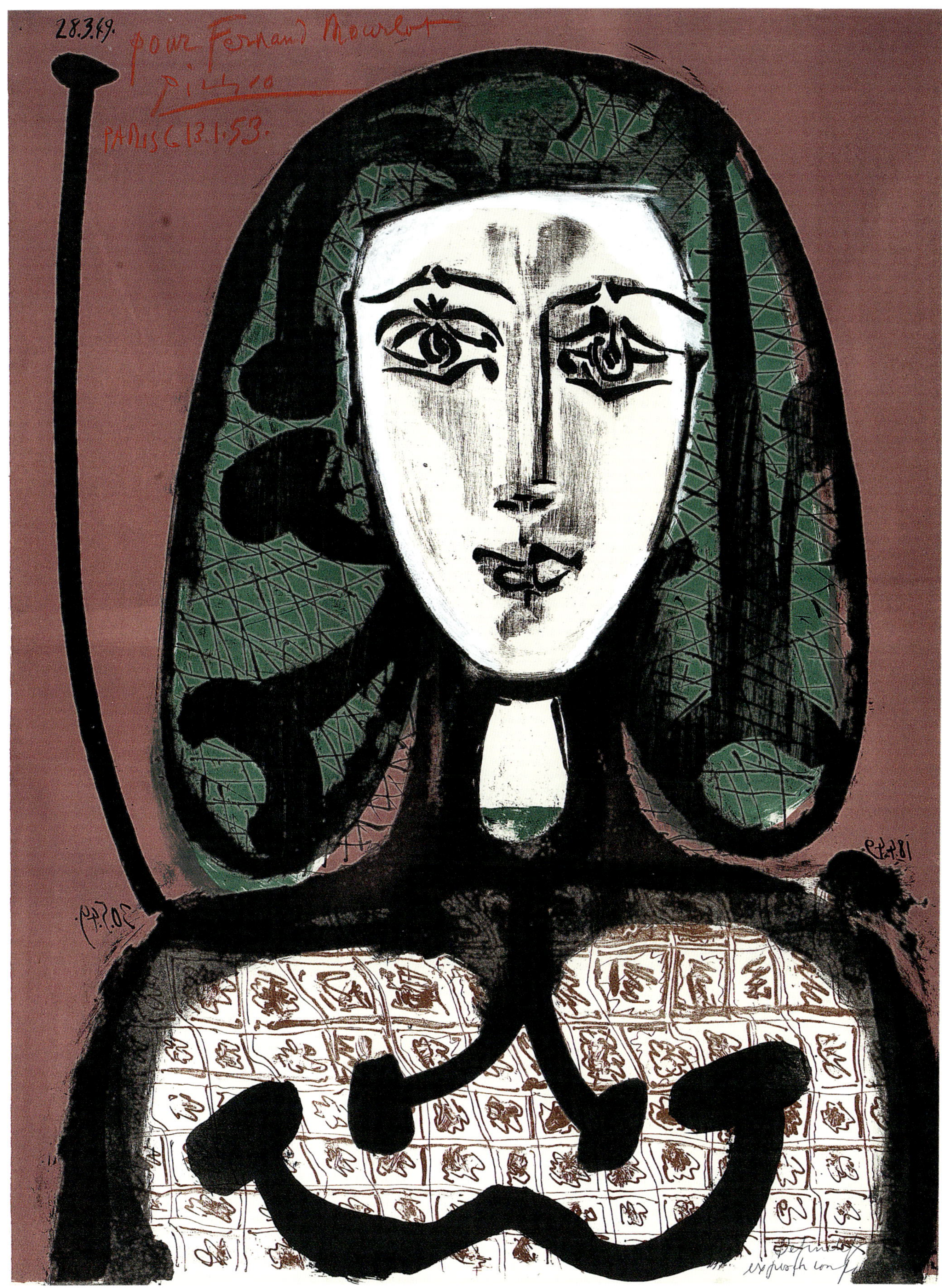
28.3.49.
pour Fernand Mourlot
Picasso
PARIS 13.1.53.

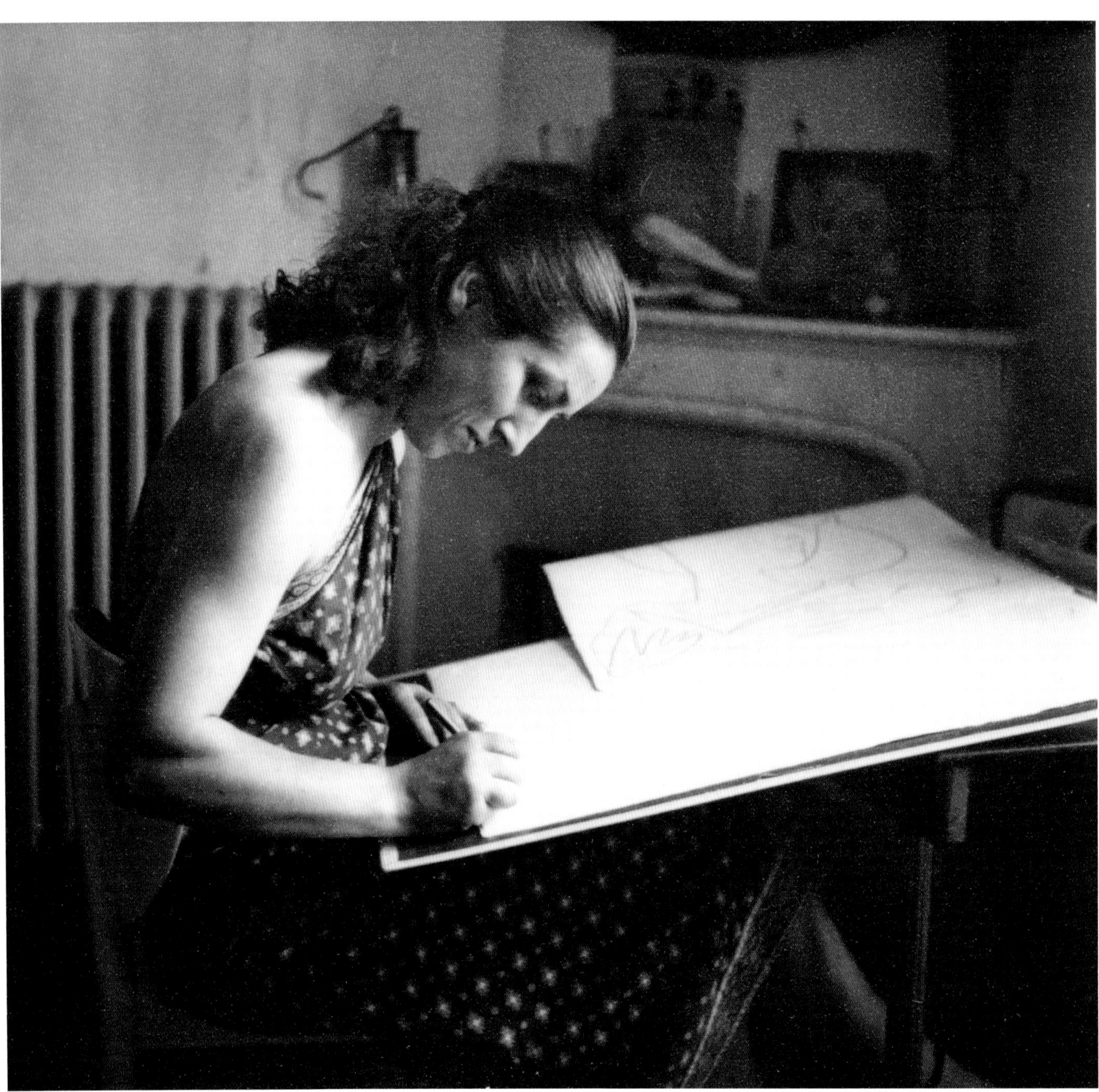

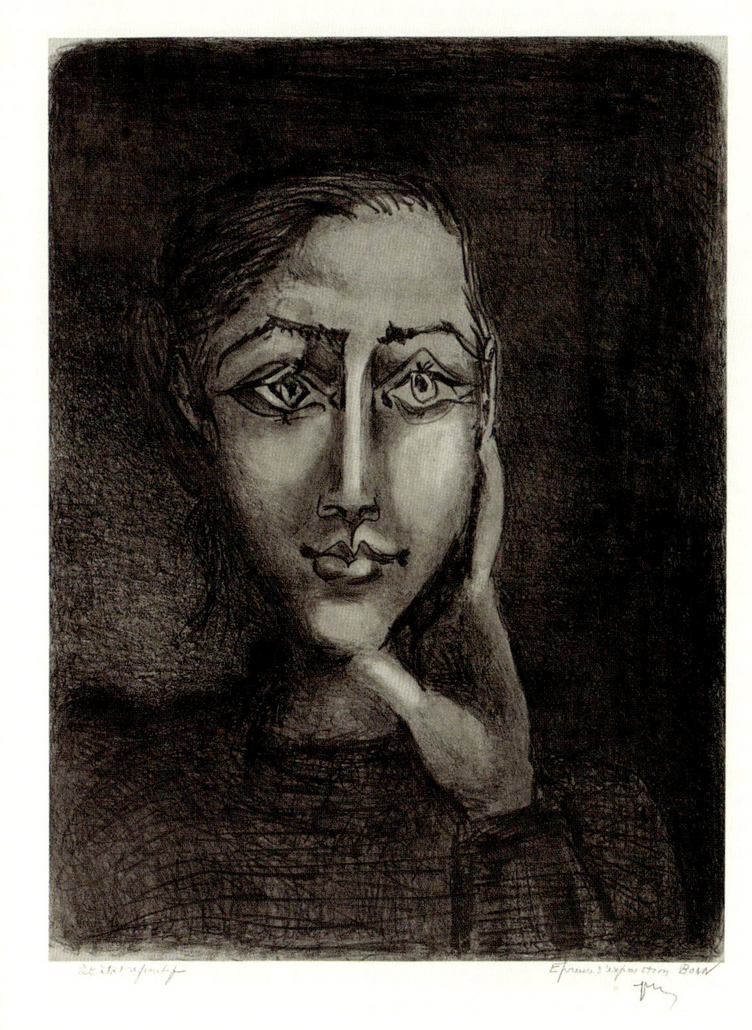

**68
Françoise Gilot
at work,
Vallauris, 1951**
Musée national Picasso,
Paris (APPH 4383)

**69
Pablo Picasso,
*Françoise
against a Grey
Background*,
19 November 1950**
Kunstmuseum Pablo
Picasso Münster

to Picasso's famous *Dove of Peace*, which adorned the posters for the World Congress of Partisans for Peace, held in Paris in April 1949. It took Gilot a long while to recover from her daughter's birth. A lithograph by Picasso dated 19 November 1950 shows a frame-filling close-up of her with her hair pinned up in a bun, looking at once battered and contemplative

(fig. 69). There is no sign here of the sublimations and stylizations of her as the 'flower-woman' or 'sun-face'. Gilot quotes Picasso as saying: 'For me, there are only two kinds of women – goddesses and door-mats',[8] and to judge by her account of his treatment of her, she must have undergone a metamorphosis from the first to the second. As the crisis in their relationship mounted in the early 1950s, Picasso claimed that it was thanks only to him that she had become someone, and when she finally left him, in September 1953, taking Claude and Paloma with her to Paris, he raged that: 'No one leaves a man like me!'[9]

In 1955 Gilot married Luc Simon, a painter two years her junior with whom she would have another daughter, Aurélia. After six years of marriage, however, that relationship likewise broke down, according to Gilot, on account of Simon's depression and his inability to

151

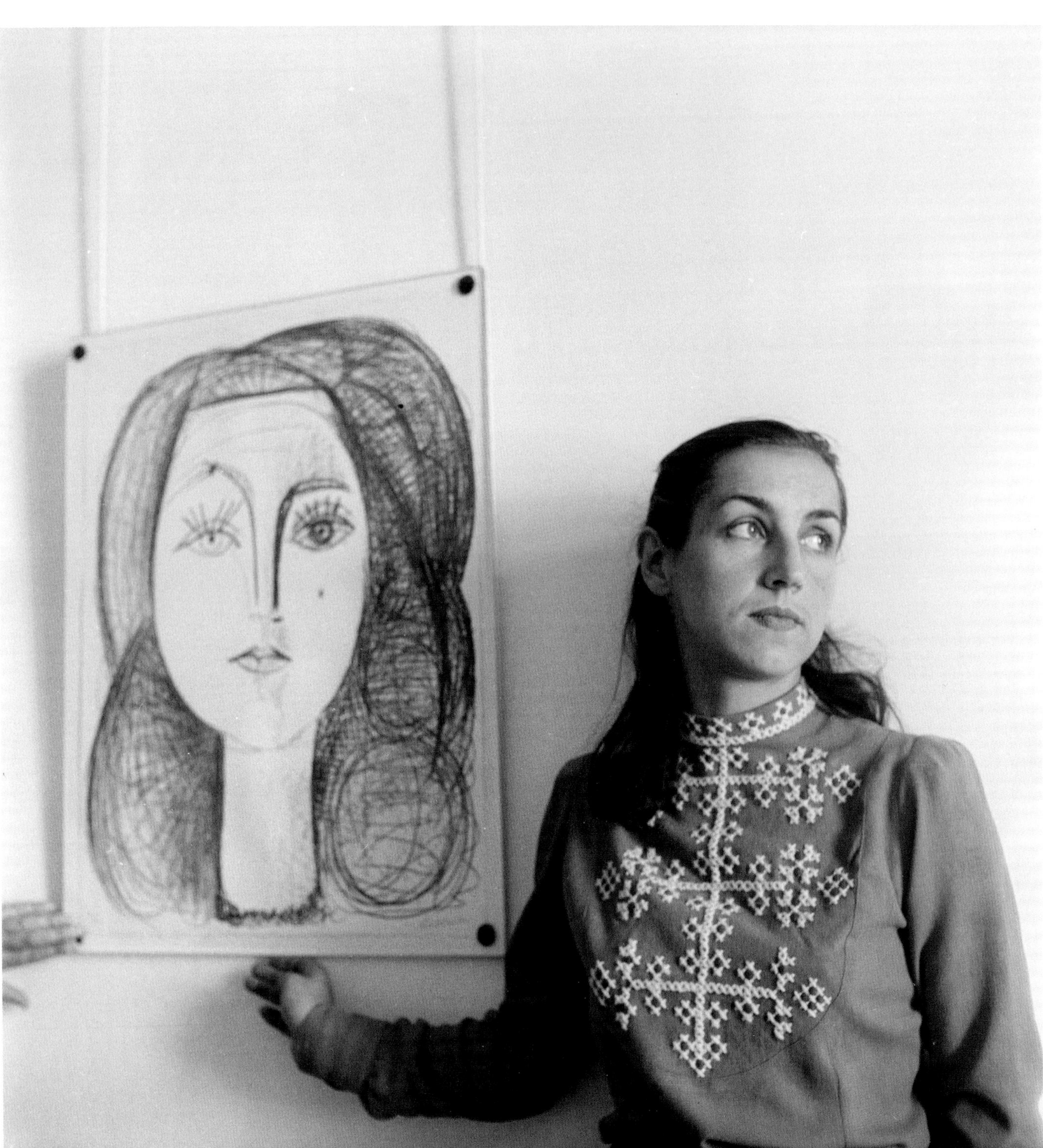

accept that Gilot was better known as an artist than he was.[10]

The book *Life with Picasso*, co-authored by Gilot and the journalist Carlton Lake, was published in New York in 1964 and hence over a decade after her separation from Picasso. Lake had been the Paris correspondent for the *Christian Science Monitor* and besides writing for such reputable publications as *The New Yorker* had made a name for himself as an art critic.

In his introduction to Gilot's memoirs, Tim Hilton describes how Gilot first met Lake in 1956 when he was preparing to publish an article about Picasso.[11] The two became friends, and in February 1961 Lake suggested the book project to her. According to Gilot's account, she had repeatedly received offers of a book contract, but had rejected them all – until Lake came along with his. It follows that far from being a long-cherished dream of hers, the book in fact came into being as a response to a series of conversations between the authors.

In his foreword, Carlton Lake praises what he calls his co-author's 'total recall'.[12] He notes, for example, the congruence between her account of her life with Picasso and the Spanish artist's own version of it. He also describes having had access to her own 'notes and journals of the period', which had until then been stowed away in three large boxes in Gilot's former home in the south of France.

In *Françoise Gilot: Monograph: 1940–2000*, Mel Yoakum, the curator of Gilot's collection, explains that starting in 1962, she dedicated three days of the week to writing her autobiography and only two to her painting.[13] By the summer of 1963, the text had gone through the various stages of editing and was ready to be handed over to Gilot's attorneys for checking – which as it happened, turned out to be a prudent measure.

70
Françoise Gilot next to Picasso's lithograph *Françoise*, 1952, **photographed by Denise Colomb**

Life with Picasso met with considerable interest among readers as soon as it came out. Such a book, one that promises to be at once both a bestseller and a long-seller, is a publisher's dream come true, and as predicted, it remained on the American bestseller lists for six months. Over a million copies of the English hardback edition were sold in the first year alone.[14]

Among Picasso's own circle, however, the book was polarising. John Richardson and Carlton Lake thrashed out their differences of opinion in a slew of newspaper articles, in which the former took the latter to task for the book's indiscreet tone and revelation of private details of the love affair between Gilot and Picasso.

The biographer also doubted the authenticity of Picasso's own disquisitions on his art as relayed by Gilot, some of them several pages long, which he felt ran counter to the dry but witty delivery for which the artist was famous. The dilemma, according to Richardson, was that for Picasso, perhaps more than for any other artist, it was his own lived experience that supplied the raw material for his art. And as the key to interpreting Picasso's works lay in his biography, Richardson complained, Gilot's work would distort his image for posterity with lasting effect. The French periodical *ARTS – lettres – spectacles – musique* argued in a similar vein, blazoning its April–May 1965 edition with the headline: 'Françoise Gilot has betrayed Picasso.'

Especially damning was the response of the French Communist Party, which Picasso had joined after the liberation of Paris, in August 1944, and which now decried the book as a character assassination of one of its most illustrious members. The mouthpiece of choice for all those vehemently opposed to the publication of the French edition was the *Lettres Françaises*, which in April 1965 ran an article by its editor,

Picasso's friend Pierre Daix, discrediting Gilot as an 'embittered gossip'. Many famous names in the world of art and culture expressed their solidarity with Picasso in his efforts to prevent the French edition of the work from ever going to press, and the list of those who signed the two petitions reads very much like a who's who of post-war French culture. Douglas Cooper, a major collector of Picasso's work, opted for a more personal, if eccentric, way of signalling his displeasure by inviting people to a party at which he ceremoniously consigned *Life with Picasso* to the flames.[15]

Gilot and her publisher fought on, however, and in the end won their case on appeal, so that publication of the French edition could at last go ahead. For Gilot personally, however, that momentous decision was as much a curse as a blessing; for while it brought her international fame, it also conditioned the public to view her merely as Picasso's muse rather than as an artist in her own right. 'Nothing grows in the shade of tall trees', Constantin Brancusi is said to have remarked upon leaving the studio of his teacher, Auguste Rodin.[16] Françoise Gilot, too, had long since left the shadow cast by Picasso for precisely that reason: in order to thrive independently as both a private individual and an artist. Even so, far from exorcising the ghosts of the past, her publication of *Life with Picasso* in fact conjured them up again and made it all but inevitable that her name would henceforth be inextricably bound up with that of her famous ex.

Towards the end of the 1960s, however, Gilot's life once again took an unexpected turn, when on a visit to La Jolla, a suburb of San Diego in California, she met the American medical researcher and virologist Jonas Salk.[17] As the developer of one of the first polio vaccines and a scientist of international repute, Salk had built up an interdisciplinary

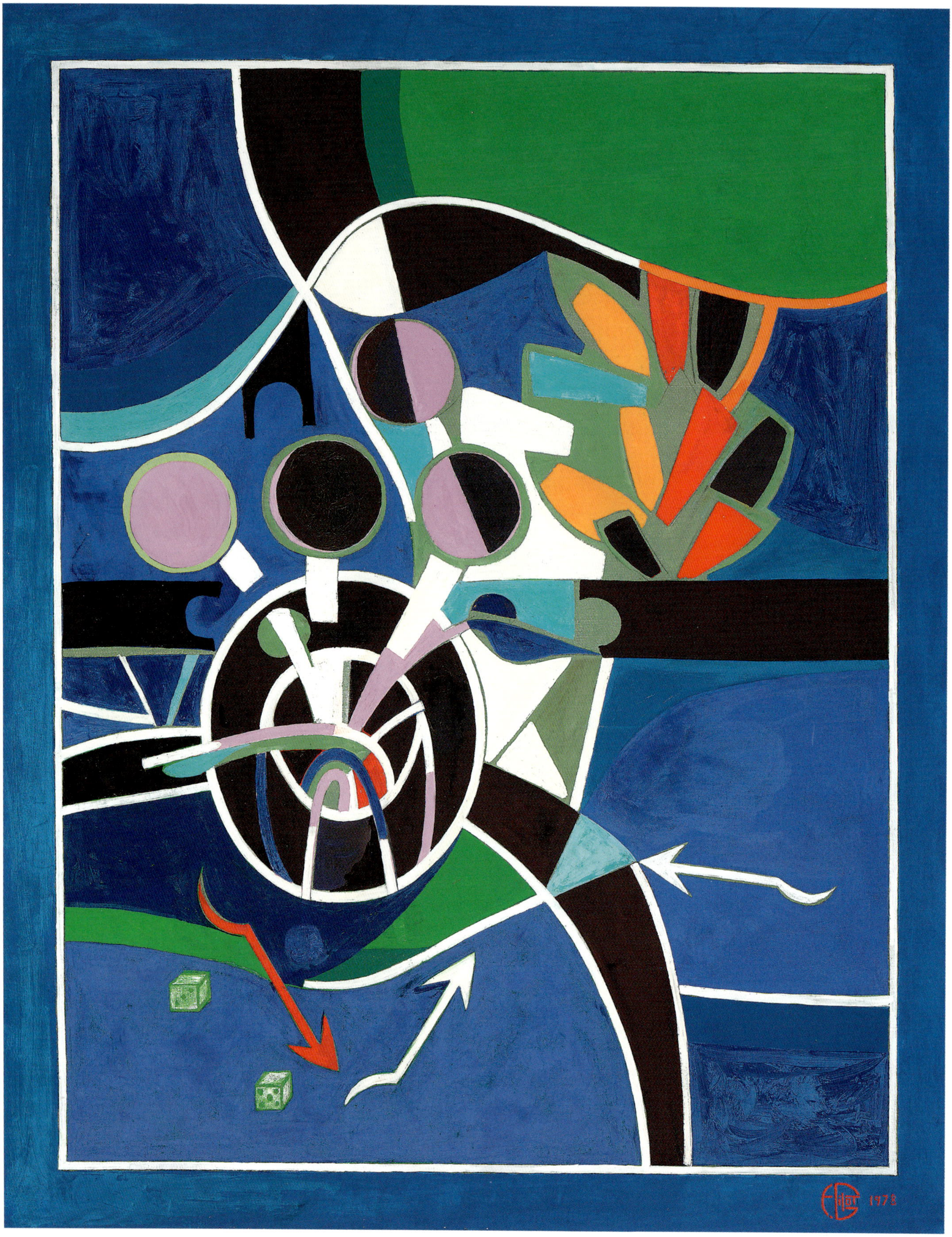

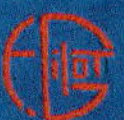

research institute in La Jolla. Gilot and Salk fell in love and married in the summer of 1970 in Neuilly in the presence of their respective children. After the wedding, Françoise moved to California, though she would henceforth spend half the year working at her studio there and the other half in Paris.[18] That Picasso had to content himself with the Villa La Californie in Cannes, which he had bought two years after Gilot left him, whereas Gilot herself was destined for the real California is not without a certain irony. Once she was happily married to Salk, Gilot seems to have been inclined to let bygones be bygones. She put the family's former home, the Villa La Galloise in Vallauris, where for years she and Picasso had lived with their two children, on the market in 1972.[19] In a similarly symbolic act of liberation well over a decade later, she decided to part with the painting *La femme-fleur*, which she sold to a gallery in Switzerland. Picasso had painted this work immortalizing his young lover as an anthropomorphic flower woman in 1946. 'You're like a growing plant',[20] she quotes him as saying to her while he was working on it. Gilot used the substantial proceeds from that sale to fix up the studio she had bought for herself in New York City in 1979.

Gilot claimed the secret to her harmonious marriage to Salk was the stimulating complementarity of their radically different professions: 'I worked on my art alone and he on his science', she told Malte Herwig in one of their many interviews.[21] After two failed marriages with other artists, she had evidently come to the conclusion that the best route to a satisfying and mutually enhancing relationship between two equal partners was to choose someone in a completely different field. Her life at Salk's side can therefore be read as the exact opposite of what she had experienced with Picasso, even if reflecting on it much later, she

71
Françoise Gilot,
Magic Games,
1978
Whereabouts unknown (formerly collection of Walter and Phyllis Shorenstein)

conceded that 'the love was more friendship than passion. It was love because I admired his commitment to the human race, his humanity, and he was a fine man. But I can't say I felt passionately about him. With Pablo it was different.'[22] Jonas Salk died on 23 June 1995, just a few days before the couple's silver wedding anniversary.

Gilot continued to shuttle back and forth between America and France for many years, long after Salk's death. A 2021 exhibition in Saint-Rémy that featured her work from the early 1940s up to her relocation to California was aptly named *The Years in France*.[23] Yet while her marriage to Salk and move to La Jolla in 1970 certainly marked a turning point in her life, it passed almost without notice in her art. Her colourful paintings would henceforth be steeped in the sunshine of California rather than that of the Midi, but otherwise, she continued much as before. Gilot's biographers have emphasised how deeply rooted in traditional French painting her art is, and it is indeed true that American avant-garde tendencies seem to have eluded her almost entirely, so that we scour her paintings and prints for signs of their influence in vain. What Gilot created were images of a world in flux, in which her own rarefied form of figuration alternates with an undogmatically abstract idiom. She skipped nimbly between these two painterly worlds without ever lapsing into a routine, crowd-pleasing style.

In 1978 Gilot designed a monogram for herself with which she would henceforth sign the majority of her works. The monogram resembling an artist's signet comprises a capital 'G' that appears to curl protectively around the other letters of her name. The monogram is unmistakably a borrowing from the Japanese artists of the great tradition, who typically changed their names several times in the course of their careers. It was while talking about them that Henri Matisse, whom Gilot so admired, said that an artist must never be 'a prisoner of a style, prisoner of a reputation, prisoner of a success'.[24] That Gilot has succeeded at this in the course of her long life is beyond doubt. Her first book of poetry in English, *The Fugitive Eye*, published in 1976, contains the line: 'My eyes were born first.'[25] And reflecting on her past work in various television interviews, she repeatedly stresses how she liked to draw and paint even in early childhood. Clearly a strongly visual person from birth, Gilot has become an artist-cum-author, whose command of the pen is as magisterial as that of brush. *Le Regard et son Masque*, of 1975, is a blend of autobiography and artistic manifesto, while the poignancy and subtle humour of her eye-witness account of the friendship – shot through with rivalry – between the two Titans of modernism, *Matisse and Picasso: A Friendship in Art*, of 1990, won her widespread critical acclaim.

Many documentary films and books dub Françoise Gilot 'the woman who said no', just as her rejection of a life at Picasso's side has made her an icon of women's liberation. Yet, even now, her very long, very productive, and very fulfilled life still tends to be eclipsed by her ten-year-long relationship with Picasso, despite the fact that decades after her break with the living legend Picasso she became a living legend in her own right.

Their biographical and creative trajectories were to converge once again in an artistic dialogue between the long-deceased Picasso and the over ninety-year-old Gilot set in motion by the Gagosian Gallery in New York in 2012. With Gilot's acquiescence, *Picasso and Françoise Gilot: Paris – Vallauris, 1943–1953*, far from looking back in anger, cast a more forgiving and more self-assured glance at the past. The curator was John Richardson, a personal friend of Picasso's, who many years previously had been fiercely critical of Gilot's *Life with Picasso*. Born of the collaboration of these two erstwhile adversaries, the show was also an affirmation of Gilot's magnanimity.

In the course of her long life, Françoise Gilot has consistently been true to herself, even as she has repeatedly reinvented herself. She had to wait until her one-hundredth year to see a work of hers – an affectionate portrait of her daughter, Paloma, dating from 1965 – break the magical one-million-euro barrier at auction; but in an age in which people are more interested in price than in value, this can undoubtedly be read as a kind of material consecration of her life's work. Her one-hundredth birthday, on 26 November 2021, was celebrated with several exhibitions of her work. Was it not Pablo Picasso himself who once said that it takes a long time to become young?

**72
Françoise Gilot,
*Sink and
Tomates* (*Evier
et tomates*),
1 May 1951**
Musée national d'Art
moderne, Paris (AM 3228 P)

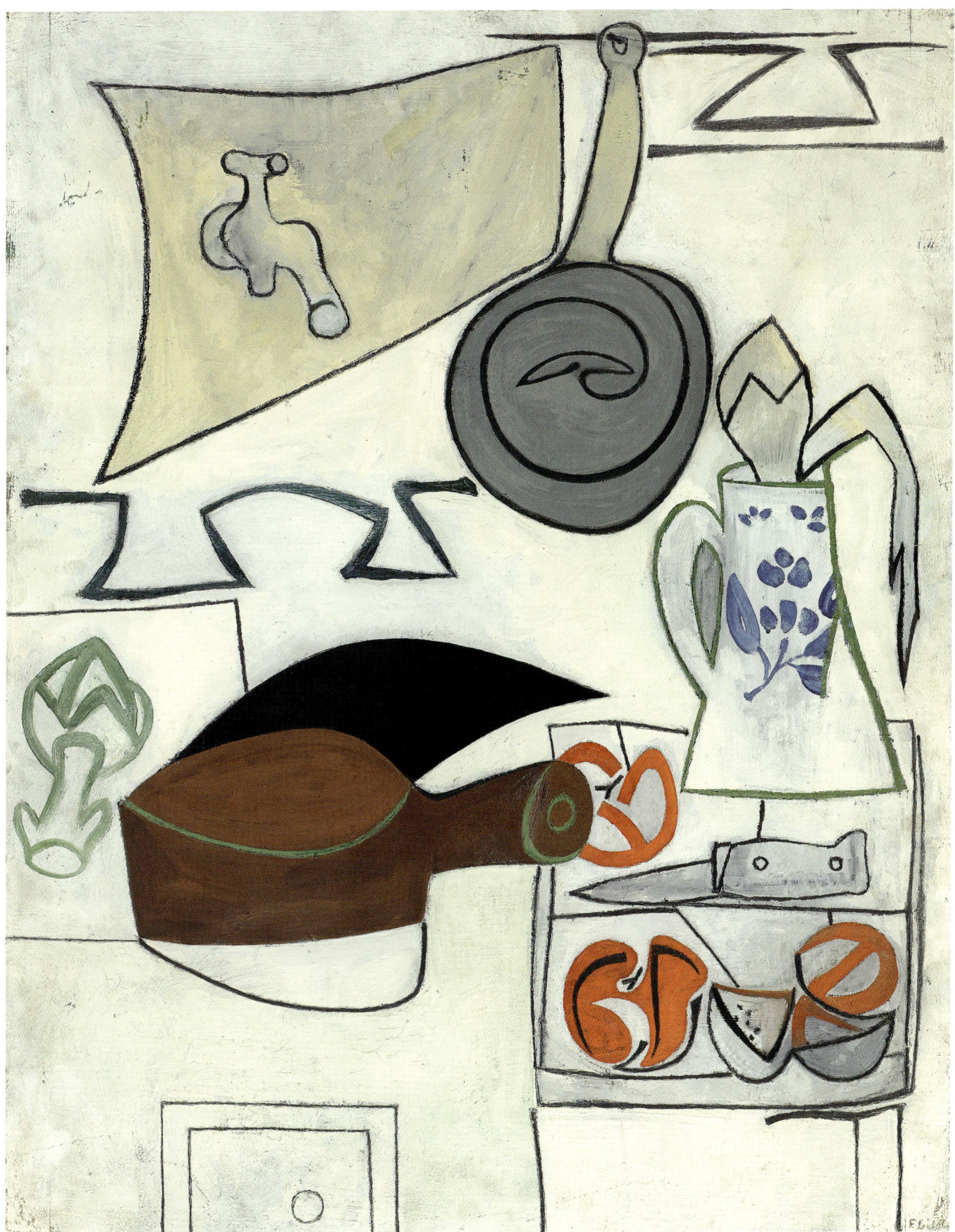

Jacqueline Roque

Markus Müller

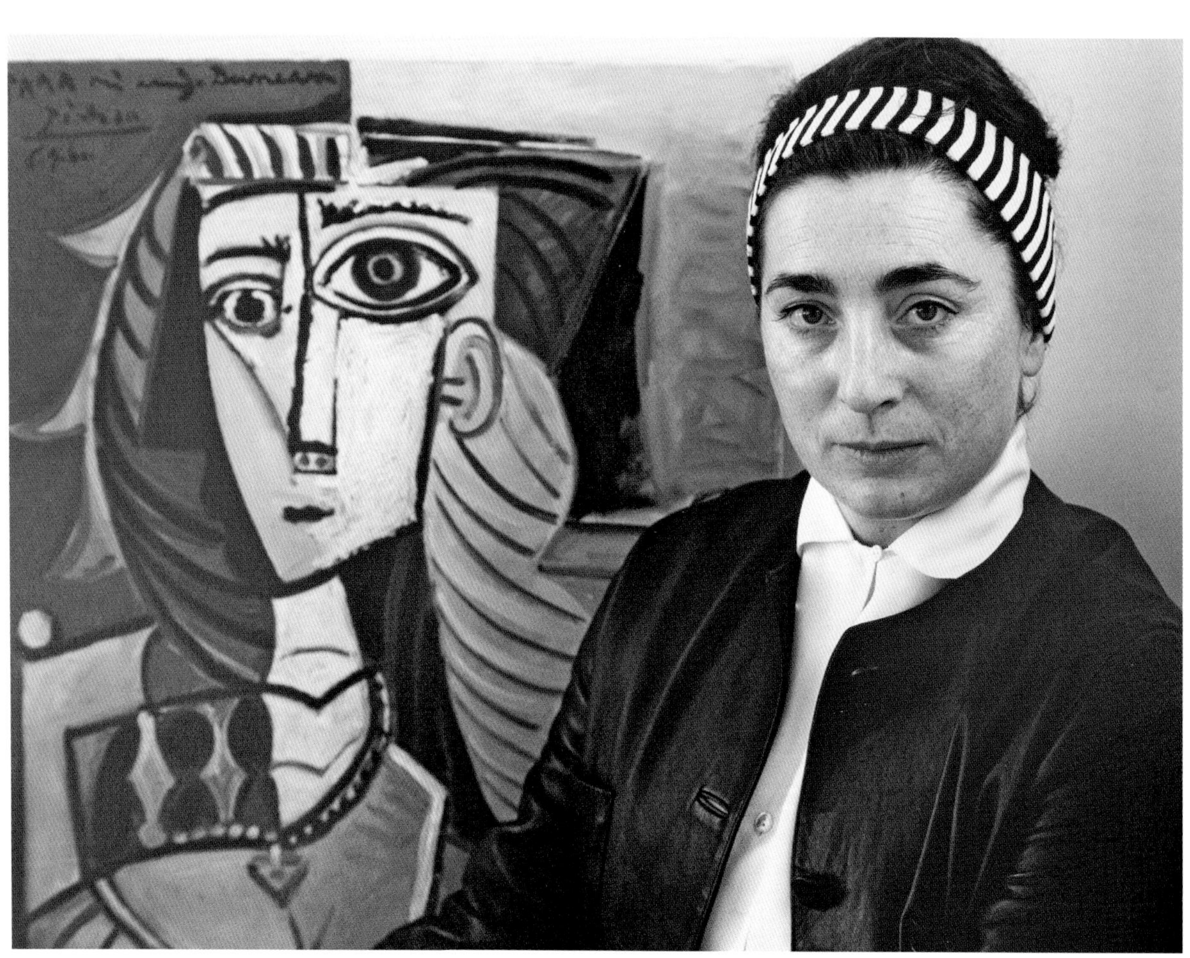

The 'Sun Worshipper'

Portrayals of Pablo Picasso's last love, Jacqueline Roque, vary greatly depending on which biographer or acquaintance is consulted. To some she is the devoted, self-sacrificing wife; to others the jealous 'guardian of the temple', shielding the deity from the outside world.[1] What everyone mentions in their descriptions of her, however, is her almost idolatrous veneration of Picasso. Several people recall her referring to him as *'Monseigneur'* (my lord) or even 'the Sun'[2] – a privilege that doubtless no other husband in French history since the Sun King himself has enjoyed. Others still characterise her as deeply ambivalent, a kind of human version of Cerberus, who guarded her husband fiercely so that not even his own children could get near him.

Doubtless the discrepancies in how Jacqueline Roque is judged are in no small part a consequence of the unusually complex family situation. She met Picasso in 1953, when she herself was just twenty-six, whereas he already had four children, two of whom were grown-up, as well as two grandchildren. An American journalist once likened this fraught family situation to one of Picasso's cubist sculptures; and given the many women in his life, not to mention the one legitimate and three illegitimate offspring, it is hardly surprising that perceptions of his last love are similarly multi-facetted. Even the most basic biological and genealogical facts about his last companion have been recorded inaccurately. Françoise Gilot, in her *Life with Picasso*, describes her as having blue rather than brown eyes, for example, and claims that she was 'a young cousin' of Suzanne Ramié, proprietor of the Madoura pottery in Vallauris, whereas in fact she was not a blood relative at all, but rather just a friend.[3] This incorrect assertion of affinity

163

Jacqueline Roque

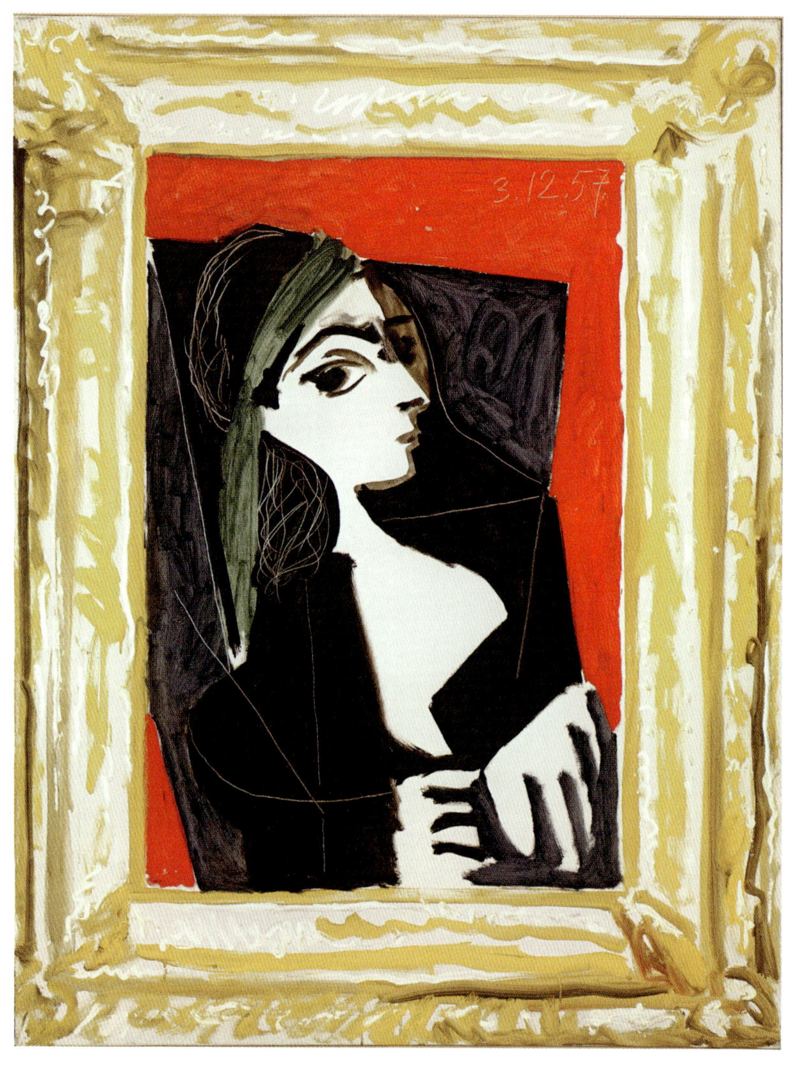

was unfortunately adopted by Picasso's biographer Pierre Daix in his own writings on the subject.[4]

What is certainly true of Jacqueline Roque is that she came late to the world of art. She was born in Paris on 24 February 1927, the second child of Georges and Madeleine Roque. Her father deserted the family when she was two and her brother four years old. As their seamstress mother was henceforth the sole breadwinner, their childhood was one of great hardship and privation. Madeleine Roque died of a stroke in November 1944, when Jacqueline was just eighteen. At war's end, she found work as a secretary at the headquarters of the Saint-Gobain industrial conglomerate in Paris and there made the acquaintance of the engineer André Hutin, who began courting her. They married in December 1946, and their only child, Catherine Blanche, was born on 4 January 1948. Later that year the young family moved to Upper Volta (now Burkina Faso) in Africa, where Hutin had been appointed site manager of a railway construction project. After nearly four years in Africa, Jacqueline left Hutin and returned to France with their young daughter. The marriage was formally dissolved two years later. Jacqueline Roque settled in Golfe-Juan on the French Riviera, where she and Catherine lived on the first floor of a house called 'Le Ziquet', the Provençal word for the little goat or kid. She was also an occasional customer at the Madoura pottery, and stood in for Huguette Ramié, Suzanne Ramié's niece who ran the pottery shop, when the former gave birth to a son in May 1953. It was there at the pottery that her path crossed with that of Pablo Picasso. After setting eyes on the new sales lady, then in her mid-twenties, he began wooing her with characteristic charm – as if he himself were an eligible young bachelor rather than an elderly man in his mid-seventies. Picasso's relationship with Françoise Gilot, moreover, was not yet over, although the tensions between them were mounting steadily, and she would leave him in September of that same year, taking their children, Claude and Paloma, with her (fig. 66).

The spring of 1954 saw Picasso create an extensive series of portraits of Sylvette David, a half-English, half-French nineteen-year-old who was visiting the Côte d'Azur with her boyfriend at the time. He produced twenty-eight paintings and almost as many drawings of her between April and June 1954. David, whose boyfriend shrewdly accompanied her whenever she sat for Picasso, wore her long hair in a high ponytail and with her pouty lips embodied the kind of ideal beauty that was to make Brigitte Bardot such a star. Most of the Sylvette David portraits show her in profile with an elongated neck. The sequence is significant as a painterly intermezzo between two muses, Françoise Gilot and Jacqueline Roque, even if the formal characteristics of the Sylvette David portraits were undoubtedly carried over into the early

depictions of Jacqueline
Roque.

The portrait *Madame Z*
(fig. 75) marks Jacqueline
Roque's spectacular debut on
the stage of Picasso's painted
oeuvre. Owing to the very visible stylistic affinities with the
Sylvette David portraits that
preceded it, some commentators have interpreted this work
as just another addition to the
former series. But not by
chance did Picasso title the
work *Madame Z*, the mysterious 'Z' being his shorthand for
the sitter's home of Le Ziquet,
and any remaining doubts are
laid to rest by the dedication to
Jacqueline Roque that he later
added on the verso. The painting is a kind of secular version
of the *Madonna of the Rose
Bower*. The subject's head
bears all the hallmarks of portraiture, despite being dominated by the rigorously and
graphically stylized facial features and hair. The woman's
head rests on a manneristically
elongated neck, which lends
the figure a look of elegance
and grace. The articulation of
the upper body follows a wholly
two-dimensional representational logic; hence the crossed
arms that are folded over like a
sheet of paper. In her 1957
book about Picasso, Antonina
Vallentin described the work
as a 'plus étrange Sphinx'.[5]
This metaphorical characterisation of Roque seems to have
rung true among Picasso
scholars, given that Pierre
Cabanne elected to head the
chapter devoted to Roque in
his own Picasso monograph
'Jacqueline, The Genius-
Guarding Sphinx'.[6]

Madame Z marks the
beginning of a love affair that
was to endure for almost
twenty years, making it
Picasso's longest relationship
with any woman. William Rubin,
then chief curator of painting
and sculpture at the Museum
of Modern Art in New York and
among the privileged few who
had contact to Picasso during
his final years, describes
the artist's relationship with
Jacqueline Roque as follows:
'Her understated, gentle, and

**75
Pablo Picasso,
*Madame Z
(Jacqueline
with Flowers)*,
1954**
Collection of Catherine
Hutin

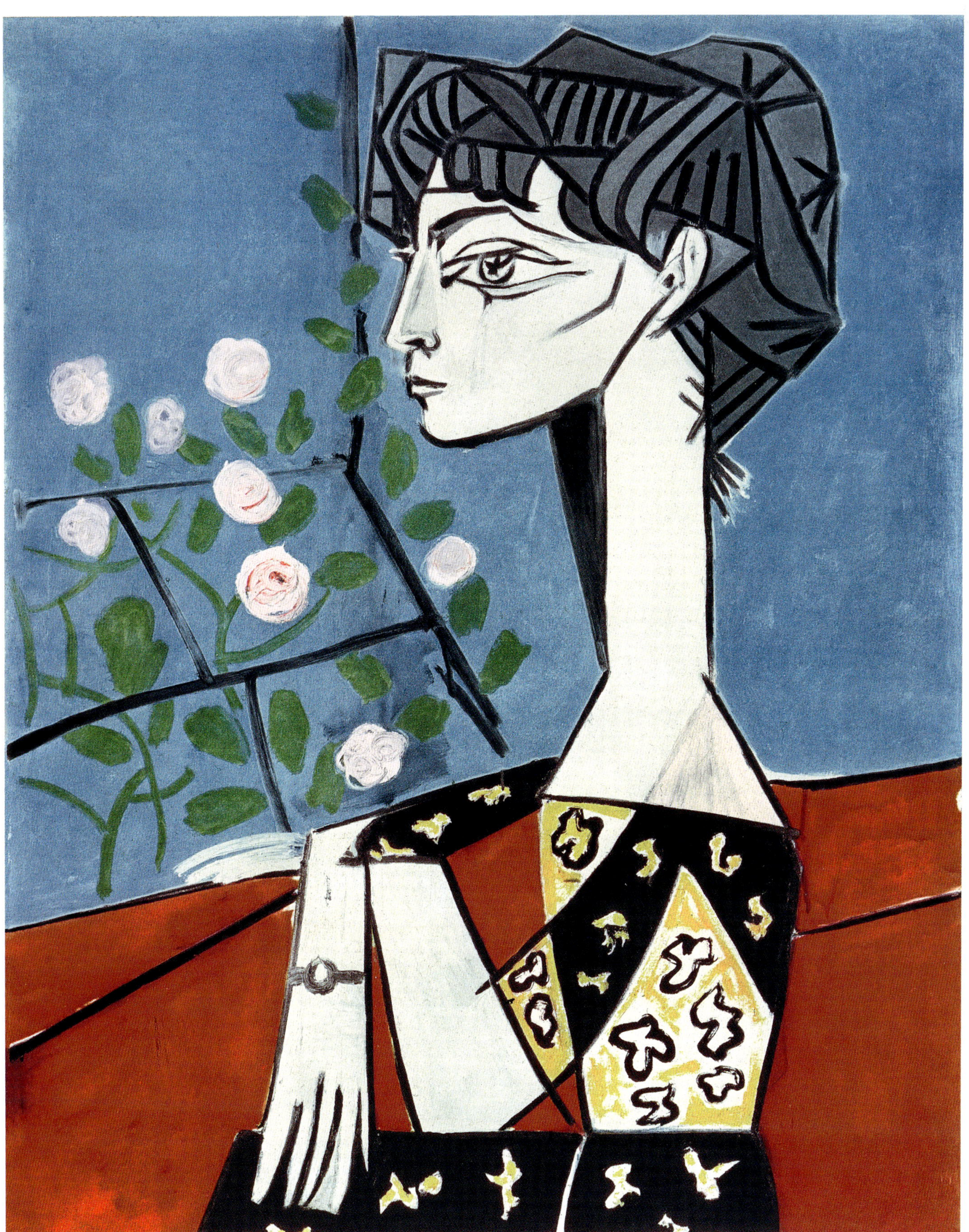

loving personality combined with her unconditional commitment to him provided an emotionally stable life and a dependable *foyer* over a longer period of time than he had ever before enjoyed.'[7] No other Picasso muse was painted as frequently as was Jacqueline. Her facial features, combined with her black hair and almond-shaped eyes, were very much those of a Mediterranean type, which is presumably why Picasso liked to call her *'l'espagnole'*. When portraying his new muse, later to become his wife, he generally preferred a profile view, which André Malraux likened to the manner in which ancient rulers had had themselves immortalized on coins.[8]

The couple moved into the Villa La Californie on a hill-side above Cannes in the summer of 1955. This very grand mansion was surrounded by a large garden and in those days commanded panoramic views of the Bay of Cannes. Picasso made the villa with its Art Nouveau windows the subject of numerous paintings and drawings, most of which show the interior of the ground floor, which served him as a multi-purpose studio and reception area as well as doubling as a dining room. Picasso never cared much for landscape painting, but made up for this with a plethora of studio paintings that he dubbed 'inner landscapes'.[9] The studio was like a second skin for Picasso; that is to say, it was a place of self-projection, but also of self-probing. The mature artist's growing need for privacy is reflected in his choice of themes and the way in which his preoccupation with his own personal domain can be seen unmistakably gaining ground. April 1956 saw him produce a whole series of paintings centred on his new studio in his newly acquired villa. One of these, begun on 3 April 1956 but completed only on 13 November of the following year (fig. 77), shows Jacqueline Roque communing silently with a studio painting still perched

76
Jacqueline Roque, 1957, photographed by David Douglas Duncan

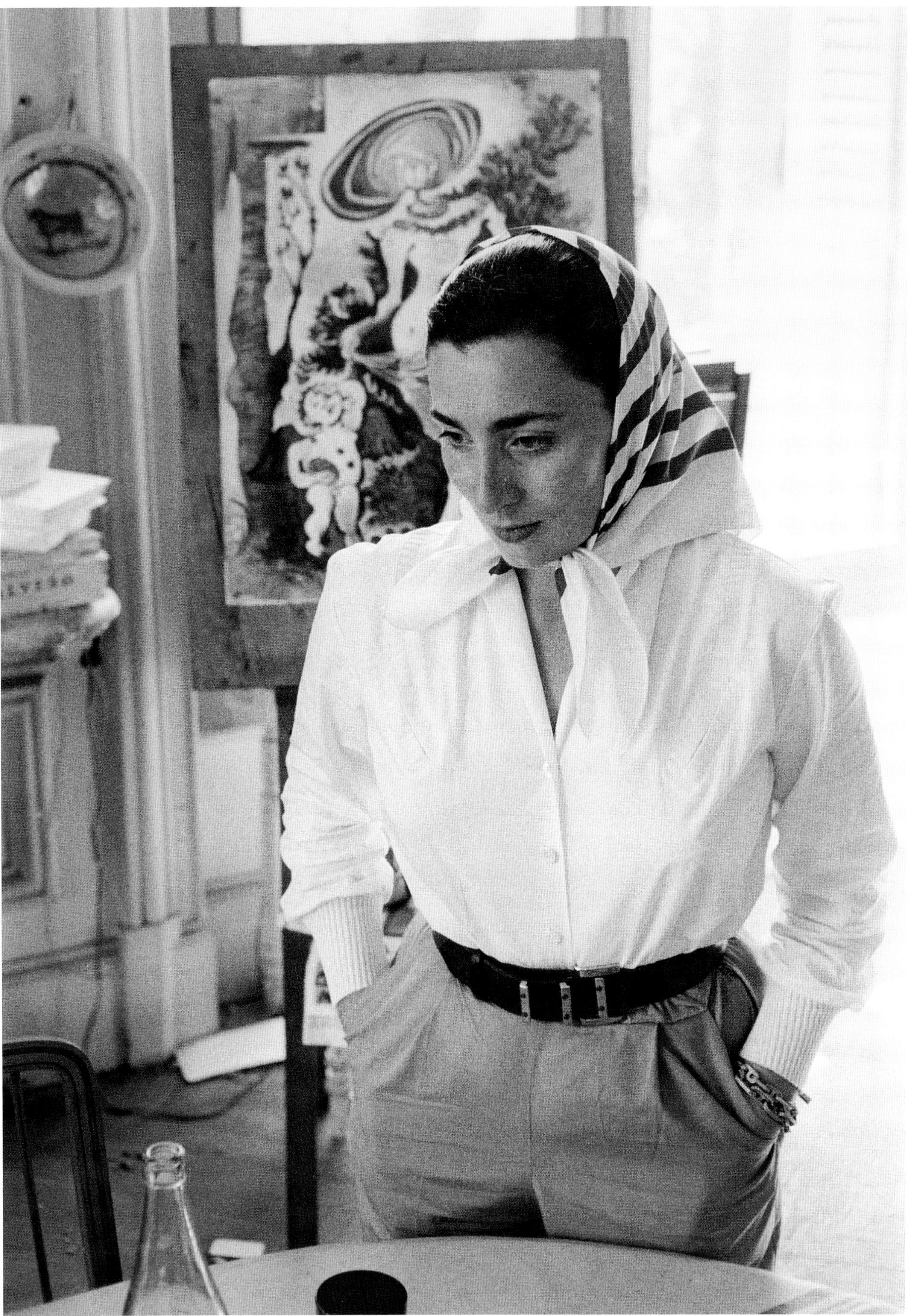

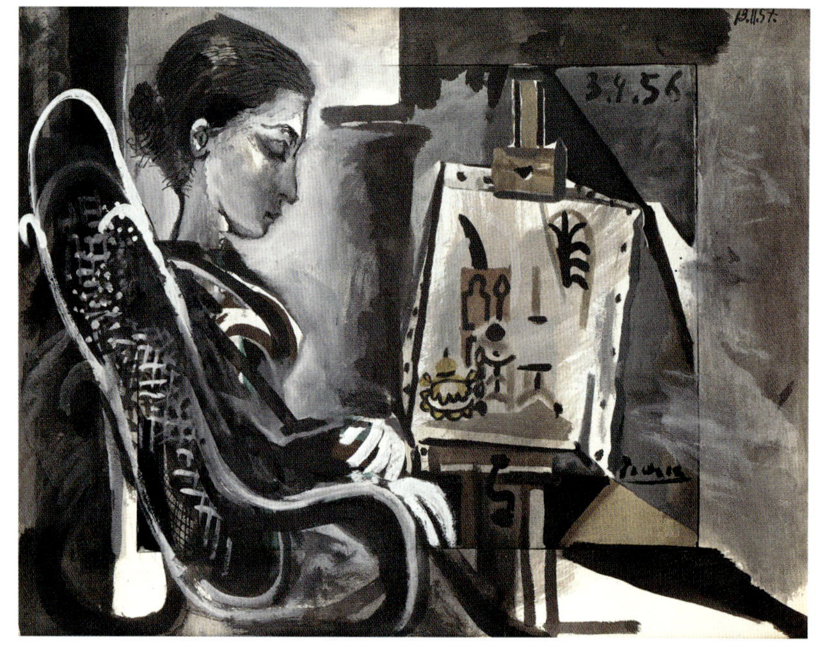

on the easel. The charm of this work lies in the tautological doubling of the real studio space and the depiction of the same in the painting. The prominent window motifs are a recurrent, cipher-like hallmark of these studio paintings evoking La Californie as the scene of the action.

When the building of some new high-rises nearby destroyed their idyllic view of the sea in 1958, Picasso and Jacqueline Roque bought the Château de Vauvenargues near Aix-en-Provence. This towering *bastide* or Provençal manor house dating from the seventeenth century was situated just to the north of Mont Sainte-Victoire, the distinctively shaped mountain that Paul Cézanne had so loved to paint. Aftering signing the contract, therefore, Picasso excitedly called his long-time art dealer, Daniel-Henry Kahnweiler, to tell him that he had bought 'the Sainte-Victoire', where-

upon Kahnweiler wanted to know which one. But the couple would only use the seat of the erstwhile Marquis de Vauvenargues between 1959 and 1961.

Jacqueline and Pablo married at the Vallauris town hall on 2 March 1961. The ceremony was performed in the utmost secrecy, with the result that the artist's children learned of it only from reports in the papers. From the legal point of view, Picasso was able to remarry only because of the death of his first wife, Olga Picasso, who after years of sickness had passed away in Cannes on 11 February 1955. In the summer of 1961, Jacqueline and Pablo moved into a new home, Notre-Dame-

77
Pablo Picasso,
Jacqueline
in the Studio,
1956–57
Musée national Picasso,
Paris (MP 1517)

de-Vie in Mougins, whose shape and layout were that of a *mas*, or Provençal farmhouse. The house derives its name from the chapel to 'Our Lady of Life' at the top end of the garden, leading many biographers to wonder whether the name alone, with its implicit promise of eternal life, might have added to the property's attractions for the then octogenarian Picasso. The property's somewhat remote, hill-top location certainly answered the couple's wish to keep journalists and other intruders at bay. As Picasso once sardonically remarked in conversation with Pierre Daix, as a living legend, he had become 'un des monuments de la Côte d'Azur' (one of the monuments of the Côte d'Azur).[10]

Picasso's rise to such Olympian heights was in part a result of the sobering fact that most of his contemporaries had predeceased him. Henri Matisse, for example, had died in early November 1954, bequeathing Picasso, or so the latter claimed, the artistic legacy of the odalisque.[11] When

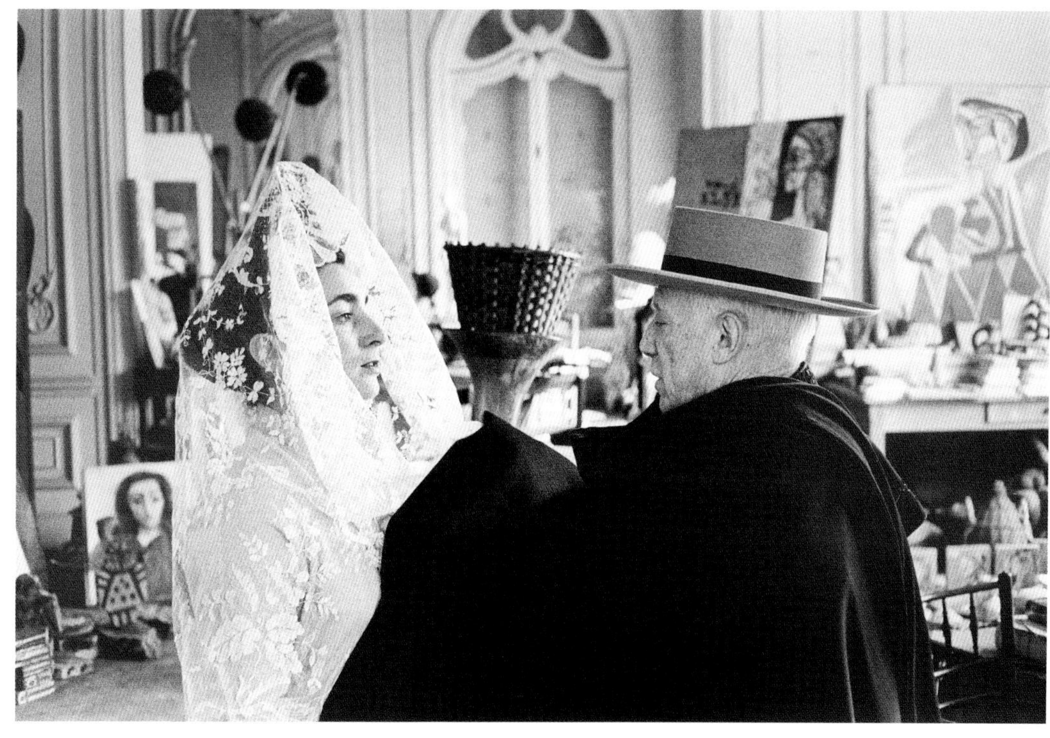

78
Jacqueline Roque and Pablo Picasso, 1957, photographed by David Douglas Duncan

Picasso began work on a major series of variations on Eugène Delacroix's *Women of Algiers* (1834) that December, however, he was following in Matisse's footsteps in more respects than just his choice of subject matter ([fig. 79](#)). Delacroix's famous painting had first caught his eye back in the 1940s, but now it seemed more topical than ever, given the striking resemblance between the odalisque squatting at front right and Jacqueline Picasso. Delacroix must have known her, too, he quipped.[12] Picasso's many paraphrases and artistic appropriations of the *Women of Algiers* mark the beginning of a prodigious series of works in which he picked apart and reimagined some of the most famous works of art history.

Contemporary trends in American art, first and fore-most among them Abstract Expressionism, were by then becoming increasingly influential, leading the famous art critic Clement Greenberg to opine that Picasso no longer counted among the revolutionaries driving the development of art.[13] Picasso nevertheless became even more prolific in the final decade of his life. One point on which he would not be budged, however, was his categorical rejection of all forms of non-figurative art, as he explained to the French journalist and writer Hélène Parmelin: 'It's a joke to suppress the subject. It's impossible. It's as if you said: "Do as if I weren't there." Try it.'[14]

'I have less and less time, and I have more and more to say', said Picasso as an old man;[15] and faced with the ineluctability of his own mortality, he developed a stenographic idiom that manifested itself largely in ellipses and a painterly *fa' presto*.

Picasso died at his home in Mougins in the late morning of 8 April 1973, in the presence of his wife and a local doctor. In accordance with his wishes, Jacqueline Picasso wrapped his body in a Spanish *capa*, the circular cape of a Spanish gentleman, and on 10 April accompanied his coffin to the

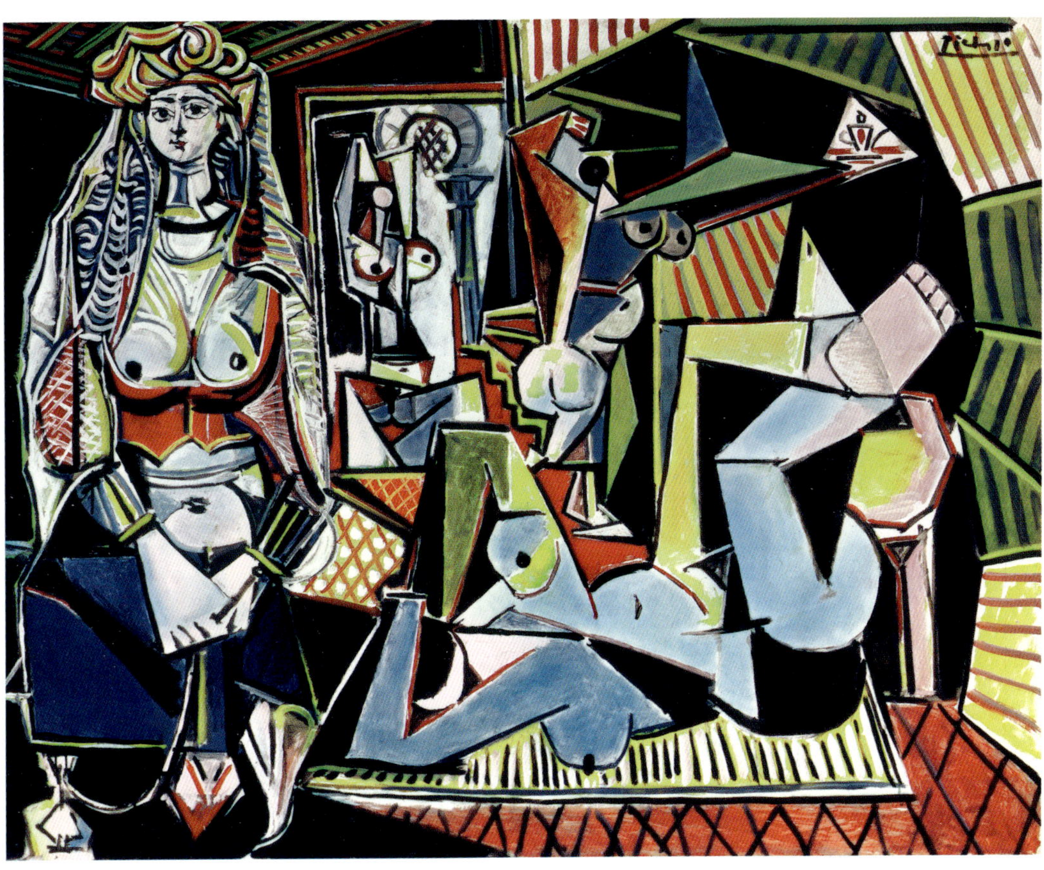

79
Pablo Picasso,
Women of
Algiers
(*Femmes*
d'Alger),
2 Februrary 1955

Private collection

Château de Vauvenarges, where she sat in vigil for six days and six nights. Picasso was buried in the garden of the château on the morning of 17 April. Only Paulo, Picasso's eldest son, was allowed to attend; Jacqueline Picasso adamantly refused to admit the other three children, along with other mourners, some of whom had travelled a long way, to pay him their last respects. She later justified her behaviour on the grounds that Picasso himself had not wanted to have a large funeral.

Picasso's death marked the beginning of a long-drawn-out legal battle between the heirs. Even just drawing up an inventory of the assets was a gargantuan task that took the auctioneer Maurice Rheims a full four years to accomplish. He later described being overwhelmed as much by the quality as the quantity of the works found locked away in Picasso's various properties. In the end, the estate in its entirety was valued at almost 1.4 billion francs (approx. 860 million euros),[16] leading the French press to hail it as the 'inheritance of the century'. As Picasso died intestate, his only legitimate heirs were his widow,

173

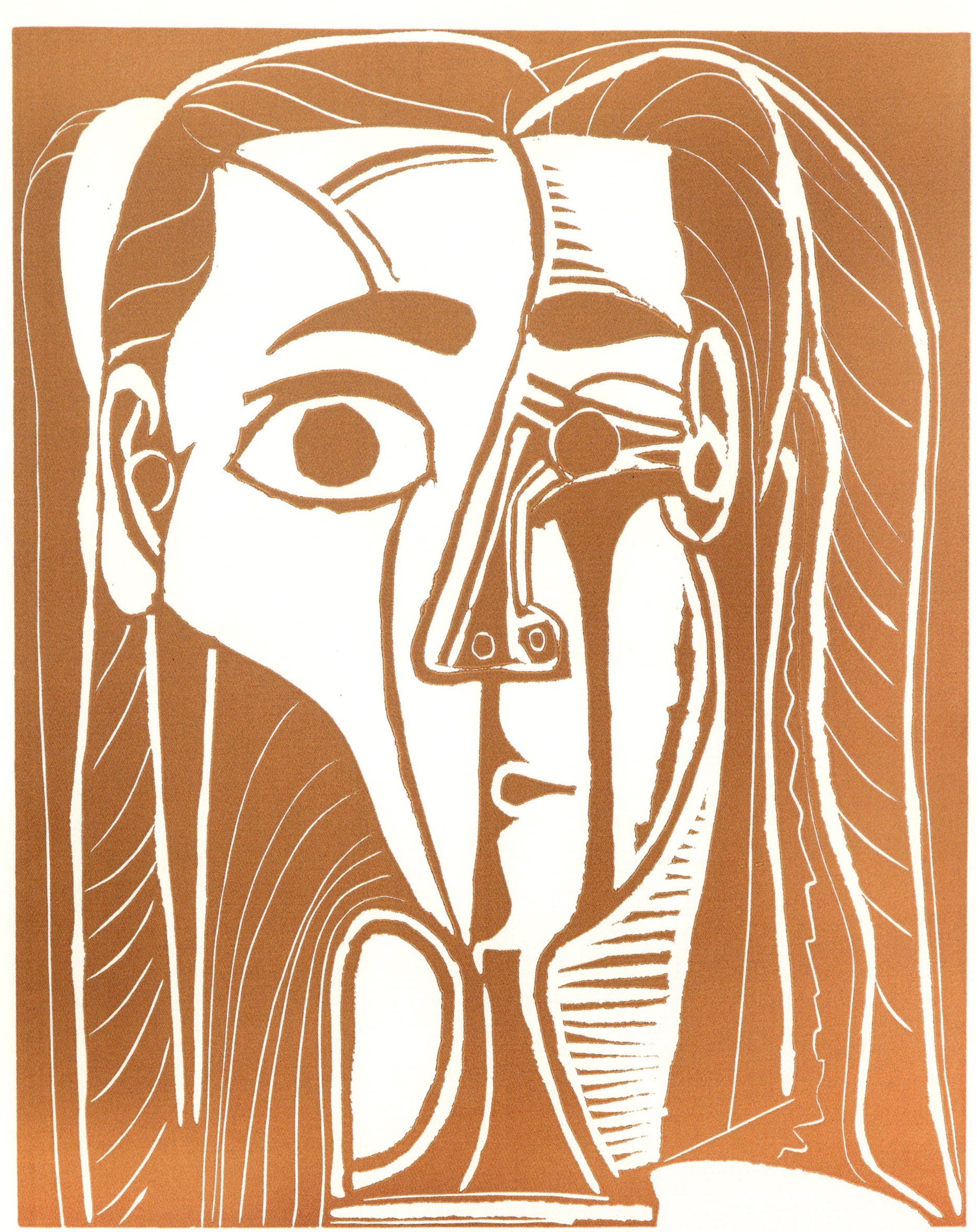

Jacqueline, and his son Paulo, the only child to issue from his first marriage, to Olga Picasso. The three illegitimate children, Maya, Claude and Paloma, sued for a share of the estate and each received half of the portion due a legitimate child. Before the inheritance was distributed, the French state also claimed a share, which it took in the form of works of art in lieu of the not inconsiderable death duties (estate tax). The museum specialists enlisted to decide what to take chose works from every phase of Picasso's

career, from the Blue Period to the late period. This colossal windfall later became the collection of the Musée national Picasso, installed in the extensively remodelled Hôtel Salé in the Marais district of Paris, which opened to great fanfare in September 1984. Two years earlier Jacqueline Picasso had donated forty-one ceramics to the Museo Picasso in Barcelona. The works had been loaned for inclusion in the show *Picasso ceramista* in the summer of 1982, and she waited until the opening event on 2 June to announce to the assembled company that she had decided to make a gift of them instead. A second gift of four sculptures, three paint-

ings, and a pastel went to the MoMA in New York. Jacqueline Picasso had evidently set herself the task of finding a suitable home for her husband's works in the museums of this world. Once the Musée Picasso in Paris had opened, however, 'she seemed to have sensed her earthly mission accomplished'.[17]

Depression dogged her throughout her widowhood and she depended ever more heavily on ritualised gestures of homage to her deceased husband to lend rhythm to her life. These included driving over to Vauvenargues on the eighth of every month in order to decorate the château with fresh flowers. She ended her life by shooting herself in the head at some point in the night of 14–15 October 1986. Her

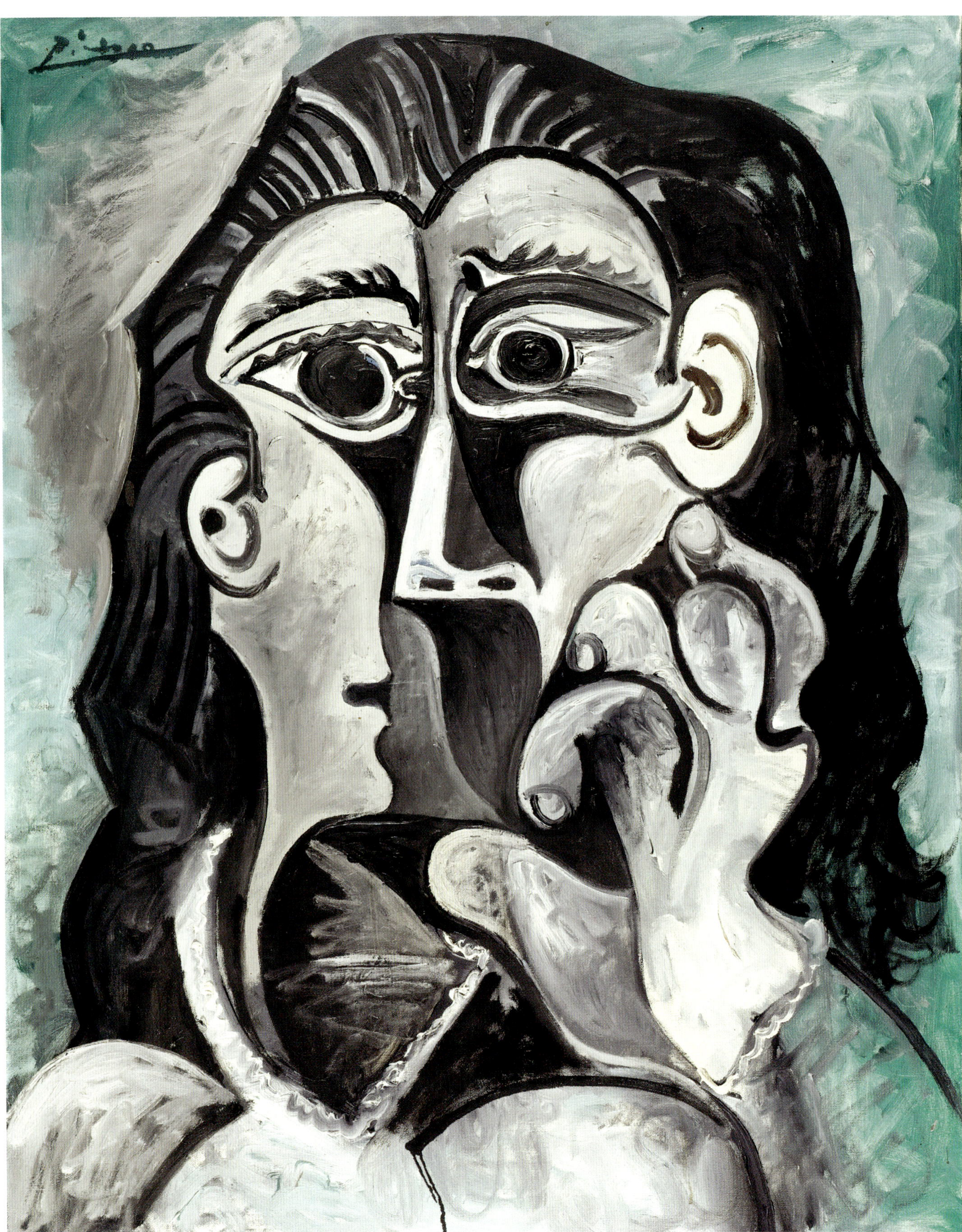

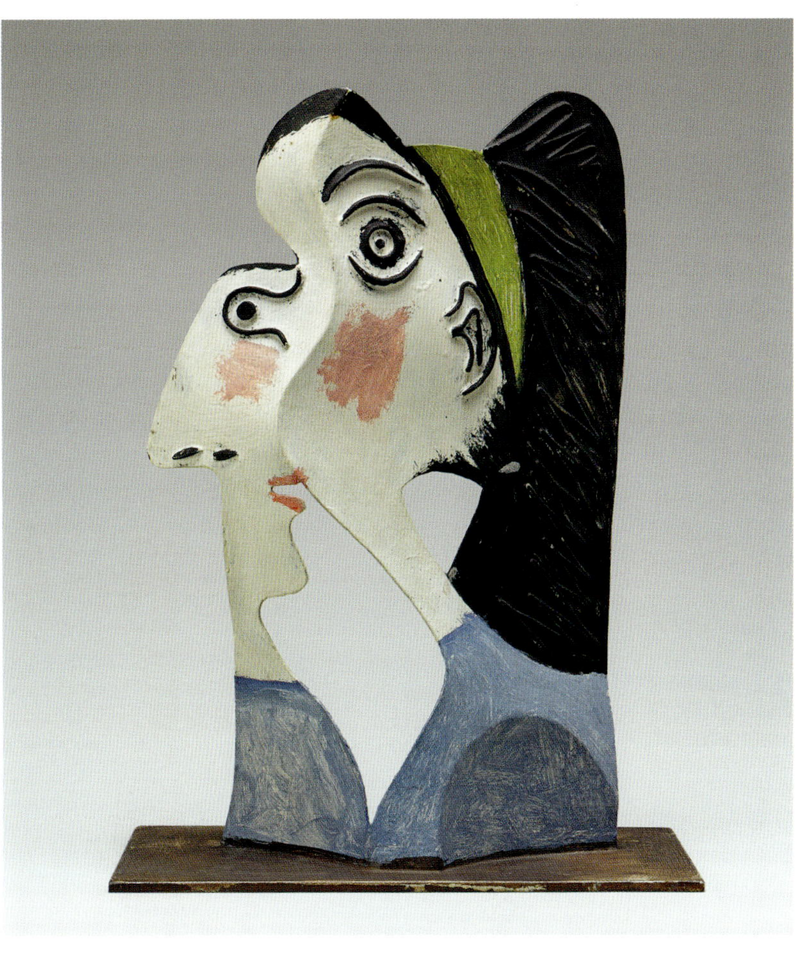

housekeeper found her in her bedroom the next morning, the pistol still in her right hand. She left no suicide note nor any other message that might have explained such a violent end.

'You have to admire your husband very much in order to be able to bear him', the German writer Hans Fallada once said. There can be no doubting Jacqueline Picasso's profound, unconditional adulation of her husband. Many of his painted 'diary pages' – which is how he viewed his paintings – bear affectionate dedications to his second wife. The secret of their apparently symbiotic bond ultimately remains unfathomable. Jacqueline's mortal remains rest alongside those of her husband under the sculpture *Woman with Vase* in the garden of the Château de Vauvenargues. The American photographer David Douglas Duncan, who made Picasso's acquaintance in the 1950s and photographed him countless times on his home territory, summarised the relationship between Jacqueline and Pablo as follows: 'They lived in a world of his own creation where he reigned almost as a king, yet cherished only two treasures – freedom to work and the love of Jacqueline.'[18]

Notes

Doña María Picasso López

1   Jaime Sabartés, *Picasso: An Intimate Portrait*, tr. Angel Flores (London, 1949), p. 12.

2   A selection of Picasso's mother's previously unpublished letters is included in French translation in Annie Cohen-Solal, *Un étranger nommé Picasso* (Paris, 2021).

3   Sabartés 1949 (see note 1), p. 47.

4   Javier Vilató, 'Los Picassos de Barcelona y los Vilató', *La Vanguardia* (3 April 1988), p. 23.

5   Françoise Gilot and Carlton Lake, *Life with Picasso* (New York, 1964), p. 148.

6   Gertrude Stein, *The Autobiography of Alice B. Toklas* (London, 1933; New York, 1960), p. 221.

7   Clive Bell, letter to Pablo Picasso, 15 October 1923, archives, Musée Picasso Paris.

8   Pablo Picasso, letter to the 'Procureur de la République', 9 May 1930, archives, Musée Picasso Paris.

9   John Richardson, *A Life of Picasso: The Triumphant Years, 1917–1932* (New York, 2007), pp. 407–08.

10 Based on the French translation in Cohen-Salal 2021 (see note 2), p. 387.

Lola Ruiz Picasso

1   Gertrude Stein, *Picasso* (1938; London, 1948), pp. 2–3.

2   *Lola Ruiz Picasso (1884–1958)*, ed. Rafael Inglada, exh. cat. Fundación Pablo Ruiz Picasso (Málaga, 2003), n.p.

3   Fernande Olivier, letter to Gertrude Stein, late August 1909, Beinecke Library, Yale University, New Haven, Connecticut.

4   Javier Vilató, 'Los Picassos de Barcelona y los Vilató', *La Vanguardia* (3 April 1988).

5   Pablo Picasso, letter to Gertrude Stein, November 1918, Beinecke Library, Yale University, New Haven, Connecticut.

6   Inge Morath, 'Lola Ruiz Vilato (Barcelona)', tr. Alvaro Aramburu, in *España en los años 50* (Madrid, 1994), pp. 25–26.

7   Additional information about Morath's visit, including Lola Vilató's comment about posing, is given in Rosamond Bernier, '48, Paseo de Gracia', *L'Œil*, no. 4 (15 April 1955), pp. 5–13.

8   Morath 1994 (see note 6), p. 26.

Fernande Olivier

1   *Souvenirs intimes* was originally published in French (Paris) in 1988; much of the journal was translated into English and incorporated into a collection of Fernande Olivier's memoirs and letters in Fernande Olivier, *Loving Picasso: The Private Journal of Fernande Olivier*, foreword and notes by Marilyn McCully, epilogue by John Richardson, tr. Christine Baker and Michael Raeburn (New York, 2000). Fernande Olivier's words in the present text are taken from that publication.

2   *Picasso et ses amis* (Paris, 1933) was published in English as *Picasso and his friends*, tr. Jane Miller (New York, 1965) and in German as *Neun Jahre mit Picasso*, tr. Gertrud Droz-Rüegg (Zurich, 1957).

3   Jean-Marie Drot, dir., *L'art et les hommes, episode 3, À la recherche de Max Jacob* (Paris, 1959).

Gertrude Stein

1 Diana Souhami, *Gertrude and Alice* (London, 1991), p. 48.
2 Ambroise Vollard, *Recollections of a Picture Dealer*, tr. Violet M. MacDonald (1936; New York, 1978), pp. 138–39.
3 Souhami 1991 (see note 1), p. 73.
4 Gertrude Stein, *The Autobiography of Alice B. Toklas* (London, 2001), pp. 52–53, 59–60.
5 Ibid., p. 64.
6 Souhami 1991 (see note 1), p. 75.
7 Ibid., p. 101.
8 Stefana Sabin, *Gertrude Stein* (Reinbek, 1996), p. 50.
9 Gertrude Stein, 'Pablo Picasso' 1909, *Camera Work: A Photographic Quarterly* (August 1912), p. 29.
10 Souhami 1991 (see note 1), p. 205.
11 Sabin 1996 (see note 8), p. 96.
12 Stein 2001 (see note 4), p. 64.
13 Souhami 1991 (see note 1), p. 192
14 Ibid., p. 231.
15 Ibid., p. 257.
16 Ibid., p. 14.
17 Mabel Dodge, 'Speculations, or Post-Impressionism in Prose', *Arts and Decoration*, 3, no. 5 (March 1913), p. 172.
18 Souhami 1991 (see note 1), p. 101.

Eva Gouel

1 Pablo Picasso, letter to Daniel-Henry Kahnweiler, 12 June 1912, in Judith Cousins with Pierre Daix, 'Documentary Chronology', in William Rubin, *Picasso and Braque: Pioneering Cubism*, exh. cat. The Museum of Modern Art (New York, 1989), p. 395.
2 Gino Severini, *The Life of a Painter*, tr. Jennifer Franchina (Princeton, 1995), p. 95.
3 Ibid., p. 102.
4 Gertrude Stein, *The Autobiography of Alice B. Toklas* (London, 1933; New York, 1960), p. 111.
5 Pablo Picasso, cit. in Cousins 1989 (see note 1), pp. 383–84.
6 Stein 1960 (see note 4), p. 111.
7 Severini 1995 (see note 2), p. 102.
8 Pablo Picasso, letter to Georges Braque, 18 May 1912, in Fernande Olivier, *Loving Picasso: The Private Journal of Fernande Olivier*, foreword and notes by Marilyn McCully, epilogue by John Richardson, tr. Christine Baker and Michael Raeburn (New York, 2001), p. 279.
9 Pablo Picasso, cit. in Cousins 1989 (see note 1), p. 395.
10 Gertrude Stein, cit. in Mabel Dodge Luhan, *Movers and Shakers* (New York, 1936; Albuquerque, 1987), p. 29. The reference to the 'late lamented' is to Fernande Olivier.
11 Eva Gouel, cit. in Cousins 1989 (see note 1), p. 414.
12 Max Jacob, letter to Daniel-Henry Kahnweiler, 1913; repr. in *Daniel-Henry Kahnweiler: marchand, éditeur, écrivain*, exh. cat. Centre Georges Pompidou (Paris, 1984), p. 118.
13 Pablo Picasso, letter to Daniel-Henry Kahnweiler, 21 March 1913, in Cousins 1989 (see note 1), p. 415.
14 Pierre Daix, 'Portraiture and Picasso's Primitivism and Cubism', in *Picasso and Portraiture: Representation and Transformation*, ed. William Rubin, exh. cat. The Museum of Modern Art, New York; Grand Palais, Paris (New York, 1996), p. 287.
15 Eva Gouel, letter to Joséphine Haviland, 12 July 1915, in *Picasso: Dessins et papiers collés Céret 1911–1913*, exh. cat. Musée d'art moderne (Céret, 1977), p. 366.
16 Eva Gouel, letter to Joséphine Haviland, 29 July 1915, ibid., p. 368.
17 Eva Gouel, letter to Joséphine Haviland, 25 October 1915, ibid., p. 369.
18 Pablo Picasso, letter to Gertrude Stein, 9 December 1915; Collection of American Literature, Beinecke Rare Book and Manuscript Library, Yale University, New Haven, Connecticut.

Olga Khokhlova

1   Mary E. Davis, *Ballets Russes Style: Diaghilev's Dancers and Paris Fashion* (London, 2010), p. 23.

2   Françoise Gilot and Carlton Lake, *Life with Picasso* (New York et al., 1964), p. 148.

3   Roland Penrose, *Picasso: His Life And Work*, 3rd edn (London, 1981), p. 218.

4   John Richardson, *A Life of Picasso*, vol. 3, *The Triumphant Years 1917–1932* (New York, 2007), p. 60.

5   John Richardson archive, The Josef and Anni Albers Foundation, Bethany, Connecticut.

6   Brassaï, *Gespräche mit Picasso* (Reinbek, 1966), pp. 11–12.

7   Cit. in Richardson 2007 (see note 4), p. 146.

8   Cit. in André Fermigier, *Picasso* (Paris, 1969), p. 132.

9   Penrose 1981 (see note 3); Pierre Cabanne, *Le siècle de Picasso*, vol. 1 (Paris, 1975); John Berger, *The Success and Failure of Picasso* (Harmondsworth, 1965).

10   *Olga Picasso*, exh. cat. Musée national Picasso (Paris, 2017), p. 142.

11   Caroline Eliacheff, 'Les vies d'Olga', ibid., p. 279.

Marie-Thérèse Walter

1   Olivier Widmaier Picasso, 'Muse, lover, lifeblood: how my grandmother woke the genius in Picasso', *The Guardian*, 8 Mar 2018, https://www.theguardian.com/books/2018/mar/08/picasso-grandmother-grandson-tate-olivier-widmaier-ey-exhibition-1932-love-fame-tragedy (accessed 28 Mar 2022).

2   John Richardson, *A Life of Picasso*, vol. 3, *The Triumphant Years 1917–1932* (New York, 2007), p. 326.

3   Olivier Widmaier Picasso, *Picasso: Porträt der Familie* (Munich, 2002), p. 60. Published in English as *Picasso: An Intimate Portrait* (London, 2018).

4   John Berger, *The Success and Failure of Picasso* (New York, 1989), p. 156.

5   Pierre Daix, cit. in Olivier Widmaier Picasso, *Picasso: The Real Family Story* (Munich, 2004), p. 56.

6   Jack Flam, *Matisse and Picasso: The Story of Their Rivalry and Friendship* (New York, 2003), n.p.

7   Cf. Pablo Picasso, interview in *L'Intransigeant*, 15 June 1932, cit. in Richardson 2007 (see note 2), p. 478.

8   Richardson 2007 (see note 2), p. 369.

9   Cf. ibid., p. 418.

10   Ibid., p. 464.

11   Pierre Cabanne, *Pablo Picasso: His Life and Times* (New York, 1977), p. 277.

12   Ibid.

13   Cf. Widmaier Picasso 2018 (see note 3), p. 59.

14   Ibid. p. 70.

15   Olivier Widmaier Picasso, in conversation with the author, 3 February 2022.

16   Cabanne 1977 (see note 11), p. 267.

17   Ibid., p. 266.

Dora Maar

1   Amanda Maddox, 'What's in a Name: The Invention of Dora Maar', in *Dora Maar*, ed. Damarice Amao, et al., exh. cat. J. Paul Getty Museum, Los Angeles; Tate Modern, London; Centre Pompidou, Paris (Los Angeles and London, 2019), p. 13.

2   Victoria Combalia, 'Dora Maar, Street Photographer: Barcelona and London', ibid., p. 54.

3   Maddox 2019 (see note 1), p. 15.

4   Karolina Ziebinska-Lewandowska, '"The Imaginary Is What Tends to Become Real": The Photomontage Period', in exh. cat. Los Angeles/London/Paris 2019 (see note 1), p. 103.

5   Brassaï, *Conversations with Picasso*, tr. Jane Marie Todd (Chicago and London, 1999), p. 51.

6   Françoise Gilot and Carlton Lake, *Life with Picasso* (New York, 1964), pp. 85–86.

7   Ibid., p. 15.

8   Judi Freeman, Picasso and the Weeping Women: *The Years of Marie-Thérèse Walter & Dora Maar*, exh. cat. Los Angeles County Museum of Art; The Metropolitan Museum of Art, New York; Art Institute of Chicago (New York, 1994), p. 7.

9   Ziebinska-Lewandowska 2019 (see note 4), p. 142.

10   James Lord, *Picasso and Dora: A Memoir* (London, 1993), p. 123.

11   Jean-Paul Crespelle, *Picasso: Seine Frauen, seine Freunde, sein Werk* (Hamburg and Düsseldorf, 1973), p. 201. English translation: *Picasso and His Women*, tr. Robert Baldick (New York, 1969).

12   Ibid.

13   Mary Ann Caws, *Dora Maar with and without Picasso: A Biography* (London, 2000), p. 187.

14   Ibid.

15   Ibid., p. 190.

16   Ibid., p. 117.

17   Ibid., p. 191.

18   Caws 2000 (see note 13), p. 198.

Françoise Gilot

1   Malte Herwig, *The Woman Who Says No: Françoise Gilot on Her Life with and without Picasso* (Vancouver, 2015), p. 27.
2   Ibid., p. 30.
3   Annie Maïllis, 'Françoise Gilot dans le miroir de l'œuvre', in *Françoise Gilot: The Years in France*, exh. cat. Musée Estrine, Saint-Rémy-de-Provence (Milan, 2022), p. 15.
4   Ibid., p. 15.
5   Ibid., p. 14.
6   Françoise Gilot and Carlton Lake, *Life with Picasso* (1964; London, 1990), p. 93.
7   Maïllis 2022 (see note 3), p. 16.
8   Gilot and Lake 1990 (see note 6), p. 334.
9   Herwig 2015 (see note 1), p. 2.
10   Ibid., p. 149.
11   Tim Hilton, 'Introduction', in Gilot and Lake 1990 (see note 6), p. viii.
12   Carlton Lake, 'Foreword', in Gilot and Lake 1990 (see note 6), p. 6.
13   Françoise Gilot, *Monograph, 1940–2000*, foreword by Dina Vierny, texts by the artist, biography and analysis of works by Mel Yoakum (Lausanne, 2000), p. 394.
14   Françoise Gilot, *Monograph, 1940–2000*, foreword by Dina Vierny, texts by the artist, biography and analysis of works by Mel Yoakum (Lausanne, 2000), p. 396.
15   Carlton Lake, *Confessions of a Literary Archaeologist* (New York, 1990), p. 175.
16   Friedrich Teja Bach, *Constantin Brancusi: Metamorphosen plastischer Form* (Cologne, 1987), p. 335.
17   Herwig 2015 (see note 1), p. 131.
18   Ibid., p. 135.
19   Gilot 2000 (see note 13), p. 406.
20   Gilot and Lake 1990 (see note 6), p. 113.
21   Herwig 2015 (see note 1), p. 133.
22   Ibid.
23   See exh. cat. Saint-Rémy-de-Provence 2022 (see note 3).
24   Henri Matisse, *Matisse On Art*, ed. Jack D. Flam (Berkeley, 1995), p. 174.
25   Sarah Wilson, 'Françoise Gilot: Autour du cercle carré du temps', in exh. cat. Saint-Rémy-de-Provence 2022 (see note 3), p. 38.

Jacqueline Roque

1   Olivier Widmaier-Picasso, *Picasso: An Intimate Portrait* (London, 2018), p. 245.
2   Marina Picasso, *Picasso: My Grandfather* (New York, 2001), p. 7.
3   Françoise Gilot, *Life with Picasso* (1964; London, 1990), pp. 334–35.
4   Pepita Dupont, *La vérité sur Jacqueline et Pablo Picasso* (Paris, 2007), p. 7.
5   Antonia Vallentin, *Pablo Picasso* (Paris, 1957), p. 354.
6   Pierre Cabanne, *Pablo Picasso: His Life and Times* (New York, 1977), pp. 6, 444–65.
7   William Rubin, 'The Jacqueline Portraits in the Pattern of Picasso's Art', in *Picasso and Portraiture: Representation and Transformation*, ed. William Rubin, exh. cat. The Museum of Modern Art, New York; Grand Palais, Paris (London, 1996), p. 458.
8   Cf. André Malraux, *Picasso's Mask* (New York, 1976), p. 26.
9   *Picasso: En el Taller*, exh. cat Fundacion Mapfre (Madrid, 2014), p. 13.
10   Pierre Daix, *La vie de peintre de Pablo Picasso* (Paris, 1977), p. 372.
11   Cf. Susan Grace Galassi, *Picasso's Variations on the Masters: Confrontations with the Past* (New York, 1996), p. 137.
12   Pierre Daix, *Picasso créateur, la vie intime de l'œuvre* (Paris, 1987), p. 339.
13   Clement Greenberg, 'Picasso As Revolutionary: Review of *Picasso* by Frank Elgar and Robert Maillard', *The New Leader*, 10 December 1956, cit. in *The Collected Essays and Criticism*, vol. 3, *Affirmations and Refusals* (Chicago, 1993), p. 275.
14   Cit. in *Picasso on Art: A Selection of Views*, ed. Dora Ashton (Boston, 1977), p. 36.
15   CM. L. Bernadac, *Late Picasso: Paintings, sculpture, drawings, prints 1953–1972*, exh. cat. The Tate Gallery (London, 1988), p. 85.
16   Olivier Widmaier Picasso, *Picasso: Portrait intime* (Paris, 2013), p. 248.
17   Cf. Rubin 1996 (see note 7), p. 458.
18   David Douglas Duncan, *Picasso and Jacqueline* (New York, 1988), p. 9.

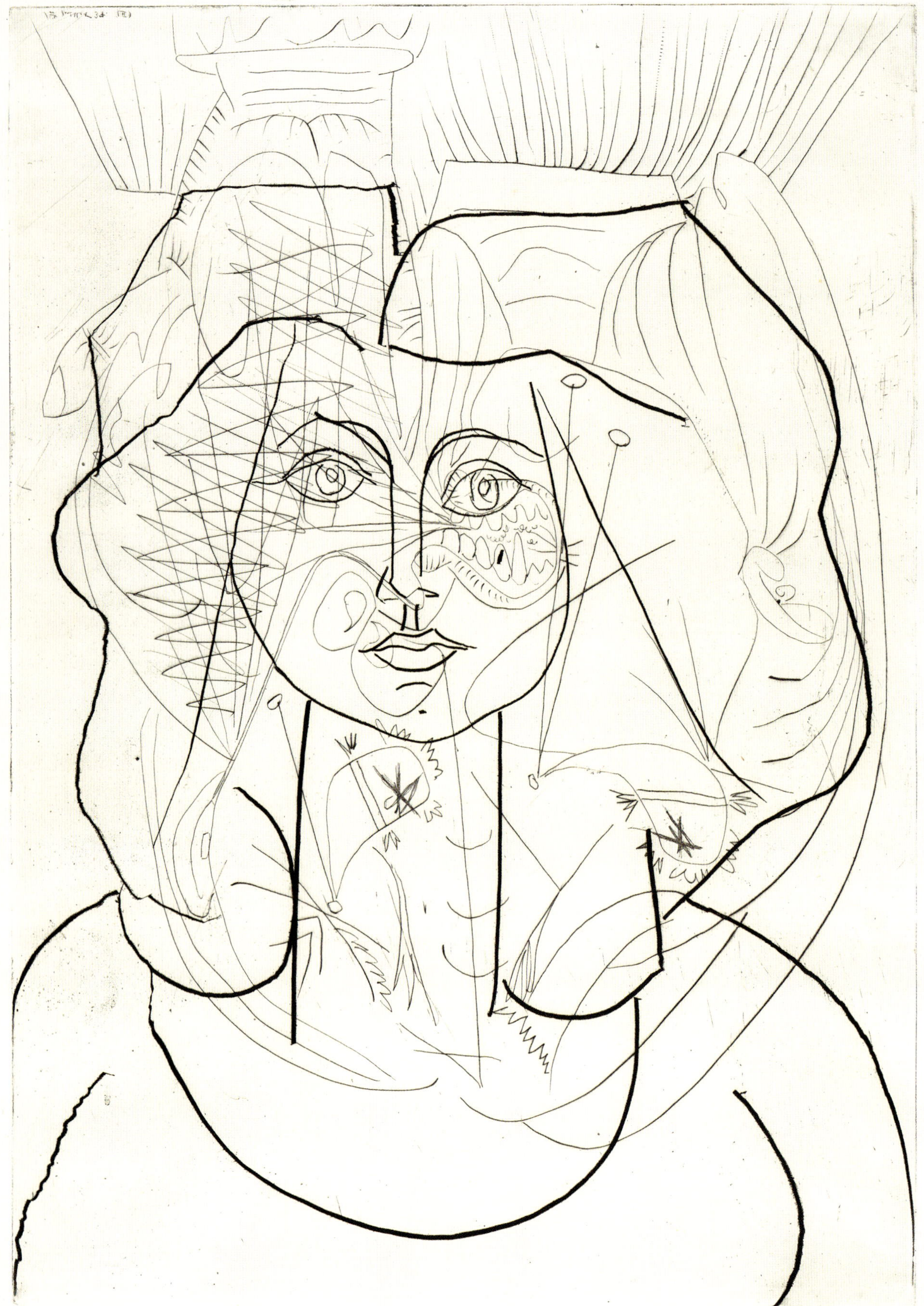

Photo Credits

Frontispiece: photo Josse/Scala, Florence

p. 4: Kunstmuseum Pablo Picasso Münster

p. 8–9: Picture Alliance/AP Images

p. 10: Museu Picasso Barcelona, Fond Joan Vidal Ventosa

p. 14: Museu Picasso Barcelona, photo Fotogasull

p. 18: © Archives Olga Ruiz-Picasso, Fundación Almine y Bernard Ruiz-Picasso para el Arte, Madrid/ photographer unknown, all rights reserved (gelatin silver print, 10.7 × 6.6 cm)

p. 19: Sara and Gerald Murphy Papers, Yale Collection of American Literature, Beinecke Rare Book and Manuscript Library

p. 21: Musée Réattu, Arles

p. 22: © Archives Olga Ruiz-Picasso, Fundación Almine y Bernard Ruiz-Picasso para el Arte, Madrid/photographer unknown, all rights reserved (gelatin silver print, 10.9 × 6.5 cm)

p. 26: bpk/RMN – Grand Palais

p. 29: FABA/Hugard & Vanoverschelde Photography (oil on wood, 35.5 × 22.5 cm, Zervos VI – 18)

p. 30: Museu Picasso, Barcelona, photo Fotogasull

p. 33: The Cleveland Museum of Art

p. 35: Museo Picasso Barcelona, Fons Joan Vidal Ventosa

p. 36: bpk/RMN – Grand Palais (gelatin silver print, 11.2 × 6.6 cm)

p. 39: Inge Morath/Magnum Photos

p. 43: Musée des Beaux-Arts, Tours

p. 44: bpk/RMN – Grand Palais/Adrien Didierjean

p. 48: Art Gallery of Ontario

p. 51: bpk/RMN – Grand Palais (aristotype, 7.9 × 11 cm)

p. 52: bpk/RMN – Grand Palais (gelatin silver print, 23 × 14.5 cm)

p. 55: bpk/Städel Museum, Frankfurt am Main

p. 58: bpk/RMN (gelatin silver print, 12.9 × 9.8 cm)

p. 62: bpk/The Metropolitan Museum of Art, New York

p. 65: bpk/Man Ray

p. 72: bpk

p. 76: bpk/RMN – Grand Palais (gelatin silver print, 21.5 × 16 cm)

p. 79: bpk/The Metropolitan Museum of Art, New York

p. 80: Digital Image, The Museum of Modern Art, New York/Scala, Florence

p. 83: bpk/RMN – Grand Palais (gelatin silver print, 23.5 × 17 cm)

p. 84: Columbus Museum of Art

p. 86: bpk/RMN – Grand Palais/ Béatrice Hatala

p. 91: bpk/RMN – Grand Palais/ Adrien Didierjean

p. 92: bpk/RMN – Grand Palais (gelatin silver print, 11.5 × 6.9 cm)

p. 95: FABA/Hugard & Vanoverschelde Photography (oil on canvas, 64 × 53 cm, Zervos III – 40)

p. 96: bpk/RMN – Grand Palais/ René-Gabriel Ojéda

p. 97: akg-images

p. 99: bpk/adoc-photos

p. 100: bpk/RMN – Grand Palais/ Mathieu Rabeau

p. 101: bpk/RMN – Grand Palais (gelatin silver print, 7.4 × 9.8 cm)

p. 102: Christie's Images, London/Scala, Florence

p. 105: akg-images

p. 106: Christie's Images, London/ Scala, Florence

p. 108: Administration Picasso, Paris

p. 111: Administration Picasso, Paris

p. 112: Christie's Images, London/ Scala, Florence

p. 113: photo Josse/Scala, Florence

p. 115: Kunstmuseum Pablo Picasso Münster

p. 116: Digital Image, The Museum of Modern Art, New York/Scala, Florence

p. 118: Kunstmuseum Pablo Picasso Münster

p. 120: Christie's Images, London/ Scala, Florence

p. 123: bpk/RMN – Grand Palais/ Jean-Gilles Berizzi

p. 124: bpk/RMN – Grand Palais (gelatin silver print, 18.5 × 12 cm)

p. 126: bpk/CNAC – MNAM/Dora Maar

p. 127: bpk/CNAC – MNAM/Dora Maar

p. 129: bpk/CNAC – MNAM/Dora Maar

p. 130: bpk/Nationalgalerie, SMB, Museum Berggruen, Jens Ziehe

p. 131: bpk/CNAC – MNAM/Man Ray

p. 133: bpk/RMN – Grand Palais/ Jean-Gilles Berizzi

p. 134: Tate, London/Scala, Florence

p. 137: The Metropolitan Museum of Art/ Art Resource/Scala, Florence

p. 141: Centre Pompidou, MNAM – CCI, Dist. RMN – Grand Palais/Philippe Migeat

p. 142: RMN – Grand Palais/Musée national Picasso – Paris/Image RMN – Grand Palais

p. 144: RMN – Grand Palais (Musée national Picasso – Paris), Mathieu Rabeau

p. 147: RMN – Grand Palais (Musée national Picasso – Paris)

p. 148: photo Mathieu Polo

p. 149: Kunstmuseum Pablo Picasso Münster

p. 150: bpk/RMN – Grand Palais (gelatin silver print, 10.3 × 11.1 cm)

p. 151: Kunstmuseum Pablo Picasso Münster

p. 152: bpk/Ministère de la Culture – Médiathèque du Patrimoine, RMN – Grand Palais/Denise Colomb

p. 156: Christie's Images, London/Scala, Florence

p. 161: bpk/ CNAC – MNAM, Bertrand Prévost

p. 162: David Douglas Duncan/ Harry Ransom Center

p. 164: photo Scala, Florence

p. 167: akg-images

p. 169: David Douglas Duncan/ Harry Ransom Center

p. 170: bpk/RMN – Grand Palais

p. 171: David Douglas Duncan/ Harry Ransom Center

p. 173: Photo Scala, Florence

p. 174: Kunstmuseum Pablo Picasso Münster

p. 176: Associates/LACMA/Resource NY/ photo Scala, Florence

p. 177: bpk/RMN – Grand Palais/ Mathieu Rabeau/Adrien Didierjean

p. 182: bpk/RMN – Grand Palais/ Adrien Didierjean

Colophon

Editor:
Margrit Bernard, Cologne

Authors:
Marilyn McCully, Markus Müller

Project director:
Kerstin Ludolph

Project management:
Karen Angne

German copyediting:
Vera Udodenko, Cologne

English copyediting:
Joann Skrypzak, Cologne

Translations English–German:
Ursula Fethke, Cologne

Translations German–English:
Bronwen Saunders, Basle

Graphic design:
Studio Carmen Strzelecki, Cologne

Production:
Sophie Friederich

Prepress and repro:
Reproline mediateam, Unterföhring

Typeface:
Neue Haas Grotesk
Bruta Pro

Paper:
GardaMatt Art, 150 g/m^2

Printing and binding:
Printer Trento s.r.l.

Printed in Italy

Front cover (clockwise, l-r):
Pablo Picasso: *Woman with Beret and Fur Collar* (fig. 51); *Portrait of Olga Picasso* (fig. 42); *Portrait of María Picasso López* (fig. 5); *Portrait of Fernande Olivier* (fig. 20); *Madame Z (Jacqueline with Flowers)* (fig. 75); *Gertrude Stein* (fig. 23)

Back cover (clockwise, l-r):
María Picasso López (fig. 1); Fernande Olivier (fig. 19); Eva Gouel (fig. 30); Lola Picasso (fig. 11); ; Marie-Thérèse Walter (fig. 44); Jacqueline Roque (fig. 73); Françoise Gilot (fig. 63); Olga Khokhlova (fig. 34); Gertrude Stein (fig. 26); Dora Maar (fig. 53)

Frontispiece:
Pablo Picasso, *Jacqueline with Clasped Hands* (*Jacqueline aux mains croisées*), 1954, Musée national Picasso, Paris

p. 4: Pablo Picasso, *The Face of Peace*, 2d version, September 1951, Kunstmuseum Pablo Picasso Münster

pp. 8–9: Picasso in his studio in Vallauris, 1953

p. 182: Pablo Picasso, *Portrait de Françoise tête-bêche sur 'La femme qui pleure, II'*, 1946, Musée national Picasso, Paris

Bibliographic information from the Deutsche Nationalbibliothek
The Deutsche Nationalbibliothek lists this publication in the Deutsche Nationalbibliografie; detailed bibliographic data are available on the Internet at http://www.dnb.de

ISBN 978-3-7774-3724-8 (German edition)
ISBN 978-3-7774-3726-2 (English edition)

www.hirmerverlag.de
www.hirmerpublishers.com
www.hirmerpublishers.co.uk